Praying Wife Healed Husband

Praying Wife Healed Husband

Marcy Myles-Clark

Your Majesty Publishing Company,
Maryland, USA

Praying Wife Healed Husband: How To Survive a Death Defying COVID-19 Experience

Permission has been obtained by Johns Hopkins Hospital for use of quotations by official hospital personnel.

Theirrien A. Clark (co-author) has given permission for his medical information to be utilized throughout this publication.

Portions of this content appeared in news media on NBC, CBS and FOX.

Printed in the United States of America
ISBN: 978-1-7365540-5-0

Cover design by: RAWDesignz.com
Book Coaching by: TheLiteraryFront.com

Library of Congress Cataloging-in-Publication Data

Your Majesty Publishing Company
6030 Marshalee Drive, Suite 214
Elkridge, MD 21075
www.PrayingWifeHelps.com

Typesetting services by BOOKOW.COM

We dedicate this book to the individuals who have been afflicted with COVID-19, the families who have lost a loved one due to illnesses related to COVID-19, and to anyone who has even been indirectly affected by this horrible virus. We know 2020 has been a year of tremendous change and pain for many.

We care about you, so we wrote this book with you in mind. We share our experiences as a reminder that if you are faced with a life-threatening struggle, you, too, can see God's miracles in the making. He never leaves us nor forsakes us. No matter the outcome, He is in control. Trouble won't last always, so this, too, shall pass! Keep the faith and watch His miracles abound. And yes, joy will come!

Although she may never see this, we wanted to extend a special dedication to Amanda Kloots, wife of deceased Broadway star, Nick Cordero. Our husbands began their COVID-19 fight around the exact same time last March. I was amazed at the similarities of their stories. Although I refrained from watching media during that time, I did follow Amanda's story during Nick's sickness and began praying for his recovery along with Tee's. Like my husband, her husband had so much to live for, but apparently God had another plan. I continue to pray for Amanda and her son's healing over the loss of Nick. No doubt, God is using her tragedy to awaken and save many beyond her reach, just like He's using our testimony for matters we can't even imagine. I pray Amanda is experiencing her silver lining like we are experiencing ours.

Blessings to all.

Testimonials

Ministers Jared & Danielle Perry, Prayer Leaders-TC Prayer Warriors
Amen! I am blessed and encouraged by your faith and perseverance during this time. Keep going and know that God is healing Uncle, even if it's not in our timeline. He will do what He said!

Chris Seymour
So excited! I'm so happy you're Tee's wife. You are the best. I got the perfect title for your book: "Behind Every Man's healing Is a praying wife."

Jill D-New Psalmist Baptist Church
Amen! You are a great praying wife! He is a miracle, but you are an inspiration! You are showing us all what a Godly wife should look like during a crisis. I just pray, if Patrick is going through like that, that I stand up like you have done this entire time.

Vera W
I'm so glad my brother is doing good. He's strong and I knew he was going to pull through. I can't wait to tell him that he has an awesome wife and how you kept praying for restoration and preservation. I am so grateful and thankful to have you as my sister-in-law—you are the BOMB. I just want to thank you and tell you that I love you so much. Can't wait to see you guys. Please let me know if you need anything; Kevin and I are here.

Kasum K RN, Johns Hopkins ICU
I just saw the video of Tee being discharged home and I just couldn't help but cry tears of joy. Your faith in God and Tee never ceased, and it moved mountains to bring Tee home to you. You are an incredible person. My joy knows no bounds! I pray that blessings will continue to shower on Tee, you and your whole family.

Ministers Jon and Kristi Gray, Prayer Leaders-TC Prayer Warriors
When I heard that Tee "Anthony" was in the hospital with COVID-19 and on the ventilator, I was devastated and knew it was time to pray. I was excited when Marcy called and asked me and my wife Kristi to help set up the Saturday prayer calls and to actually be one of the prayer leaders on the Saturday prayer calls. Watching the POWER of God in action through the good and bad days and then to see Anthony come home in May was a true testimonial to the power of PRAYER. I am thrilled about how Marcy represented a praying wife and never stopped believing that my brother was going to be healed.

Chaplain Dr. Monica Andrews, Divine Order Foundation
I know the power of God very well and I was most honored to watch and participate

with a woman of God using what I call her "daughter power" while her husband was on a ventilator fighting COVID-19. Watching Marcy's faith at work, calling on prayer warriors and reporting details to the warriors daily for our individual and powerful group prayers weekly, and as needed based on the daily reports of Tee's status, brought the words in the Bible to life. As the Bible says (and I paraphrase) in James 2:26 "...faith without works is dead also." and in Mark 11:24 "...whatsoever things we ask when we pray, if we believe that we will receive them, then we will." If everyone operated in this way, the world would be a better place. Thank you, Marcy for including me in one of the miracles that our Heavenly Father allowed.

Janet Jeffreys
I'm so grateful for your leadership. You helped to bring me closer to God and bring our family closer together this year.

Megan Hosey, PhD, Johns Hopkins
Working alongside Tee and Marcy during illness and recovery was a true joy. Although Tee was very sick, it was clear that his connection to Marcy and to his family brought healing, especially in the darkest and hardest moments. Their story reminds us all that in the worst of times, we find our strength by coming together.

Sandra Draper Stewart-New Psalmist Baptist Church
Just want to say "Thank You" for sharing your Testimony and being Transparent! You and Anthony (Tee) are Blessed to have each other. Your LOVE, FAITH, DEVOTION, STRENGTH, and HOPE are all GOD'S GIFTS he has bestowed in YOU. Giving GOD All The Honor, All The Glory, and All The Praise!
Peace and Blessings!

Diane Taylor (Aunt Di)
When we learned of the severity of Tee's COVID-19 battle we had no idea how much your formation of a prayer line was going to bring to life the passage of scripture in James 5:16 that reads, the effective fervent prayer of the righteous availeth much. As Tee endured each Health Challenge during his hospital stay, your persistence that we unite In prayer during each of those pivotal times gave evidence that you were a true believer in the power of prayer.

Glossary of Abbreviations

ATC – around the clock

CDC – Centers for Disease Control and Prevention

COVID-19 – coronavirus disease 2019

CT-scan or CAT-scan – computed tomography scan, or computerized axial tomography scan

ECMO – extracorporeal membrane oxygenation

EMG – electromyography

ICU – intensive care unit

JH-HCGH – Johns Hopkins – Howard County General Hospital

LFT – Liver Function Tests

OT – occupational therapy

PPE – Personal Protective Equipment

PT – physical therapy

PTL – praise the Lord

SLP – speech-language pathologist

TGBTG – to God be the glory

FOREWORD

There is a big difference between an interruption and a crisis. In March of 2020, Marcy and Tee were hit with a crisis. Their married life was hit with the newly discovered Coronavirus (Covid-19), and no one knew what to expect. Those early diagnoses that progressed to hospitalizations were a scene that no one wanted to see. In a matter of days, they went from a couple enjoying each other to a couple fighting for life itself.

Their story is a marvelous odyssey about the power of prayer and the need for unfaltering faith. Their story is made rewarding because they express the highs and the lows of the journey, the FaceTime calls, and the alerts that things were not looking good. Yet, that indomitable faith in God kept them pressing, pleading, and believing. Tee came out of intensive care, and now is a witness to all that this can be beat.

Their story will open your eyes to the power of faith and the intensity of it that one needs in the time of crisis. This moment claimed every aspect of their lives. While Tee fought to live, Marcy fought to keep him alive and you will read about that and all it entailed as you chronicle with them through their journey.

As you read these pages, I do believe that you will come to understand what this virus is capable of doing and not doing. You will understand the unique struggles of African Americans in the health care system, and you will understand why we love the Lord our God. I know when the doors of the church open again, there will be two faces that I will see who will be thanking God for moving them from crisis to celebration.

–Bishop Walter S. Thomas

Bishop Walter S. Thomas has been pastor of the New Psalmist Baptist Church in Baltimore, Maryland since 1975. Under his leadership, the church body has grown from 200 to more than 7,000 active members. Bishop Thomas is also a highly regarded executive and personal coach, and Myers Briggs Practitioner, with over 30 years of experience leading workshops and seminars across the country, preparing church leaders, pastors, church staffs for their next level.

Bishop Thomas is known as the "Pastor's Pastor", he was the past President of the Hampton University Minister's Conference 1999-2002. He currently serves as the Presiding President of the Kingdom Association of Covenant pastors.

Disclaimer

The information, including opinions and analyses, contained herein is based on the author and co-author's personal experiences and is not intended to provide professional medical or spiritual advice. The author and the publisher make no warranties, either expressed or implied, concerning the accuracy, applicability, effectiveness, reliability, or suitability of the contents outside of the period of time in which the events occurred.

While it is our intention to offer enlightenment and inspiration, if you wish to apply or follow the same measures mentioned herein, you take full responsibility for your actions. The author and publisher of this book shall in no event be held liable for any direct, indirect, incidental, or consequential damages arising directly or indirectly from the use of any of the information contained in this book. All content is for information and inspiration only.

CONTENTS

Special Insight for Reader

For many of us, the term "pandemic" is a word that creates both intellectual and emotional distance. To be sure, we have all read about epidemics that have taken place in other countries. We think about widespread death in faraway third world nations. The news reports of extensive tragic death counts in places that suffer from the lack of sufficient science and health care are nothing new to us. But pandemic? A worldwide plague of disease and death in highly developed western civilizations? That reality is so far-fetched most of us readily dismiss the possibility.

Then COVID-19 happened. Suddenly, life changed for the entire planet. No corner of the globe was protected from this deadly pathogen. In the year 2020, we have seen untold members of humankind infected and seen unimaginable loss of life. As I write this, in the United States alone, we have seen over 30 million people infected and over 480 thousand people die in the U.S, alone. This book is the journey of one of those persons, Marcy Myles-Clark. It is a journey of understandable fear, but it is also a journey of unwavering faith in God.

I have known Marcy most of her adult life. Our paths crossed in the workplace. She was a bright, energetic young woman just a few years removed from college. Determined, enthusiastic, and sharp-witted, Marcy is just one of those people you naturally gravitate to. As a young lady among corporate veterans, Marcy is someone who became everyone's "little sister."

As the years went by, our journeys took us in separate directions. I eventually left corporate America as God called me to the ministry. I will never forget the day Marcy showed up at my church and introduced me to her new husband, Tee. They looked truly happy, and I thanked

God that they were linked together for this journey called life.

Then COVID-19 happened. Tee was infected and the grip of fear entered their lives. I became one of the many people that prayed for Marcy and Tee in 2020, and I watched the unshakeable faith in Marcy as she declared that God would get them through this. Surely enough, the healing power of God has answered Marcy's prayers, and this couple is a living testimony to be shared with the world.

Why did God allow Tee to survive this ordeal? I believe there is another Marcy and Tee out there that need to hear their story. This book will open up the day-to-day journey of a praying wife. A young woman who fought through this still ongoing pandemic with tears, and a circle of loved ones who stayed close to her in both presence and spirit.

But most of all, this is a story of someone who prayed that God would carry both she and her husband through the valley of the shadow of death. She prayed, God answered, and their journey through life as praying wife and healed husband continues to the glory of God.

We love you, Marcy and Tee.

– Rev. Brian Murray

Rev. Brian E. Murray, MA Theology, is a Doctoral Candidate and Senior Pastor of New Covenant Community United Church of Christ in Baltimore, Maryland. He is also Co-Chair of BRIDGE Maryland, Inc., a relationship building, organizing and intensive leadership development program to strengthen congregations and faith leaders for the advancement of justice.

Our Story Begins

Don't procrastinate. Read this now.

This coronavirus disease 2019 (COVID-19) that caused a pandemic in 2020, or any major illness for that matter, quickly and unbearably puts matters into perspective—in many ways. Take procrastination for example.

Studies by psychologists and other specialists have associated the characteristics of those who procrastinate with conditions such as low self-esteem, anxiety and neurological disorders such as ADHD. However, those who engage in it may simplify their habit of deferment as having too many items on their to-do list or perhaps just not feeling up to the task. Medical justification or not, there is nothing like a pandemic to bring urgency, not complacency, to every action you consider. Ask me how I know!

With this worldwide outbreak of COVID-19, urgency suddenly became the order of the day for everyone around the world. Can you imagine that? The entire world! Thanks to the speed of this virus' transmission, some patients have been going from being ok to feeling only a little sick, to being totally unable to breathe in the span of just a few hours. It's so baffling! Not to mention how overwhelmingly taxing this has been on physicians, nurses and other essential hospital personnel—to an extent never seen before in modern history.

In many cases, especially where the demand for proper equipment is not being met, these first responders are coming up with on-the-spot, critical therapeutic decision-making, on a larger scale than perhaps they were trained. In life, as we knew it before the pandemic emergency room personnel had time to delay (yes, procrastinate) seeing certain patients—those with lower-grade pain issues—while they attended to patients with more critical needs. Well, not anymore! Since COVID-19, everyone who is even allowed in the ER requires immediate attention.

Patients have been rushed into intensive care units with little, if any, time to say goodbye to loved ones. Those loved ones have had to spring into action with no plan whatsoever to prepare them for the next hours, let alone the next weeks and months.

Well, that's exactly how it happened for me and my husband, Theirrien (Tee). If you had told us six months earlier that our lives would be turned upside down following the occurrence of a few cold and flu like symptoms, we would've sent you on your way to get your head examined.

We were your typical, basically healthy, 47-year-old sales professional and 56-year-old law firm senior manager, fun-loving, suburban, empty-nester couple. Although we had demanding careers, we attempted to maintain balance between our work life, family life and, most importantly, our spiritual and meditative life. Not that either of us was a big procrastinator to begin with, but what this nasty virus has dictated to the world, and what it has certainly taught us personally, is that there is no time like the present to live your life to the fullest! That is, of course, without infringing on the lives and well-being of others.

In the following chapters, you'll learn what brought us from that life-changing day in March 2020 to our continuing health challenges of today. We've made miraculous strides, yet there are many steps ahead to be accomplished. That life-changing day I speak of was Monday, March 16, 2020, when we decided to go to the urgent care center called Patient First (PT First) in Columbia Maryland, not far from where we live. Both Tee and I had begun to feel sick a couple of days earlier with flu-like symptoms—nothing out of the ordinary. My symptoms remained pretty mild, sort of like a sinus infection, whereas Tee's symptoms worsened, accompanied by a persistent cough and fever over 101.

Once at PT First, they tested us for the flu and RSV. Both tests came back negative; however, given the circumstances of this new coronavirus outbreak, as well as Tee's symptoms, they referred us to neighboring Johns Hopkins Howard County General Hospital (JH-HCGH) for COVID-19 testing.

The following day, Tuesday, March 17, we both tested positive for the virus. Tee still had flu-like symptoms with a fever, accompanied by a cough, that got progressively worse throughout the week. We called Dr. Nyanjom, our adopted uncle and Tee's pulmonologist, who instructed us to go back to JH for a CT scan to make sure his lungs were OK. We did and that's where our miraculous story begins.

Finally, when that 46-day scare was behind us and I was able to breathe again, I wrote a letter to Dr. Sarkar, the doctor who headed up the team that helped save Tee's life. I'm not sure if Dr. Sarkar is, or was, ever a procrastinator, but I was very impressed with how quickly he responded to my letter. After all, this has been an extremely busy time for all medical staff, not to mention the simple fact that letter-writing usually gets pushed down on the bottom of my to-do list with so many other important things crowding it out.

As I mentioned before, I believe this pandemic made so many of us realize the importance of NOW. Dr. Sarkar knew how close Tee was to not pulling through. He knew that waiting to respond to us was not an option. Following are the letters Dr. Sarkar and I wrote to each other via email.

Part I

My email correspondence with Debjeet Sarkar, M.D., Attending Emergency Physician, Johns Hopkins Howard County General Hospital, Columbia, MD

FIRST EMAIL FROM MARCY TO DR. SARKAR

—– Sent: Fri, Jul 3, 2020 10:34 am

Subject: GRATEFUL HEARTFELT THANKS FOR YOUR LIFESAVING MEASURES @ JH HCGH ER-T CLARK FAMILY

Dr. Sarkar,

On Friday 3/21 at approximately 7:00 PM, my husband Theirrien (aka Tee) Clark was admitted into the ER at Johns Hopkins HCGH per Dr. Nyanjom's instructions for what we believed to be a "Diagnostic CT scan of the lung". Dr. Nyanjom firmly ordered me to bring Tee to the ER after several days of persistent coughing, as a result of COVID-19. I was unable to accompany him into the ER because I was also recently diagnosed with COVID-19, so I dropped him off at the front door of the ER where your nurses met us outside, they had been previously notified by Dr. Nyanjom that we would be coming within the hour, and they were expecting us. I would like to point out that my husband and I were in the first 5 COVID-19 patients diagnosed in Howard county, so this was very new and scary to all of us! I can only imagine how many lives you've saved before and after us (both COVID-19 and Non-COVID-19) ...

We would later find out that apparently once my husband got inside you decided not to wait for the time that it would take to prep him (Due to his COVID-19 diagnosis) for a CT scan, and you opted to do a chest x ray which would be enough to determine that he was in acute lung failure. You made the quick decision to do an emergency Intubation and admit him into the ICU which ended up saving his life that day! You delivered this information to me over the phone while I was sitting in the parking lot waiting for my husband to return, after what we thought would be a quick diagnosis and discharge. This chain of events would be the beginning of a traumatic 46-day hospital stay at Johns Hopkins Main hospital (in Baltimore, MD), including 28 days on the ventilator.

We were extremely GRATEFUL and delighted with the quality of treatment and medical care that Tee received during this time, starting with Dr. Nyanjom's assistance in getting us into the ER, the ER nurse's ability to quickly triage him professionally and effortlessly, and of course your quick diagnosis and decision to immediately intubate him.

It has been a little more than 3 months since the day that you admitted him into the ICU, and we are overjoyed to report that my husband is ALIVE, WELL and RESTORING WONDERFULLY! Dr. Nyanjom has been a long-time physician turned friend/adopted uncle and he has contributed to saving my husband's life for the second time in 5 years. We first encountered him back in 12/2015 when he helped to save my husband's life as he battled a severe case of Pneumonia, there at HCGH. He has been a God send to us, and we can't thank him enough!!

I also wanted to let you know how highly your staff thinks of you. I remember talking to a few of your nurses that evening, who continued to sing your praises, telling me how Tee was in the hands of one of the best ER Doctors around. At that time, I didn't know just how true this was! We also wanted to let you know just how much we appreciate all that you've done for us as well. Tee is an amazing, husband, father, son, nephew, boss, colleague, etc. He is loved by many, and we couldn't imagine life without him. Words cannot express how Thankful and Grateful we are to God for putting you, Dr. Nyanjom, and all of the JH-HCGH and main campus HCP's into our lives to care for him, during his time of dire need. The Clark family is "Team Hopkins", and we can't Thank and Praise you'll enough both privately and publicly. WE have and we will continue to do so, whenever possible. It is important that people know the value of your service. May God continue to Bless and keep you and use you as a vessel to help and save lives, as you'll have done for us.

Lastly, on a personal note we have two grown kids (24, 34) and (2) 7-year-old twin grandboys. I'm attaching a few family pictures including. Marcy and Tee cute older couple, old pic of Tee and the grandboys, our son and daughter-looking like young models to further solidify our appreciation for your efforts in saving this Amazing Family man's life. Blessings, to you and yours!

Gratefully,

Marcy and Tee Clark

FIRST RESPONSE FROM DR. SARKAR TO MARCY

—- Sent: Sat, Jul 4, 2020 2:34

Subject: Re: GRATEFUL HEARTFELT THANKS FOR YOUR LIFE-SAVING MEASURES @ JH HCGH ER-T CLARK FAMILY

Dear Mr. Clark and Clark Family,

Thank you for such a heartwarming email and the beautiful photos—what a lovely family! I read the email mid-shift tonight and was welling up with tears.

I am cc'ing two of the ER nurses that helped saved your life—Sean and Kelly. Doctors are nothing without nurses. I know I am leaving out others that were involved that shift, for sure.

I'm also very grateful to have Dr. Nyanjom on staff here. Howard County has been lucky to have his skill and compassion for so many years. He is a role model and mentor to the physicians and beloved by all his patients and our staff.

I am ecstatic you are doing so well, sir! I followed your care daily via our medical records system from 20-Mar to 17-Apr when the breathing tube was removed. I was not sure what direction your care would go, and both the ICU doctor and I knew we needed to get you to Johns Hopkins by the next day.

I am an Army Veteran of Iraq and Afghanistan and my time overseas in combat taught me how precious small moments in life can be. Speaking with Marcy for even just a few minutes gave the team the confidence and comfort to know we were proceeding with the right steps. After that conversation, I made it a priority to use Zoom, Bluetooth headsets and iPads to improve on how we communicate with patients and families in the pandemic.

I know the road ahead is long, but you being alive and beating this virus is a testament to your individual strength, the power of collective strength and love and the ability of the human body and spirit to overcome even the longest of odds.

Please keep in touch and let me know if there is anything we can do to help. Thank you for sending this note!

Please remain safe and in good health. V/r,

Debjeet

SECOND EMAIL FROM MARCY TO DR. SARKAR

—- Sent: Sat, July 4, 2020

Subject: Re: GRATEFUL HEARTFELT THANKS FOR YOUR LIFE-SAVING MEASURES @ JH HCGH ER-T CLARK FAMILY

Dr. Sarkar,

Thanks for reading and acknowledging my email. I definitely remember Kelly; I spoke to her quite a bit during the first night. She was the one who told me that Tee was in the hands of one of the best ER Docs. Special thanks to her and Sean for their assistance as well!

SECOND RESPONSE FROM DR. SARKAR TO MARCY

(Marcy's comments are in *Italics* Font & Bold)

—- Sent: Sat, Jul 4, 2020 2:34 am

Subject: Re: GRATEFUL HEARTFELT THANKS FOR YOUR LIFE-SAVING MEASURES @ JH HCGH ER-T CLARK FAMILY

Dear Mr. Clark and Clark Family,

Thank you for such a heartwarming email and the beautiful photos—what a lovely family! I read the email mid-shift tonight and was welling up with tears.

I am cc'ing two of the ER nurses that helped saved your life—Sean and Kelly. Doctors are nothing without nurses. I know I am leaving out others that were involved that shift, for sure.

For sure and we Thank them ALL!! BTW, I am a 20+ yrs. veteran Pharmaceutical Sales Rep and I've also been a patient, caregiver etc. I PERSONALLY LOVE NURSES and highly respect the profession!

They should get an automatic entry into heaven.

I'm also very grateful to have Dr. Nyanjom on staff here. Howard County has been lucky to have his skill and compassion for so many years. He is a role model and mentor to the physicians and beloved by all his patients and our staff.

Yes, he is A-M-A-Z-I-N-G! He's our adopted uncle.

I am ecstatic you are doing so well, sir! I followed your care daily via our medical records system from 20-Mar to 17-Apr when the breathing tube was removed. I was not sure what direction your care would go, and both the ICU doctor and I knew we needed to get you to Johns Hopkins by the next day.

That is so GREAT, WE are so grateful that you had this insight!

I know that you treat many patients, and I wasn't even sure if you would remember him, I truly didn't expect you to follow him! I know Dr. Ny did the same, but again he's our Uncle. THANK YOU!!

I am an Army Veteran of Iraq and Afghanistan and my time overseas in combat taught me how precious small moments in life can be. Speaking with Marcy for even just a few minutes gave the team the confidence and comfort to know we were proceeding with the right steps. After that conversation, I made it a priority to use Zoom, Bluetooth headsets and iPads to improve on how we communicate with patients and families in the pandemic.

That was one of the most traumatic and helpless moments of my life-to get that devastating unexpected news and not be able to communicate or visit. I had faith in you and God, that you were doing the right thing for him, and I remember telling you how valuable Tee's life was to us, and to do whatever you needed to do keep him alive, and you did. To God Be the Glory! You are Amazing, and you will continue to be Blessed.

I know the road ahead is long, but you being alive and beating this virus is a testament to your individual strength, the power of collective strength and love and the ability of the human body and spirit to overcome even the longest of odds.

WOW DOC, THIS IS WONDERFUL! We are writing a book along these lines and you'll will definitely be inclusive. We have also begun to give local interviews and we will most likely be giving national interviews in the coming weeks and months. We will continue to Give Thanks to the JH family whenever we have a chance. We may not be able to always mention you by name, but please know how much we appreciate you and your staff!

Please keep in touch and let me know if there is anything we can do to help.

For sure, and please feel free to pass this along to your higher ups, whomever needs to know about the good work that you'll are doing!

Thank you for sending this note! Please remain safe and in good health.

V/r,

Debjeet

Part II

My journal entries and intimate thoughts, along with a firsthand account of matters from Tee's perspective

I've always found writing to be therapeutic, which is why I've kept a journal for many years. Writing has also been the best outlet for me to communicate my innermost thoughts with others from time to time, and with God all the time.

Naturally, I journaled throughout this ordeal since it was one of the toughest periods in recent years. Later, as I received numerous requests to share the details of Tee's miraculous recovery, it made perfect sense to transform my journal notes into a book. I pray that these moment-by-moment notes let you see—if only at a glimpse—just how horrifying this Coronavirus is, changing one's condition from good to critical in the blink of an eye. But most importantly, I pray my notes of triumph allow you to learn or confirm just how mighty and truly amazing our God is when you pray and believe.

Chapter 1

A Parable About Life (GOD speaks victory to me)

What is a parable? A parable is a simple story used to illustrate a moral or spiritual lesson as told by Jesus, in the Gospels. I hope you understand the significance of this parable about OUR Life:

We were at the beach on a nice sunny day (Enjoying Life). We both got into the water together and a storm came over us and a huge wave came in and tried to overtake us (COVID-19). We got separated (Marcy on the outside and Tee on the inside of the hospital). I was safely able to make it back to the shore (Healed). Tee was still out there in the ocean clinging for life (Tee's fight for his life). I couldn't see him or hear him, but I knew he was in imminent danger (Tee in peril on the ventilator in the ICU).

I know that my life partner is in trouble, but I cannot physically help him, so what do I do? Do I stand there and hope, cry or wish for the best? Or do I go to the Lifeguard (God), the one who's certified in lifesaving with a proven track record, and tools and resources to help, who's knowingly helped save so many before us? Naturally, the answer for us was, and always is, GOD.

I graciously asked the Lifeguard (GOD) to save my husband. He told me that HE was using us because we were the glue between a lot of people, and he needed us to bring each other closer to ourselves and ultimately closer to HIM through this experience. God told me that I needed to be faithful, obedient, and prayerful, as if our lives depended on it.

HE told me that HE would see Tee through, however there were a few things that he needed me to do in the meantime (test of faith and obedience). HE told me that I needed to get a few close friends and family members (some who did and didn't know Him), and to pray for Tee's safe journey back to shore (arrange a prayer group of faithful family and friends to unite in collective prayer), and I did (formation of the TC prayer warriors, a group of 100+ national and international praying angels). God told me that if we united in prayer and believed in his healing power that Tee would be safely rescued and brought back to shore unscathed (healed). He told me that once Tee was brought back to shore, everybody on the shore who prayed and witnessed this miraculous rescue (friends and family, believers and non-believers) would know that it was our prayers and faith that brought Tee through.

So, after 28 days of praying, God sent out a life raft and freed Tee from the waters that could've taken his life (removed from the ventilator). He pointed the life raft toward the shore and sent him on the scenic route (journey through various floors) post ICU, at Johns Hopkins (JH) back to the shore. While on the scenic route Tee would be able to become mentally, physically and emotionally (various therapies) restored from being in the water for so long.

Finally, 19 days after being freed from the waters (removed from the ventilator) and being reconditioned (therapies) in preparation for his arrival, Tee arrived safely back to shore (made it out of the hospital and back home). His friends and family greeted him on the shorelines with lots of love and excitement. They were overjoyed to see him after 46-plus days, knowing that it was only by God's grace that he made it back safely and unscathed. To God be the Amazing Glory for doing what He said He would do!

Chapter 2

THE EMERGENCY ROOM

Our unsuspecting trip to the ER

As we left the house late on that brisk March afternoon, my husband spoke in a weak and barely audible voice. I could hear the trepidation in each word, which was truly uncharacteristic for this typically confident and strong man. "What are they going to do to me?" He and I both knew it was a rhetorical question. No answers could possibly come from me, as we faced the possibility of a seriously unfamiliar virus that confounded the entire world. No, all I could offer in response was a positive word of encouragement to ease his fear. Wait, who am I kidding? To ease BOTH our fears. Because while I was not experiencing the physical discomfort in *my* body that Tee had been dealing with all week long in his, I *was* feeling his pain in my spirit. We were in this together as we vowed to be—in sickness and in health. Up to that point, we had enjoyed nine and a half years of bliss: good health, good fortune and lots of fun. But now, along came the sickness.

I knew better than to ask God: "Why?" "Why Tee?" "Why us?" But just because I knew better doesn't mean that question didn't creep up in my mind a time or two during that week, especially when seeing Tee clutch his chest in agony each time he coughed or sneezed.

How could I answer Tee's question when I was fielding hundreds of my own? All remaining unanswered, mind you. Nevertheless, I summoned my best reassuring tone and told him they were just routinely following up with him to make sure his lungs were OK. I followed that assumption with another one: that he would be fine.

Another tablespoon of cough medicine to suppress Tee's cough and we were on our way to Johns Hopkins Howard County General Hospital (JH-HCGH) in Columbia, MD. I looked back uneasily at the lowering garage door as we pulled away. Would this be the last time we leave the house together for a long time? Or at all? I quickly dismissed those horrible thoughts conjured up, no doubt, by all those crazy medical news reports flooding the media. No one knew anything for certain, yet every time you turned away there was "breaking news" giving more speculative information, instilling deeper and deeper fear in the millions plugged in to get the latest.

I forced myself to remain calm and optimistic, telling myself he didn't have a fever anymore, a symptom that concerned the experts. So, he's not as bad off. We're just going to get a quick CT scan and be back home to battle this virus together for the coming days until it passed. Tee slept peacefully all the way to the hospital, while I fed my spirit with good worship music like "Jesus Is My Help" by Hezekiah Walker. I also prayed and rubbed Tee's leg the entire time, finally feeling a sense of extreme peace.

An ER visit turned unimaginable

When we arrived at the ER, a nurse met me at the curb saying she was waiting on us. I thought, "Yes, we're off to a GREAT start. No ER drama, so everything is going to be fine."

I couldn't go inside, as they weren't letting anyone other than patients in—especially not me with a recent COVID-19 positive diagnosis. As the nurse and I helped Tee out of the car, he realized he didn't have his phone charger with him. I promised him I would get him a charger if he ended up being longer than planned. I kissed him, told him I loved him and reassured him he would be OK. I watched them put him in a wheelchair and wheel him toward the ER entrance. I climbed back into my car to head to the parking lot. I glanced back and noticed they were taking his vitals at the entrance. So, I looped back around and asked the nurse if he had a fever. She said, "No, he's normal."

I thought to myself, "Great, still no fever, we are good!" Driving off, I looked back one last time and took note of the back of Tee's head and his gray and orange sweatsuit. That last image replayed in my mind over and over in the weeks to follow.

I sat in the car for about 45 minutes without hearing from anyone. Finally, I dialed Tee's cellphone and he didn't answer. He called me back about five minutes later and put the ER doctor on the phone (the heroic, angelic, incomparable Dr. Sarkar, whom I introduced you to earlier).

"Things are a lot worse than we envisioned here," Dr. Sarkar began. "We are going to have to do an emergency intubation, and we need your permission." My mind rapidly grappled with that information to formulate a suitable response. Emotion took over as I spewed sentiments of how special Tee was to me and how he had so much to live for. Through a teary and shaky voice, I gave permission—no, it was more of a command—for Dr. Sarkar to do whatever he and his team needed to do to save Tee's life!

Next, I begged him to let me in to see my husband. "Please, I will wear whatever you need me to." Dr. Sarkar's chilling but truthful words struck as a reality check to me regarding the severity of the coronavirus in those early stages of the pandemic: "I can't let you do that; you will contaminate my whole staff."

They handed the phone back to Tee and I spoke to him briefly. His slurred speech indicated he was succumbing to his pre-intubation sedation. I told him I love him and that he was going to be OK. I assured him he was in God's hands.

That would be the last time Tee and I would speak for more than a month. With all the peaks and valleys, and trials and testimonies that were about to take place, that one month felt more like a year.

WTH just happened?

I sat in the parking lot feeling like I had just gotten dragged to the ground and kicked in the head again and again while still down. My thoughts were racing. There were so many mixed emotions to contend with. I was scared, alone, confused, shocked. I couldn't believe what was happening.

Was my husband going to die? Was *I* going to get sicker? Was this the beginning of the end for us after just nine and a half short years together?

The past week flashed before me, as I pondered how it all happened. Why us? HOW DID WE GET HERE?? My body felt numb. All I knew to do was pray—so I prayed. Next, I cried. My brain felt numb as well.

Several minutes into my pity party I realized I didn't have time for that. My husband was in the fight of his life and I had to notify family, as well as solicit as many immediate prayers as possible. I sent out a few texts and made some urgent calls. The first person I called was our cousin Lawanda, a native of Prince George's County, who lives in Howard County. She was at the hospital in a flash. I just needed someone to intervene and be a presence for us during this time. I thought she may have a better chance of getting inside the ER in my place since she was presumably COVID-19-free.

Lawanda has also battled her own share of health problems, so upon her quick arrival I had to make sure she was in a healthy state, with a mask. She immediately stepped up and went into the ER. She wasn't allowed to see Tee, but she was able to talk to Kelly (the ER nurse extraordinaire who works with Dr. Sarkar), and gather relevant contact info for me. Nurse Kelly later became my point of contact and new BFF for the next few hours while Tee was in the ER. I'm still extremely grateful to both Kelly and Lawanda for their assistance during this time.

The phone calls and texts poured in as word spread. I ended up talking to our niece, Minister Danielle Perry, who sprang into action with a MIGHTY prayer that gave me just the strength I needed at that time! I am forever grateful to God for sending her when He did.

Finally, I mustered up the strength to take the long, dark drive home alone. I had to pee profusely, and no one was allowing entry into their establishment to use the bathroom. After two unsuccessful attempts to find a bathroom, my overtaxed bladder could no longer wait, so I drove to a long, dark back road in Clarksville (Ten Oaks Road) and relieved myself physically and spiritually, just letting everything go that just tried to overtake me. How refreshing!

Normally, I would've been too afraid to do that, but given my current state of mind, I had NO FEAR! God guided me peacefully and safely up the dark roads. I talked to my Aunt Marilyn most of the way home and fielded several other calls, as well. I stopped for gas and took my time, as I was in no hurry to face my new possible reality of being "Home Alone" indefinitely. Finally, a little more than an hour and a half after leaving the hospital, I pulled up to our peaceful sanctuary we built together, realizing that for the first time in our 10 years together, I was thrust into solitude, bracing myself for the unknown.

I couldn't help but think, is this how Kobe Bryant's widow, Vanessa Bryant, felt each time she entered her home now void of the love of her life? The day before the death of her 13-year-old daughter, Gigi, and beloved basketball superstar, she lived a life of envy, one that would cause any woman to want to walk in her shoes. Then, news broke of that horrible helicopter crash and nobody wanted to be her and walk through those moments of tragedy.

Negative thoughts now flooded my mind. Was Tee going to die? Was I also going to be a young widow like Vanessa with such an abrupt loss of my husband? Lord, please say it isn't so. Please God, not my Boopy! We're just getting started, we still have so much left to do!

Transition to Johns Hopkins Main Hospital-Baltimore (JH)

JH-HCGH kept Tee in the ER for a number of hours that night, until he eventually got a bed in its ICU. I was notified in the morning that the medical staff wanted to transfer him to JH's main hospital in Baltimore that afternoon with my consent. They had established a central ICU unit for COVID-19 patients downtown at the main hospital. I knew this was the best thing for him, but there were so many unknowns. He would be in a huge and strange institution without Dr. Nyanjom's immediate care. I had called on JH as a pharmaceutical rep, but I didn't know anything more about them than what I needed to know for my job. I certainly didn't know its staff personally. Furthermore, I was extremely nervous about his transport because he was so fragile, and patients can die during transport. JH assured me he would be safely and professionally transported, and that his transfer was necessary for the best care for him during this time! A period of time that would end up being 46 days!

The hospital did an amazing job keeping me abreast of his condition and pre-transfer details. I was inclined to follow the ambulance from Howard County (Columbia) to Baltimore, but decided I didn't need the unnecessary stress, nor did they need my assistance. This was a LET GO, LET GOD moment and boy, have I had quite a few of those lately!

Before Tee's arrival, I received a call from the nurse at JH. I had to give consents for ports and PICC lines to be used for life-saving measures. I had my smart sister friend Marisa (Risa), who is also a nurse, conferenced in to help me make these crucial decisions. She assured me these were good proactive signs of good medicine, which significantly helped relieve some of my concerns. I was forever grateful for Risa's help during this time. I had so many mixed emotions, and I really wanted to make sure I was doing the right things. JH confirmed Tee's arrival around 2:00 PM and Dr. Nyanjom confirmed it with me as well. There, Tee began the next phase of his journey.

There are so many unknowns about COVID-19, especially at the beginning stages, but what I *do* know, and have never doubted is that "My God is in Control." I'M BELIEVING IN FAITH THAT HE'LL SEE US THROUGH THIS!

Wednesday 3/18 @ 5:00 AM (First journal entry)

OMG! What a week! This is definitely one for the records! Tee started feeling bad Friday night, March 13. He got progressively worse with severe fatigue, cough and fever over the weekend. By Saturday afternoon, he had a persistent fever in the 99-100-degree range. I nursed his fever and cough all weekend with Tylenol, cough syrup, etc., and we invested in an expensive head scanning thermometer that we ended up breaking from excessive usage. I told him over the weekend if his fever reached 101 degrees, we would go to the urgent care center.

Meantime, we were both fatigued, which is not unusual after a long workweek. I felt nasal discomfort similar to a sinus infection. By Monday morning, his fever reached 101 degrees, so we headed to Patient First in Columbia (PT-First). It was déjà vu from December 2015: this was the same care facility that diagnosed Tee with severe pneumonia when he ended up in the hospital for four days after our trip from Mexico (which is another story entirely).

We arrived at approximately 8:30 AM, as I wanted to be there bright and early. We had on our masks and gloves, and they were extremely grateful for this. They tested us both for flu, strep and RSV. We were negative for all three, however they were suspicious of Tee's symptoms, so they (thankfully and intuitively) referred us to JH-HCGH for COVID-19 testing.

When we arrived at JH-HCGH, they treated us like aliens and quarantined us in a room in the back of the ER for over an hour before they came in with their hazmat space-looking suits on. They gave us both painful nasal pharyngeal swabs (I know about this from selling a rapid Flu & RSV test previously) and sent it out to their lab. I asked to go to the bathroom, and I was told "I'd rather you wait until you get home." *"How nice,"* I sarcastically thought.

We were told to quarantine until we got our results within the week. We got negative flu and RSV results on Monday night and Tee's positive COVID-19 results Tuesday morning via JH electronic medical records. I got my results Tuesday afternoon. We were both positive for COVID-19! Interestingly enough, we saw the numbers go from two to five new cases in Howard County on the news that afternoon, and we knew we were a part of those numbers. I figured the sickly-looking man getting tested behind us in the ER was one of those numbers as well.

Tee was really bummed by his results. I was kind of relieved in a weird way because I knew something was wrong with him because of his severe cough, his fever and flu-like symptoms. He was obviously sick, so I was eager to find out what was going on so we could deal with it accordingly. I had a feeling that Tee was COVID-19-positive, but I prayed otherwise.

In all seriousness, I wasn't afraid of COVID-19 because God had already delivered me from more challenging trials in my life. I figured once we could identify the devil, we would know how to fight it. I was, however, surprised when I got my "RNA Detected" positive results because I didn't feel sick. I now know it's almost impossible for one spouse to get COVID-19 without the other having it, since we share life so closely. When I shared my results with Tee, he wasn't as surprised that I was also COVID-19-positive. I told him I had good news and bad news and he gave me an irritated glare. "What? Just tell me!"

I disclosed, "OK, the bad news is that I am also positive, the good news is that we're in this together and we'll get through it." He didn't seem impressed. Instead, he was really looking and feeling awful. We had decided earlier in the week we were going to get through this week quietly without sounding the alarm unnecessarily to family and friends at that time.

I've been OK and trying to keep it that way with supplements, rest, gargling, mask, etc. I am also trying to keep my mind right by refraining from hysteria and CV reports, and more focus on getting helpful information. I'm resuming my work schedule as much as possible as a welcome distraction to keep from focusing on our current reality. We finally decided to notify Tee's family as well as church friends, and a few other close friends. We figured we may as well let some folks know; no need to carry this burden alone. After all, the most important thing we need is prayers for healing. There is power in numbers!

Sunday 3/22 @ 5:52 AM

OMG, a lot has happened over the last week. I've been fine, with no noteworthy issues after being diagnosed with COVID-19 last Tuesday, March 17. I worked Tuesday, Wednesday, Thursday in a virtual training class, but I had to take off Friday. Tee was feeling bad and I couldn't focus on anything else but him. He had a bad cough and a fever; I had been nursing his fever and cough all week, but his cough was terrible. Tuesday, I got a prescription for an antibiotic and some cough medicine with codeine to give him some relief so he could sleep.

Dr. Nyanjom (our adopted uncle and pulmonologist who helped to save Tee's life in December 2015 when he was hospitalized with severe pneumonia) told me to consider finding an outpatient imaging center that would service a COVID-19-positive patient, or to bring him into the ER for a lung CT scan if things continued to persist. I expressed our reluctance to encounter the ER again after our testing experience last week, and Dr. Nyanjom told me to call him beforehand if we chose to come into the ER.

Tuesday and Wednesday were rough; by Thursday he seemed to be feeling better and asked me to get him Chick-fil-A, always a good sign when my fat boy (mutual term of endearment) wants to eat. Thursday, we toughed it out; he ate better, but he was still battling intermittent coughing and sleep deprivation. He would spend hours sleeping on the toilet and sleeping upright on the ironing board. In fact, leaning on that ironing board became his favorite position.

I couldn't understand this at the time. It scared me because I know family members who perished on the toilet after a heart attack, so I constantly badgered him all week to get into the bed, but he would find solace in those two positions. Later, I would come to understand that the upright position aids in breathing when patients are in respiratory distress.

Also, on Wednesday and Thursday, I had reached out to a few outpatient imaging centers, but they fearfully declined taking in a COVID-19-positive patient. By Friday it became painfully obvious that we were going to have to go to the ER at some point for further observation. Friday morning Tee's fever had broken but he still had the lingering cough. His cough was so bad I could hear it playing over and over in my mind for days after he left the house. The weekend was approaching with no relief in sight. My intuition told me we could not let this linger over the weekend; we needed to address it TODAY!

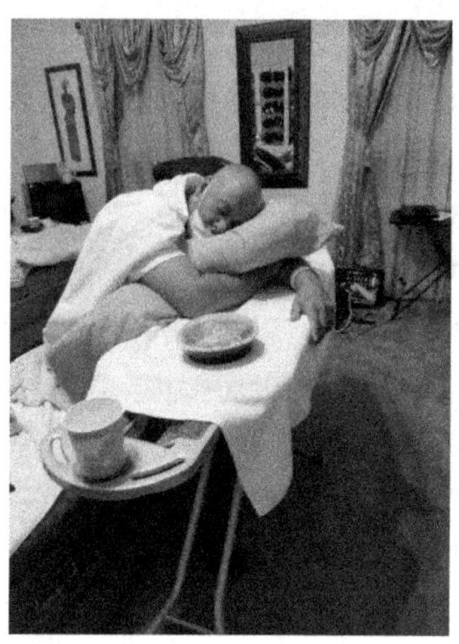

Tee on Thursday 3/18/20, in a position that brought him relief.

I decided to take Dr. Nyanjom's advice and arrange going to the hospital today. I reached out to Dr. Nyanjom earlier in the day, but we didn't connect until late afternoon around 5:00 PM, at which time I gave him the update. He spoke pointedly, "People are dying by waiting too long. You need to get Tee to the ER immediately!" He asked me how quickly I could get there and told me that he would call ahead and notify the staff that we were coming. I told him we would be there within the hour and we arrived at 5:55 PM, just under an hour.

Chapter 3

HEAVEN HELP US NOW

There were so many things going through my mind during this time. It helped that I stayed busy. I continued to work virtually while also trying to maintain a healthy mental, physical and spiritual balance. I would continue to journal whenever time allowed throughout this journey. I also kept a binder full of detailed records of Tee's daily progress notes. These progress notes started on Tuesday, March 24, after his Friday, March 20 admittance to Johns Hopkins Howard County General Hospital (JH-HCGH), including the Saturday March 21, transfer to Johns Hopkins (JH) main hospital in Baltimore.

Once he was situated at JH, I would call in daily (five to six times a day) always tracking his fever, physical position (*i.e.,* prone on his stomach), oxygen saturation levels/oxygen pressure (aka PEEP), and other vital signs, etc. I called whenever relevant and whenever possible.

What I am sharing here corresponds with daily progress notes that I kept (see Part III) illustrating the roller coaster of clinical and physical changes from March 24 throughout the entire 28-day journey on the ventilator. Who knew that I would be tracking the unveiling of a living miracle or creating a platform for this book at that time? I was simply trying to stay organized and sane. Once again, God had another plan!

In addition to journaling and keeping progress notes during this journey, I also sent out a myriad of daily texts to our friends and family who became our prayer warriors during this time. I am sharing some of these communications with you as well (also in Part III).

Monday 3/23 @ 6:12 AM

Saturday was tough. Tee had on-and-off fevers. Marisa talked with me and the nurses and doctors to further assess their plan of action and to ensure he was getting the right care. I had a good day on Sunday, as good as it could be without my Boopy. I did virtual church, listened to some Fred Hammond music, read scripture and fielded a bunch of texts and phone calls.

The word is still getting out about our situation and inquiring minds want to know things. I also spoke to my sister in Christ, Marie Therese, whom I affectionately refer to as my personal chaplain. Marie has a major anointing and always knows how and when to deliver a mighty prayer!

Aunt Barbara Ann's famous homemade soup

I ended up meeting Big Sister Dee Dee Sunday afternoon to get some homemade soup from her that Aunt Barbara Ann made for me. When I picked up the soup, Dee Dee kept raving about how good the soup smelled, and I couldn't smell it at all. I didn't think anything of it, but I cataloged this in the back of my mind. When I got home, I devoured that soup even though I didn't have much of an appetite for anything. I certainly didn't feel like cooking. While I couldn't smell what I was eating, I surely could taste it! It was delicious with meat and real veggies (including corn, greens, etc.). I'm so grateful to Aunt Barbara Ann's homemade soup. I lived off that soup and her amazing seafood gumbo for days and even weeks!

I drove around and looked at some houses so that I could breathe in some fresh air. I called and checked on Tee afterward. He was requiring less oxygen and had no fever, praise God! I also got a personal call from Bishop Thomas. He was really surprised and intrigued by our story. He had a lot of questions about our situation, like where we sat in our last church service. He then gave words of inspiration and prayer. I was overjoyed. I know that Bishop is TRULY anointed, and his prayers coupled with Marie's, my own prayers and those of everyone else who's been praying for us just really helped my spirit.

I decided sometime on Saturday that Tee was healed, and that I was rebuking COVID-19 in the name of Jesus, because it couldn't take him! I commanded No more negative thoughts, as I prepared for his progress and looked forward to seeing him soon, when he was on the healed side of all this!

I had a thought later after speaking to Bishop Thomas, since he was quite interested in where we sat during our last in-person church visit on March 8. We sat in the balcony in a row by ourselves. We had begun social distancing, spreading out and not touching during this service, as COVID-19 was just becoming mainstream, so we didn't have direct contact with anyone, but none of us were wearing masks either back then.

In hindsight, I vividly remember a woman sitting behind us harboring an ugly cough. Tee and I gave each other a look that clearly signified our disgust. UGH! Later, after Tee's ordeal, he also recalled this episode and told me she actually sprayed his neck with droplets from her cough. (Why didn't he tell me that right then and there so we could we have sanitized ourselves to keep from getting sick?) Thinking about all this now is, as my dad would say, a Monday morning quarterback moment (hindsight is 2020).

Could that woman have been one of many possible sources of our COVID-19 infection? There are just so many unanswered questions. Unfortunately, we will never know. If she was infected, we're sure she didn't know it, nor did she know she was spreading it. Prayerfully, she fared well! This is the reason it is so important for people to abide by all Centers for Disease Control (CDC) guidelines that we NOW know and have to help protect us—guidelines we didn't have back then!

So many people have called and prayed with and for us. Jon and Kristi Gray, Chris Seymour, our friends in Aruba, Glenda and her church folks, colleagues, family, friends.... Just a magnitude of prayers going out and up. I'm feeling confident that this is a test—just part of my testimony—and that we're going to be OK.

I've been sleeping in my spare bedroom; it's too painful to go into our bedroom without Tee. Our bedroom is just as he left it and will remain that way until it's time for him to come home. I keep hearing him coughing and seeing him sickly, the way he was right before we left for the hospital. I was feeling vulnerable about being home alone in this big empty house, so I safely moved my firearm into the spare bedroom with me.

Using Facetime, I got a gun refresher crash course from my little brother, Kyle, who's a professional weapons instructor (among other things). I feel so much safer knowing I'm protected by JAS (Jesus Christ, ADT, and Smith & Wesson). Neither my Earthly nor Heavenly fathers have given me the spirit of fear! THANK GOD FOR THAT!

Tuesday 3/24 @ 10:39 PM

I felt as though I was getting sick earlier but I'm fine now, just tired. I'm planning to ease back into work tomorrow. Tee's been stable today. I started off with scripture, then this song, "Power Belongs to God," by Hezekiah Walker. That helped to start my day off right, to keep my mind and spirits in the right place.

I had lots of calls and text messages all day. I spoke to the nurse, and she put me on the phone to talk to Tee through speaker phone. I prayed, offered words of encouragement and sent him my love. I prayed that he could hear me and that he is not scared inside.

This is so hard! I just keep thinking positively, trying to think ahead. I miss him so much; at night, it seems like he should be coming in at any minute after a long day's work and commute. I conferenced our daughter Kaelyn in today with the doc so she could get her questions answered and it went well. There have been lots of prayers and words of encouragement sent to me.

I joined Bishop's prayer call at 7:00 PM and invited a bunch of people. All that transpired was relevant and timely, indeed! People are scared and searching for answers. Prayerfully, we'll all get closer to God during this time and not depart when things improve.

I participated in a virtual investor training, as a welcomed distraction, giving me something to look forward to. Once things calm down, I can revisit my real estate business, but for right now I'm praying for mine and Boopy's healing. Everything else is secondary and doesn't matter!

Wednesday 3/25 @ 7:05 AM

I'm trying to establish a morning routine that includes waking up by 5:00 AM; engaging in prayer, music scripture, a TC status check-in call before 5:30 AM (and before the shift change); and then sending out daily AM/PM text updates. Tee held his own overnight, and I'm remaining faithful. I have great comfort in knowing that he's in God's hands. I've plead the blood of Christ on him; therefore, I know he's covered!

Friday 3/27 @ 5:55 AM

In a group text to my prayer warriors, I shared that one of Tee's nurses was nice enough to let me speak through speakerphone again this morning. I said a mighty prayer for his continued healing and for the minds and hands who are treating him, and she appreciated it!

Remember, Tee was still heavily sedated; yet I prayed he could hear me speak and that he was feeling the power of all our prayers!

Soon after, I got confirmation of answered prayer. I had called right back to ask the nurse something else, and she was still in Tee's room. She put me on speaker a second time and I spoke to him again. She told me Tee began to cough twice when he heard my voice!! I could just scream; I know GOD'S hand is on this situation. He's working for our benefit from the inside out!!

Monday 3/30 @ 5:00 AM

God told me to get closer to Tee, so I drove down to JH yesterday around 4:30 PM. I sat outside Tee's building and read scripture and prayed for him. Of course, I know God's prompting could have also meant "get closer emotionally and spiritually to Tee." Well, this whole situation is taking care of that, so I interpreted God's message as "get closer *physically*." Therefore, I hopped into my car and went and, boy, am I glad I did. It helped me visualize where he was and to learn where to pick him up when this whole ordeal completed itself and he was ready to come home.

The word from the nurses was he was doing well, still holding his own, His fevers had been pretty low, and some of his meds had been decreased or discontinued altogether, including the Vecuronium paralytic. Praise the Lord!

They were rotating him on and off his back to aid with his breathing. His breathing levels continued to fluctuate, sometimes forcing him to need as much as 90-100% oxygen from the machine, then back down to 70-80% a few hours later. We prayed that he stabilized so he can start requiring less of the machine, and more of his own oxygen, as his lungs rejuvenate.

I remember praying for my God-mom, Polly, to come off a ventilator before we left for our wedding in Aruba in 2015, and she did. My prayers were the same for Tee. We prayed specifically for him to be off the ventilator by April 6, in one week, or shortly thereafter—God willing!

Monday 3/30 @ 11:22 AM

I experienced a hectic past 48 hours. Lots of phone calls, paying bills, organizing our personal and business affairs and such. All of that was a job in and of itself. Frankly, I needed a personal assistant to help keep all the balls juggling in the air!

On the other hand, Tee's been rather stable, his vitals normal. No fever but his oxygen levels still fluctuated some. He had been on 100% support most times and other times as low as 80%.

However, last Friday truly overwhelmed me! The nurse casually told me they had to paralyze him. What? I just spoke to the doctor and he didn't mention a thing about it! I demanded he call me back immediately and explain to me what happened. THAT REALLY STARTLED ME!

As it turns out, they often use a paralytic drug called Vecuronium to keep patients breathing in sync with the ventilator. This prevents further unnecessary respiratory distress on the lungs. This is super scary stuff that left me feeling so alone sometimes having to absorb so much heavy and disheartening information. After I took it in, I had to regurgitate it with a positive spin so that others wouldn't get freaked out. Many times, I wanted to keep things to myself because I felt others wouldn't quite understand it all, or that they just couldn't help anyway so why bother? Clearly, this is a life-defense mechanism for me.

I explained to the doctor and nurse how I was taken aback by their casual use of the term "paralyze." Obviously, the frequency to which procedures are performed by medical personnel desensitizes them to how scary it all sounds. However, they need to remain cognizant of the fact that hearing that word in the context of a loved one is not an everyday occurrence and is therefore very frightening. I told them our daughter, Kaelyn, would have totally freaked out if she were on the line when the nurse delivered that information. I could just imagine her only hearing "He's paralyzed," and nothing else. That would NOT have gone over well at all!

This current condition of Tee's is the beginning of a potential multi-week process. The day was still young so there was lots of time left to continue praying for his healing and for things to rapidly change for the better moving forward.

I love how Bishop Thomas is so insightful! He reiterated exactly what I was thinking about information being disseminated. God had spoken to me vividly that morning in the shower and told me I should highly respect the opinions of the medical doctors; however, I shouldn't get bogged down with their details and reports. Ultimately, they know what they know, but I know *who* I know (The God of Everything!). That was so liberating for me! Because my spirit is truly aligned with God's power, I began to really feel victorious for Tee.

Our first Saturday prayer call invitation

God assured me pretty early on that Tee and I would make it through this test. He told me we were the glue between many people, and he was using us and our situation to bring us closer to each other and closer to Him. I hadn't had a chance to speak to everyone live, so I had been doing a lot of texting. There were still a lot of unanswered questions and speculation swirling around our current situation.

God laid it on my heart to arrange a prayer conference call for Tee, which we had yesterday. My baby sister Dakota, aka Didi Cakes, a beautiful and talented millennial with skills, made a beautiful invitation with Tee's picture, which we distributed electronically.

Jon and Kristi Gray (Tee's best friend and best man, and his wife) helped set up and moderate. We had an amazing lineup with four prayer warriors (including three couples—the Perrys, Overtons, and Grays). We prayed, sang, and read scripture. Bishop Thomas made a surprise guest appearance and led us in a timely and mighty scripture and prayer!

When it was time for me to speak, I addressed the elephant in the room: How did this all happen—as in, how and where we contracted COVID-19—and where do we go from here? I shared what God had spoken to me about us being the chosen couple for the test, and that we were going to be victorious in Tee's recovery. I assured everyone on the call that if we were obedient and did what God told us to do, we were coming out of this victoriously. Just before we closed with Diana Ross' legendary song, "I'm Coming Out," I performed a little tribute to Tee that God placed in my spirit, sung to the melody of "Ain't No Mountain High Enough":

Ain't no devil big enough,
Ain't no virus bad enough,
Hopkins isn't far enough,
To keep me from you!

The call was a huge success. The feedback was that everyone loved how it was factual, compelling, uplifting, testimonial, etc. I felt God was pleased with me, and that I had officially recruited an army of prayer warriors. It inspired me to repeat the process, which brought about the "TC prayer warriors prayer call." As of the publishing of this book this prayer call still takes place on Saturday at 4:10 PM.

Chapter 4

DEATH IS NOT AN OPTION

Thursday 4/2 @ 4:28 AM

Yesterday was Bud's 34th birthday. I know Tee was there for his son in spirit from his hospital bed. He's such a great dad and truly loves Bud and Kaelyn. Tee's family threw Bud a virtual Zoom party, but I was unable to make it. The three-hour time zone difference didn't work well for me. My days are long, so I'm exhausted by early evening. I'm up by 4:30 AM or 5:00 AM, and I try to be in bed by 9:30 PM-ish, sometimes earlier and definitely not later. Early in the morning, I'm conditioning my mind with prayer and scripture, as well as mental, emotional and sometimes physical exercise, in preparation for the day.

When routine gets interrupted

I usually make my first nurse call by 5:30 AM or 6:00 AM (before their shift change) to get a recap on Tee's overnight status. Most days, I check in again between 11:00 AM and 1:00 PM, between 3:00 PM and 5:30 PM, and then lastly before bed between 8:30 PM and 9:00 PM. I kept meticulous notes on almost all those calls, as you will see in Part IV, where I share those progress reports chronologically. In my ongoing text messages with family, friends and prayer warriors (see Part III), along with relevant and inspirational messages to and from everyone, I gave very accurate updates on Tee's condition because of those notes.

During this entire time, I maintained my same work schedule with my job, but now I'm working from home, thank goodness. I am a busy bee by nature, so after work hours, I still managed to fit in a few real estate tasks. I also kept managing my G'mom's affairs as much as I could. Thank God for her companion, Aileen, who took up a lot of the slack there for me and for my friend and real estate partner, Miki, for her contributions on my behalf. Otherwise, I don't know how I would've made it. There's never a dull moment around the house.

This morning, I started with my journal entry, prayers, scriptures, etc. Within an hour's time, my normal morning routine became anything but normal as I received the most terrifying words that I have heard thus far. My phone rang at 5:30 AM and I saw "Johns Hopkins" on the caller ID. My heart dropped to my stomach in anticipation of terrible news. Within 10 minutes, I was praying, texting the prayer warriors, making necessary phone calls and heading to the hospital.

Brush with death

A doctor from JH somberly explained that Tee's oxygen levels had dropped to critical levels and that he was on maximum ventilator support. They told me if his oxygen levels dropped any further, there wasn't anything else they could do to save him. They asked me about implementing lifesaving measures if necessary, including CPR and chest compressions. My heart sank some more—this time to my feet, it seemed!

My mother had died in a hospital (Hahnemann University Hospital-Philadelphia) in 2001. They unsuccessfully performed chest compressions on her. The thought of now going through the same thing with my husband overwhelmed me beyond measure.

I asked the doctor if they would let me visit Tee since he was critical. As soon as I heard "probably," I immediately said, "I'm on my way!" I don't remember much else about that conversation as you can imagine. I remember hanging up and pleading with God, "Please do not take my husband."

I laid prostrate before God on my bedroom floor and cried and prayed with every ounce of strength in me. Once again, I knew I did not have time to fall apart. I had to reach out to the family and activate the prayer chain—IMMEDIATELY.

I made a few key family phone calls and texts. I wasn't sure I could drive to the hospital alone, so I reached out to two of our closest friends, Jeff and Stacey White. I asked if they could take me to the hospital and they agreed.

Next, I sent a group text to the family informing them Tee was in trouble: "Just got a call from hospital...Prayers for a miracle right now!!! Heading there shortly!!"

I then called my prayer warrior friend, Marie Therese, in New York, whom I affectionately call "my chaplain." Marie has prayed me through some hard times previously, but this one was the hardest thus far. She had always told me I could call her anytime and she would pray for me. I needed to take her up on that offer at that very moment. She prayed for me in her calmest, most faithful and powerful voice. She reminded me that God would take care of us, and He did!

Marie Therese's prayer equipped me with the power I needed to drive myself to the hospital. I quickly showered, dressed, and headed out the door. I called the Whites and told them to meet me at the hospital instead. I was on pins and needles during the whole drive, praying I wouldn't get a call saying it was too late and he didn't make it.

I got there in record time, arriving at JH around 7:00 AM. Tee's immediate family and the Whites met me there. Once inside, I called up to the nurse's station to see if we could get in. They informed me Tee's oxygen levels had actually stabilized and they didn't need to invoke lifesaving measures after all! I was so relieved and ever thankful to God and JH for saving my husband's life once again. Oh, the mighty power of prayer!

We ended up sitting around for hours praying and talking from our cars while waiting for hospital administrators to grant us approval to see him in spite of the COVID-19 visitor lockdown. I did get periodic updates from the nurses' station as we patiently waited in our cars for updates on his condition and our visitation approval from JH administration.

They finally granted us approval around 2:30 PM for three immediate family members to go in two at a time to visit. Our daughter Kaelyn and I went in first. We had to suit up in unimaginable layers of uncomfortable PPE armor. We stayed with Tee approximately 45 minutes, then Kaelyn left, and my sister-in-law, Anita (Byrd), came in with me. Mom Lulu (Tee's mother) was too distraught to come inside the hospital. Understandably, she was also concerned about being exposed to the virus in the ICU (aka Biocontainment Unit, where they housed all the COVID-19 patients), so Anita took her place. During her time at her dad's bedside, Kaelyn Facetimed her grandmother, family members who remained outside in their cars, and her brother, Theirrien (Bud), in San Diego. It was a very troubling sight for everyone to see Tee this way. We all knew from the reports that he was deathly ill; seeing it firsthand, though, made it more real.

This is what we saw. Tee's body and lips were swollen, he had tubes coming out from every area, and he was connected to the machine that sustained his every breath. Even my man's fine straight hair had become beady beads (mine and Tee's inside joke). I had to check for familiar body marks to assure myself it was really him.

Yes, Tee was in bad shape, but he was still alive and fighting the good fight. I'm sure that Anita and Kaelyn have their renditions of their visit, but for me it was both scary and comforting. I know it sounds crazy to harbor two such polarizing emotions simultaneously but that's how I felt.

The comforting part was that as bad as my baby looked, I expected him to look worse. I knew that as long as he had breath in his body, he still had a fighting chance. Furthermore, I hadn't seen him in almost two weeks, during which time he had been transferred to JH's main hospital.

All I could do was imagine how he looked and try to envision his surroundings while loving on him, and praying for him, from afar.

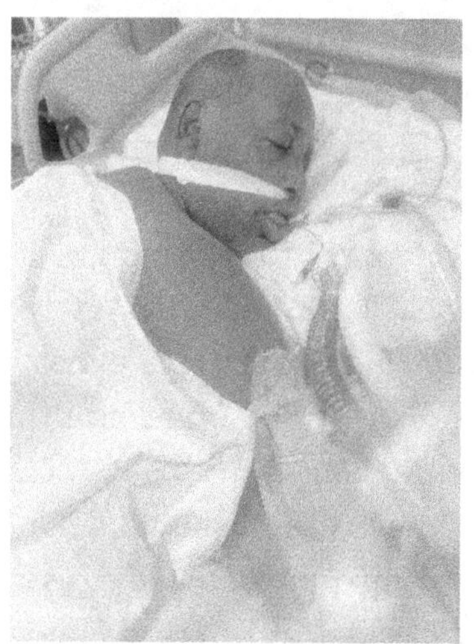

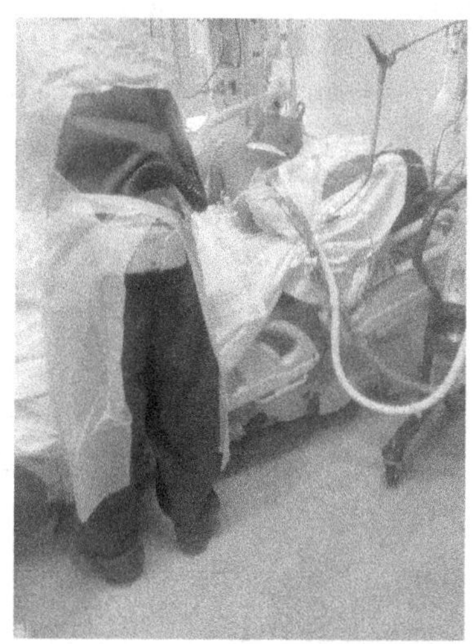

Tee on ventilator - April 2, 2020.

We are a close-knit family, so I was wondering if he was feeling alone and missing us and wondering where we were. I prayed that he could feel our love and concern from afar, and that he didn't give up, thinking we had abandoned him. I would often hear the stories of people who were dying alone in hospitals and nursing homes, and I could not help but think this was largely attributed to feelings of loneliness and abandonment. Despite the circumstances, I was glad to be able to see him up close and personal, and I know that my sister-in-law and daughter felt the same.

Thursday 4/2 @ 5:00 PM

(SCARE!) FLASHING LIGHTS, SIRENS! That's figuratively how my day started.

- At 5:30 AM, I received an alarming call from the JH-ICU doctor stating that Tee's oxygen levels dropped to critical levels, and he was on maximum ventilator support

- Questions about life saving measures — CPR and chest compressions
- I bolted to Johns Hopkins arriving around 7:00 AM with family — waiting hours to get approval to see Tee. We finally went in around 2:30 PM and stayed with Tee over 1 hour (Marcy, Kaelyn, then Marcy and Byrd)
- Tee has a lot of fluid — He's definitely in trouble with swollen lips — fully intubated VERY TOUGH TO SEE! — But I was just strong, prayed up and Faithful!

We loved, read scriptures, prayed and laid hands on him. I talked to him and tried to kiss and hug him. OMG, I love and miss my husband.

- During our visit, Nurse Julie (very sparky) informed us that Tee responded to the medicine they gave him to stabilize him when his Oxygen levels tanked-Praise God!
- The doctor/nurse also told me earlier (No CPR/Compressions were needed. Thank God!)
- She also told us that they've had 1 COVID-19 patient get off the ventilator thus far, and the average recovery time for Ventilator has been 2-3 weeks — sometimes longer.

During our visit with Tee

- Prayers for Healing-Luke 8:40-48 (Daughter be of good cheer; For your Faith Has Healed you).
- We conveyed Feelings of love and joy.
- We reiterated A reason to live, Great life, family, travel, future goals including retirement, etc.

End of day reflection

Today was different. We were able to love Tee, pray for him, and speak life into him up close and personal. I knew in my heart if my husband could feel our touches and hear our voices that it would give him the push he needed to fight on. I believe in my heart of hearts that this crisis was all a part of God's plan to get us closer to him on that day!

Side Note: Tee has since reiterated a conversation that Kaelyn had with one of the nurses during our visit. He remembers hearing her voice and thinking that she worked there. It is true that people can often hear conversations in an unconscious state!

We met the medical staff who were taking such GREAT care of him. I was able to put names to faces for the angels whom I talked to several times per day. It gave us great comfort to see that he was in good caring hands.

We also saw that they had received the family pictures I emailed to them earlier in the week, and they let Kaelyn tape them to the wall during our visit. We wanted the hospital to know that Tee had a loving and supportive family, and we also wanted him to see these pictures when he woke up. These pictures would end up moving with Tee as he changed locations throughout his entire hospital stay!

Side Note: Remember I had driven down to Hopkins one or two times before this visit and sat outside the building to pray from afar. I guesstimated where I thought his room was located based on the building and room number. During my visit I was able to confirm the exact location, and I had been positioning myself correctly. More Divine Intervention!

Other people's brushes with death

Because COVID-19 was so new and extraordinarily perplexing—and still is to some degree, as of the printing of this book—I would follow a few similar stories of recovery and determination during our journey. I was really moved by Broadway actor Nick Cordero's story, and his wife,

Amanda Kloots' love and determination to stick by her husband. I could totally relate to many of his clinical updates and her spiritual mindset during the time when both of our husbands were in this sudden fight of their lives.

I also followed the story of a Virginia man named Titou Phommachanh. Recently, he miraculously recovered from COVID-19, after weeks of love, family, prayers and great medical treatment. When Titou was at his worst, his wife, Amanda (a fellow Realtor), proclaimed that she was too young to be a widow. I completely agreed and added my own flair to that statement. I declared I was too young *and* sexy to be a widow. Sometimes, you must bring your own sunshine when the skies are gray.

When Titou recovered, I would often humor myself by saying if God could heal Titou, then He could heal Tee too. And He did!

Virginia man's miraculous recovery from COVID-19

Virginia man's COVID-19 recovery after medically induced coma 'nothing short of a miracle.' [1]

MANASSAS, VA. (WJLA); A 44-year-old Northern Virginia man who was put in a medically induced coma after contracting COVID-19, is awake and talking after his wife says he was "knocking on deaths door." Titou Phommachanh of Manassas is a father of three daughters and a Capital Hilton employee. His wife told ABC7 News the couple took a trip to New York City the weekend before Phommachanh developed flu-like symptoms.

Johns Hopkins is the best

Can I just tell you how pleased I am with JH? All the nurses have been wonderful and very accommodating. Kaelyn even observed that her dad

[1] **Va. man's COVID-19 recovery after medically-induced coma 'nothing short of a miracle.'** Fox 42. WJLA, MANASSAS, VA. Victoria Sanchez.
https://fox42kptm.com/news/nation-world/coronavirus-recovery-nothing-short-of-a-miracle.

always gets good nurses. It's because he has a great spirit and draws good people to him. In hindsight, I know it's also part of God's protective covering over him, to make sure that he has GREAT people in his midst.

I was informed that patients now have iPads in their rooms, which is how we were able to get the gospel music playing in the background. They are working on getting us access to virtual meetings (such as with the Zoom app) since we couldn't be there. That would allow us to bring our prayer calls right into his room.

We truly thank God for the staff at JH and how they continued to take great care of Tee, while at the same time keeping me informed regularly. Just think, during this pandemic, they are coordinating all these accommodations between patient and family as much as they can, for hundreds of patients simultaneously! What is being expected of these front-line workers, and what they are delivering every single day, is nothing short of amazing. Even more awe-inspiring is that some of them are going through much of the same hardship on a personal level with their *own* families, while putting our families first. Remarkable, to say the least! Tee and I will be giving back to JH as best we can.

But first and foremost, I had to just focus on praying for Tee. I encouraged everyone—family and prayer warriors and anyone else who inquired about Tee—to just keep praying with fervency. My battle cry was, "Hold On! Change is Coming. We're looking for a miracle. Just believe it and receive it. God will perform it today!" Those became two of our many survival and inspirational themes.

Chapter 5

Easter Miracle – Our Prayers Answered

Saturday 4/4 @ 1:00 PM

We just completed a wonderful Noon-hour prayer with Tee and his immediate family through speakerphone. We showered him with love, prayers and words of encouragement. We continue to believe that he is feeling and hearing our prayers!

His doctor said he's still stable and holding his own, he has overcome some major obstacles over the last 48 hours and his body cannot afford any more setbacks. While we remain mindful of the fragility of which the doctors speak, we will only use it as a springboard to escalate our prayers, ultimately remembering that God is in control!

I was prepared to pray Tee through this if we had to do a call every day! I started a 24-hour nationwide Christian-based fast starting on Good Friday at midnight until the following Saturday at midnight, fasting and praying for God to release the coronavirus, which has affected us personally and has plagued our nation and many parts of the world! The time is now for us to unite as the body of Christ to rebuke this devil in the name of Jesus!

Escaping death

Within a 48-hour period, Tee escaped death three times: on April 1, with a 108-degree temperature (cytokine storm syndrome); on April 2, due to critically low oxygen levels; and on April 3, due to an irregular heartbeat (atrial fibrillation); each time, prayers went up and out, as the JH team responded with immediate interventions. As we prayed, Tee responded. Death was not an option! TGBTAG!! (To God Be The Amazing Glory)

God had brought us through several close encounters the last few weeks, and we were determined to stay unified in prayer as the journey continued. The more we prayed, the more Tee responded. Our momentum was at an all-time high, and we were watching a real-life biblical miracle unfold right before our eyes. We were all hunkered down and sheltered in place because of the COVID-19 shutdown, and God had our full attention. We all watched curiously and optimistically to see what God would reveal next!

Sunday 4/5 @ 9:49 PM

This past week and weekend have been a blur. I had a full day at work on Friday. Saturday, I didn't go out, but we had an amazing second prayer call co-moderated by our good friends, (prophets) Jon and Kristi Gray, with Marie Therese ("my personal chaplain"), Pastor Julius, Ministers Danielle and Jared Perry (niece and nephew), and Deacon and songstress John and Lorraine Overton (our aunt and uncle). I closed it with Hezekiah Walker's "I'm Waiting on the Lord". The words say, "I got a change coming. Everything's gonna be all right!"

Afterward, I remained on the line and received an overwhelming amount of love and support from both sides of the family for my demonstration of strength, love and support for my husband. I thanked everyone and told them this was what I was supposed to be doing. I was doing what I thought Tee would do for me, and most importantly doing what he would want me to do.

Tee has seen me in the trenches, so he knows my dedication to my loved ones (to a fault, but that's another story). It felt great to openly receive the love from my side and from the in-laws. God has brought me, individually, and our relationship, collectively, a mighty long way. That's a miracle in and of itself. LOL. We've been rolling pretty tight the last few weeks since Tee's been in the hospital. We all have much love for Tee, so we're all definitely going through this time together. I am truly GRATEFUL for all who have been there for him and me! God spoke to me early on and told me that we were going through this time to bring us closer to one another and closer to Him, and once again He did what He said he would do!

Yesterday morning, before our prayer call, we did a group family conference call where we spoke and prayed with Tee through speakerphone. It was GREAT! I committed myself to a fast, beginning Good Friday for 24 hours, and encouraged others to join in.

My sister-in-law, Vera, actually serenaded me with a poem earlier and she shared it on the call. It was beautiful! Vera loves her brother to life and has always been in his/our corner and vice versa.

Holding On to survive

By now, Tee had been on the ventilator almost two and a half weeks. He had also survived three MAJOR crises. We were feeling optimistic about his progress and remaining faithful that he would beat the 15% chance of survival that he was given. Dr. Nyanjom (Tee's pulmonologist) told me if he was going to leave us, he would've been gone by now after he overcame three death-defying experiences last week.

Easter Sunday was less than a week away. My prayer warriors and I were in full swing with multiple weekly unified prayer calls and daily communications. We were preparing to do a 24-hour fast led by the First United Church of Washington on Friday, April 10. Until this week, Tee's reports were still very iffy. We were told he was "taking baby steps in the right direction." On April 7, Tee began showing his first signs of stabilizing. Around Noon, I was told his oxygen pressure (Peep score) dropped three points from 18 to 15. I knew 5-10 was normal range, so he would only need two more 3-point drops to be in the normal zone. This was so exciting! The prayer warriors continued to pray accordingly!

We held our fourth prayer call last night and it was awesome! We reinforced the power of prayer and had a few testimonies of recent miracles (thanks, Aunt Bunny and sister Jackie for sharing). We heard "I'm Looking for a Miracle", by the legendary Clark Sisters. We asked God specifically for full restoration, and complete preservation healing for Tee and we closed with a positive song, "Hold On (Change is Coming)" by the mighty gospel group "Sounds Of Blackness."

Tuesday 4/7 @ 8:06 AM

Kai "Moogie Poo" (Daughter niece's 21st birthday)

I have so much to say but so little time right now. We had an awesome prayer call last night, reinforcing the power of prayer. Sometimes, just prayer alone has to be enough.

Friday 4/10 @ 7:00 AM

Today is Good Friday, it is also week 3 for TC on the ventilator. Me and The TC prayer warriors are embarking on a 24 fast which started with a 24-hour prayer call which began at midnight. Watch what happens over the next week starting with Good Friday!

Sunday 4/12 @ 8:09 PM (Our Easter Miracle!)

OMG what a week! TC's oxygen has been stable for the last few days and they've decreased the ventilator air pressure (peep) from 18 down to 5. Yes! He is in the normal range zone now so they're going to be trialing him in the coming days to make sure he can sustain himself without the ventilator.

Oh, my goodness! We have been praying without ceasing for this news over the last three weeks, since March 20! Along with praying, there have been miracle testimonials, as well as praise and worship, at least two to three times per week, and it has been awesome! I've been blessed by the support, love, praise reports and miracle testimonials. People are amazed at my God-given strength during this time. Isn't it so amazing how God's strength is made perfect in our weakness?

Tuesday 4/14 @ 10:12 PM

Quick entry, I'm really tired. Tee is doing well; he's getting stronger each day. Doc said that he is constantly improving. Praise God, this is music to my ears!

He's had some issues with anxiety which was predictable. It looks like he's been stabilized and they're decreasing his IV meds and ventilator settings. His ventilator settings are at their lowest now! Prayerfully he'll be getting extubated over the next 24 to 48 hours, barring no setbacks, God willing!

This is so exciting to think that I may be able to talk to him and possibly see him in the coming weeks after almost a month of being apart! I'm just forever grateful for his progress and the miraculous turnaround he's made over the past few days. It has been so much of a roller coaster and he's seemingly weathering the storm. This is definitely a NOTHING BUT GOD (NBG) experience.

God is pleased and Tee is responding to our prayers. I am so thankful and grateful. God told me to be faithful and watch Him deliver, and I did. He is doing just what He said he would do.

I believe it and I receive it!
God will perform it today!
Hey, hey!

Friday 4/17 @ 6:45 AM

Tee is doing very well. He is seemingly physically ready to be removed from the ventilator, but he needs more cognitive awareness. I have no doubt he'll be there soon. Today marks four weeks (28 days) on the ventilator. I gave the analogy this morning that he's in the sky circling and waiting for God to give him the cue for a safe and timely landing. So, we're praying for that safe and timely landing. I thought it was going to be yesterday but I'm waiting on the Lord patiently, which is not something that comes naturally. LOL

God is continually stretching me. I think He is pleased with my overall progress and obedience! It's been a good week! We're on the road to recovery and restoration; prayerfully the ventilator will come off today or soon and he'll be able to step down and be home by the middle to the end of next week, God willing!

Chapter 6

The Landing. 'I Made It!'

Saturday 4/18 @ 8:39 AM

Tee did well his first night off the ventilator, praise God! They say the first 12-24 hours can be the hardest. Boopy is rolling like a champ! His heart rate is a little elevated. They started meds for him, prayerfully he'll normalize soon…he usually does. I don't have too many concerns or fears right now seeing how God has brought us a MIGHTY long way in the one week alone, not to mention what He's done collectively since this all began almost a month ago. This time last Saturday (the day between Good Friday and Easter) we were praying for a miracle for Tee's oxygen levels to stabilize.

Easter Sunday, he made a drastic improvement and they talked about preparing him as early as Monday to extubate. Throughout the week, they kept observing him to make sure he was ready and then Friday it happened. Just one week from our Good Friday fasting prayers! Last Saturday, a group of us virtually and simultaneously watched Sight & Sound Theaters' *Jesus, Reenactment,* and The Clark Sisters' movie.

I cannot express how grateful I am for my prayer warriors. We've had over 10 prayer calls in four weeks, an average of 2.5 calls per week. Most of the calls were planned, and a few have been spontaneous when encountering various crises. Yesterday around Noon, I had a phone conversation with the JH doctors. They told me they would attempt to extubate again within the next one to two hours. As usual, they gave me best and worst case scenarios if extubation was unsuccessful. They told me if he was not ready to be extubated today, that they would have to consider doing a Tracheotomy (Trach) in his throat. I thanked them as usual and I reassured them with confidence that I believed that they would be successful. I thought to myself, "you all are not putting a hole in my man's throat!" I immediately assembled the prayer warriors for an impromptu prayer call. Within 15- 20 minutes, a group of us assembled including a few "old faithful's" such as, but not limited to, Aunt Di, Uncle Johnny, the Grays, Perrys, Aunt Barbara Ann, Sharee, Uncle Jim and Aunt Diane, Leroy and Cynthia, (too many to name, but God bless them all), and prayed for a successful extubation.

I peacefully proceeded with my workday knowing that everything would be OK. From 1:00-2:30 PM, I was on a work Zoom call. I expected my meeting to be interrupted with a call from the hospital giving me good news. If not, I already settled in my mind that I would call them around 2:30 PM, as soon as I was finished with work.

Instead of a call from the hospital, I received a couple of text messages from Bud and Kaelyn.

"Did you know my dad was off the ventilator? We just called to check on him and they told us casually that he's been off the ventilator for 1.5 hours. His throat was sore, he was drowsy, but we were able to talk to him!"

I was overjoyed by the news. Another PRAISE GOD moment, for sure! Oh, what a happy day that God has done it for us, once again!

I called the hospital around 5:30 PM when Kaelyn, Bud and I could all be on the Zoom call. We couldn't really hear him, but we could see him. He looked GREAT! He looked much more like himself, except for that mini-Afro and gray beard. I assured Tee, I'd help him take care of those two matters over the next week, just as soon as I could get some clippers and his hair color and other beauty products to the hospital.

The fight wasn't over with that exciting news. We kept praying he would recover quickly and be released to come home. I wasted no time preparing for such. I set up housecleaning and landscaping services for

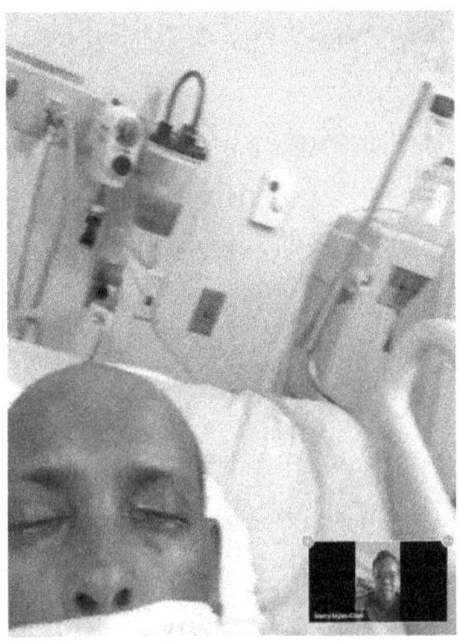

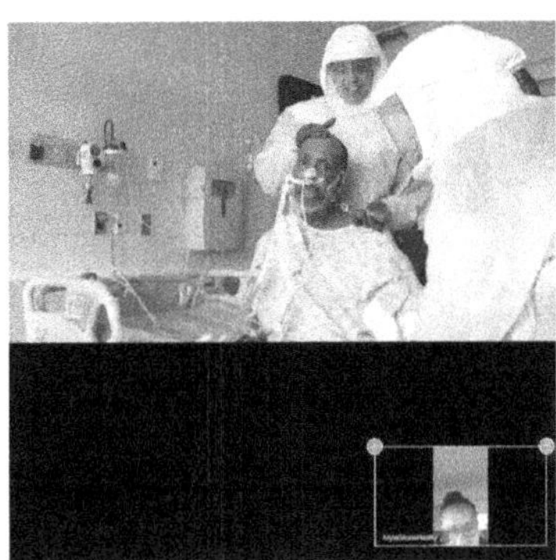

Early post extubation photos captured through Zoom

the upcoming week. I wrote out a long to-do list of so many tasks that needed my attention.

Donnell and Priscilla B donated their services and installed a railing in the garage and bars in the bathroom to help Tee get in and out easily. We were extremely grateful for that gift, which was such a *needful* adjustment following a long and near-death ordeal in a hospital. During a time like that, the thought of what adjustments to make, let alone *how* to make them, can be nothing short of overwhelming. Their gift was right on time to help eliminate any anxiety that tried to rise up in me.

Monday 4/20 @ 7:31 AM

Tee had a good weekend in the hospital, while I enjoyed a rare and much needed lazy day on Saturday. I went out and got some Chick-fil-A, conquered some work around the house and held one successful prayer call Saturday night.

The calls have been awesome. Because of them, I'm seemingly blessing others and they are most certainly blessing me. The calls help me to not feel so alone, despite being physically alone for 32 days so far. So, I'd been home alone but not alone. Praise God!

Most days have been very much a blur with sending out updates three to four times a day. Everyone has been in awe of Tee's miraculous progression so I couldn't let up on the updates. Hearing how well he's doing is half the battle for keeping our praying going strong.

Tee's been talking a little, he has sat up on the side of the bed, and he's even been undertaking the bed bicycle. He knows what year it is and where he is. Those are huge accomplishments, yet they tell us he has a way to go for full recovery. Nonetheless, we are all sleeping more soundly knowing he's come that far.

Tee has been receiving a great amount of physical therapy (PT) and respiratory therapy (RT). Prayerfully, his improvements would allow for his return home in one to two weeks, God willing! My prayer was for a May 1 release, two weeks post-ventilator. That would be the best five-year anniversary present I could ever imagine!

Thursday 4/23 @ 1:57 PM

Tee looked good and appeared to be doing very well on a quick Zoom call. He was very psyched to see us. I greeted him with, "Hey, Boop!" To which he weakly responded, "Hey, baby."

Ugh! Restraining myself was extremely difficult. I wanted to reach through that screen, kiss his forehead and hold him for a very long time. Lord knows I longed for that moment every day!

Tee's doctor just assured me his heart rate normalized as expected. Praise God! He was being introduced slowly back into solid foods. He could consume thick liquids and Jell-O-y type of food now! He was getting water ice (our funny way of saying Italian ice in Philly). I know he was incredibly grateful to be able to quench his thirst—another huge milestone for him.

Tee was also doing well with his oxygen intake and was expected to have the oxygen tube out of his nose soon. Prayerfully, the feeding tube would be next to come out once he demonstrated the ability to tolerate enough food to give him nutrition.

The doctor assured me Tee was making huge strides, yet he had a little way to go to exit the ICU. That would be the next step, then Tee would enter inpatient rehab for a few weeks.

As much as I wanted him home, like yesterday, I know it is important that he got everything he needed while there; otherwise, I could be faced with bringing him back due to a rapid heart rate episode or something. My sentiments were, "We love you, Johns Hopkins, but once we roll out, it's going to be a wrap!" Therefore, I bit the bullet and remained tolerant for full restoration to take place.

We continued to pray for his progress and waited on the Lord to take us through the next steps: our preparation for Tee's homecoming. The better he got, the more independent he became. He was now able to talk on the phone more regularly. Waiting didn't seem as hard once I began communicating with him more directly.

Tee has been totally on God's clock. God hadn't disappointed us yet, so we continued to trust Him, like the song we played on the phone for him last night said to do: "Trust Me" by Richard Smallwood. Seemed like God was telling us all something through that song. We humbly received His message.

It thrilled me that we could begin having conversations about future plans, when just a few weeks earlier matters were so fragile, we could only process issues in my mind day by day. TGBTG!! One of those future plans, albeit short term, was Tee's spectacular homecoming celebration! No doubt, it needed to be huge!

Moving Out and Onward

Tee graduated out of the ICU on the afternoon of April 24, 2020, after 35 days. Praise God! They gave him a hero's send-off down the ICU halls and onto his next ward. I couldn't be in there, of course, but the doctors and nurses told me what they did, and Tee later confirmed it. They all lined up, clapped and sang to "Eye of the Tiger," the theme song of the movie *Rocky*. The nurses and doctors really took to him there because he had been there so long and had progressed beyond their expectations. Everyone inside and outside the hospital were elated!

The event proved bittersweet. Of course, we were glad he was moving on to the next, and final, phase of his hospital stay, but we'd come to know the ICU staff who were so attentive and responsive. Many of them became extended family and friends since I would talk to them several times a day over the past month. They were so comforting that I had to admit I was a bit concerned if the next group of medical personnel could and would match the level of care on the next floor. Like a mom on the first day of school, I was scared and excited for his progression. Once again, I had to LET GO, and LET GOD!

Tee was entering an intermediary care floor where he would receive more care than a regular floor, but less care than an intensive care unit. More prayers answered regarding continued attentive care.

During a previous Zoom visit with me and Kaelyn, Tee's voice was still very low, and he appeared weak as he attempted to chug some water through a straw. Because he would tire easily, our visits were brief, but each one gave us realization that the days were getting shorter until his release.

The next day, a Zoom call with several of us along with Tee was longer and much more emotional. He kept trying to tell us something, and we couldn't exactly get it. Finally, we understood him to say he wanted us to pray. I told him we could definitely do that, as we had gotten plenty of practice doing so over the last month.

We delivered a very emotional prayer to him. What an uplifting and gratifying moment to pray with him at his request. We were so overwhelmed; my spirit was overcome with emotion and I just wept with an outpouring of tears of joy—the ugly snotty kind of cry that comes from the soul and creeps up on you. But it was all good! I just kept stressing to him how much of a miracle and a blessing it was for him to still be with us on this earth!

My heart was so incredibly full after that call. It reminded me of just how important it will be moving forward to make time to pray with Tee at least once a day. He needs it and now, as never before, and he wants it. Glory to God!!

It was so funny to see Tee physically resembling Bishop Thomas with his black glasses and his now gray beard that we weren't used to ever seeing. I teased him that he was looking very pastoral-like. At least for the moment because he was supposed to be getting a shave today.

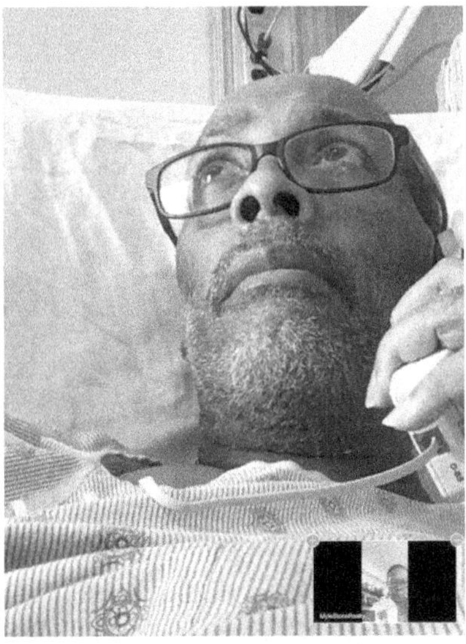

Post ICU Pastoral look

Another day playing out in this great, modern-day biblical miracle. God's healing has been ever-present, and Tee has been responding. Yet, I urged our prayer warriors to keep the prayers going as we would now be communicating with a whole new set of rules and medical staff in the new unit.

The JH ICU personnel were simply phenomenal. They have become friends. Afterward, I still talked to a few of them several times a day. The new group had huge shoes to fill to perform up to par, so they needed to bring their A game to meet this praying wife's satisfaction!

Chapter 7

We Made It This Far (Preparation for Home)

We made it this far by faith! Tee was discharged from the ICU on April 24 and transferred to the step-down intermediary floor for four days.

Wednesday 4/29 @ 6:27 AM (Day 40)

Tee has been moved to the Inpatient Rehab floor. God is SOO AMAZING AND WORTHY OF ALL PRAISE! Tee is doing great! He came off the ventilator April 17, out of the ICU April 24, went to the Immediate Care floor until April 28, and lastly, he transferred to the Inpatient Rehab floor flawlessly. He'll get evaluated and assessed today, then we'll have a better idea of his release timeline. I'm believing by faith, and planning accordingly, for his arrival home on or before Friday, May 15.

Prayerfully, he'll arrive between Wednesday and Friday so I can take a long weekend to arrange around-the-clock nursing help, possible stairlift, and whatever other equipment or assistance he'll need. I have a lot to figure out over the coming days and weeks in anticipation of his arrival, but I've already started putting wheels in motion. I'm so excited to think that he could be back home in the next few weeks!

Tee is physically progressing, talking louder and better than since arriving here. His mind is definitely sharp because he's giving commands. He's worried about money, house, trivial things. He wants Kevin W (bro-in-law extraordinaire) to come over and do a few things around the house. I'm constantly having to calm him down and refocus him on worrying about his health and recovery! He asked me to call his job and start a "Go Fund Me" page because he's worried about his medical bills.. (Really, Tee, after all you've been through??)

I reassured him that we have good insurance. (See Part V for more information on this subject) I also had to inform him that the entire country—excuse me, the entire world—is suffering through a pandemic to some degree thanks to the coronavirus. Almost everything here in the United States has been paused. Most importantly, as I reiterated to Tee, is the fact that the same God who just saved him is the one who's going to see us through this mess. So, there's no reason to fret or fear!

It takes more than just *telling* someone not to fear when they've been through this level of trauma. Therefore, we may have to get some good anxiety meds for him to temporarily relax. He's got to calm down and have faith in order to heal thoroughly. He literally cannot afford to be stressed! It feels like he's been asleep for over a month, so I know his mind is racing trying to make up for lost time. I reassured him all bills have been paid and the house is being maintained. I reminded him that I've owned a few houses before he and I married, so I do know how to do some things. I got this, and God's got us!

This is a new day for us. We're putting our material things second and on the back burner and seeking HIM first! While we all love our worldly possessions, this ordeal has taught us all a great lesson: that none of our houses, cars, jobs, etc., could save us or keep us healthy during our recent storm. There were times when I would look into our driveway and garages and just see our cars sitting for weeks at a time, not being driven. I would trade my husband's good health and presence for all of it. I loved my big house much more when I wasn't home alone. There are rooms (including our bedroom and his man cave in the basement) that I haven't even been able to go into during his absence.

It is my prayer that Tee, like me, truly realizes the magnitude of what we've been through and loses his strong need and desires for worldly possessions and acquisitions.

Sunday 5/3/20 @ 2:02 PM

Thank You, God, for all You've done for us! What a difference a week makes! Tee landed on the rehab floor earlier this week. He's getting rehab three times per day (OT, PT, SLP) and doing well. They said, "He's working so hard." He told me it's a "Good Tired." Praise God! His spirits are high. He's made friends with all of the nurses and therapists, typical Tee Clark style. The nurses have been making him strawberry smoothies from his Ensures. He thoroughly appreciates this, but he's so ready to go.

The doctor and nurses told me Friday; that he'll be ready to go home by Sunday, May 10. Tee is saying Wednesday, May 6. We'll see. I'm so ready emotionally for him to come home. I'm working diligently to prepare for him physically and mentally. I still have a lot to do, including getting his bed and relevant equipment, and I need to secure a home nurse. I'll talk to the social worker and home care coordinator tomorrow to confirm all of his services and missing pieces. I have a lot of good leads from family and friends that I just need to follow up on.

The doctors told Tee he retested positive for COVID-19 on Saturday AM (almost two months from the original diagnosis on March 17). Of course, he was nervous and thinking it would delay his release. They called him back that evening to let him know he should still be OK to leave next week. Praise God! Now, I just have to find someone who wants to come into our war zone to help, UGH!

I'm praying I can get retested and we'll both be negative ASAP! I think Tee had a higher viral load, so he probably has lingering traces. Nevertheless, I don't believe he's still infectious, but we have to take precautions. That means NO unnecessary visitors, and everyone must wear a mask and gloves. NO EXCEPTIONS!

This time next week, my Boop will be back home with me after 42+ days!

I asked our cousin Lil Jack to help me spearhead the homecoming celebration. We're all wearing royal blue. He came up with this idea and some other good stuff already. He suggested doing a parking lot drive-by instead of one on the street. Participants may have a banner, balloons, etc. I'm completely overwhelmed with coordinating his home care and equipment needs so I greatly appreciated the help in this area.

Monday 5/4 @ 5:36 AM

Sunday was a productive, yet quite peaceful and restful day. I have to enjoy such moments when they come, since I don't know if I will be afforded a restful day once Tee's home. I got a lot done; always more to do, though. I posted ads on Care.com.

Tee and I, together virtually, watched a previously recorded church service. It was a right-on-time "I'm OK now" story of Mary being OK once she realized Jesus rose again. Always quite relevant and prayerfully, it resonated with him. I'm committed to reading the scripture and praying with him when he gets home. (How sweet this sounds.) I will also include him in all weekly virtual services at New Psalmist Church, including Tuesday night prayer call and Thursday night Bible study.

Today is going to be super busy. I must try to get some work done and get Tee's follow-up matters situated in time for his arrival back home. I also must get all his medical resources coordinated early today so I can pick him up from JH on Wednesday afternoon.

Wednesday 5/6 @ 5:11 AM (Day 46)

TEE IS FINALLY COMING HOME TODAY!

Quick entry due to a very busy day. I have to get prepped and ready to pick up my Boop this afternoon. Everything is working out. I got the lawn done, got his bed delivered yesterday, and a tentative caregiver is scheduled to start Thursday or Friday. It looks like there may be some news coverage, CBS WJZ Baltimore, and Fox 45.

I'm ready mentally, physically and emotionally for today. I've ordered car magnets, got balloons, videographer scheduled, and the family is planning to do the car/garage parade. We're super psyched and grateful. I'm sure there will be lots of tears shed today, Praise God!

Chapter 8

HALLELUJAH! HE'S HOME!

And just like that, he was outta there, folks!

In Chapter Ten and Chapter Eleven, we captured the events and excitement of Tee's exit from JH on Wednesday, May 6, 2020. The Homecoming Celebration we put together for him could not have happened any smoother than it did, starting with when he emerged from those hospital doors. So many details had to be coordinated with the hospital staff. I am forever grateful for their diligent cooperation. They were real troupers in the midst of their busyness and stress due to so many other patients being in critical conditions and even dying.

I was led to reach out to a few local media outlets to share Tee's survival story, since it was still early on in the pandemic and he was JH's sickest COVID-19 patient at that time. Fox News and CBS News Baltimore agreed to cover his release. I also hired my own personal videographer to capture every moment, as I knew it would be a humbling and emotional homecoming to treasure for years to come.

Thank goodness it was captured on video by our local news station, because I was so caught up in the moment that I don't think I could've relayed after the fact what all transpired. It was beautiful and surreal, that I know.

Wednesday 5/13 @ 5:37 PM (Tee's been home one week)

Tee's been home one full week, Praise God! I must say, it has been a good week. It has certainly gone by fast. He is all settled in—has his nurse, PT, the works. He's getting stronger and seems happier, as long as he's busy and interacting. He's becoming more independent, walking with and without his walker. He's gained 5 pounds back from the 52 pounds he lost, and a few upcoming virtual appointments this and next week. We've been out for a few safe car rides to give him fresh air and a change of scenery. Maryland's governor is lifting our stay-at-home order in phases starting soon. We're still not pressed to do so, as we believe it's a little too soon. We're still in the struggle, so it's like they're opening up a Pandora's box.

Saturday 5/16 @ 2:51 PM (Tee's been home 10 days)

Another stellar week. Tee is doing super with PT. His spirits are good. The weather has been nice, so they've been walking around outside sometimes. He's still very fatigued and gets winded, but he's been up and down the house and all around. He went up the steps yesterday during PT and that was it! He slept in our upstairs bed for the first time in 54 days. Glory!

Sunday 5/24 @ 8:17 PM (Memorial Day weekend)

Sadly, my aunt Debbie O passed this weekend and my brother-cousin, Merv, is fighting for his life, (both from cancer-related illnesses). I've done a tremendous amount of reflection and praying. It makes us further appreciate life every day that we're blessed with it!

Tee is doing fantastic! We had an excellent prayer call yesterday. My prayer calls and texts have been reduced to once a week, as it became next to impossible to keep up the previous momentum with all my hands-on attention to Tee. Frankly, there's less to report now anyway.

We've been chillin' most of the weekend with the greatest activity being a trip to the supermarket together for the first time in two months. I was nervous for Tee, but thankfully, there weren't a lot of people out and about. I'm very protective of him because I know he's extremely vulnerable. He's got a serious professional mask, and we keep our masks and gloves on continuously, as well as staying safely apart from other people. We concluded our supermarket spree with a basket full of tasty food, including seafood, which we cooked and enjoyed all by ourselves. Much different from Memorial Day celebrations of the past.

Thursday 5/28 @ 7:16 AM

Tee and I had a nice heart-to-heart chat. He has a lot of concerns and anxiety about his recovery, his future, the possibility of getting sick again. He probably could use some anxiety meds, and possibly counseling. JH told me these feelings would be normal and to expect them as a result of the PTSD associated with the long-term ICU stay and ventilation.

I'm looking forward to putting our story into words to share and let others know about the goodness of God, which saw us through this traumatic time. I pray that God will continue to give me the courage, wisdom and insight to bless others the way we've been blessed through telling our story!

Sunday 5/31 @ 7:15 PM

I think I'm going through a post COVID-19 midlife crisis. I'm asking God to give us direction during this time. I don't want this experience to be in vain. I colored my hair Ronald McDonald red last week, as an act of liberation. It is something I always wanted to do but I didn't think it was appropriate for the workplace. Now that I'm working virtually, and now that I also don't really care, I figured it may be a good time. I am also thinking about doing a short natural style since I can't get to the hairdresser on a regular basis right about now—nor do I want to pull an all-day marathon at the hair salon. (I can't really blame that one on COVID-19 since I've always felt this way.)

I'm really tired and temperamental. I want to desperately escape but there's nowhere to go. Also, Tee is still in the midst of his therapies and appointments, so I can't interrupt his schedule. I keep proposing renting a Winnebago and driving to Canada, but I just heard Canada shut down its border to us. Everybody but us knows that Americans are being considered stupid and uncool right about now! Before this time period, it was cool to be an American. Now, we're seen as idiots globally. SMH.

Monday 6/1 @ 11:27 AM

We had a nice and hot weekend. We took a car ride to Virginia to handle some business, then we went to get carryout from Timbuktu (seafood restaurant). It was a lot of driving, Tee tried to persuade me to let him drive. He's doing very well, but I'm not ready for him to drive yet, and we're surely not starting on the highway.

I'm trying to patiently wait for the doctor's clearance. Tee still has some spasms in his hands and he's unable to completely raise his right arm due to suspected nerve damage from being in the prone position on the ventilator. I know he's getting antsy and truthfully, I would have to hide his keys or do something drastic to try to stop a grown person from driving his own car! Prayerfully, he'll hold on a little longer and at least settle for local driving until we can figure out what's going on…

Tee is getting stronger. We're doing good overall, hanging in there, while watching the rest of the world go to hell after the killing of George Floyd—another unarmed black man killed senselessly by a white cop. There is never good timing for this kind of thing and it's on the heels of frustration from the pandemic. People are tired, and losing their minds, rightfully so.

We must figure out how we can help without being physically present. It doesn't help the situation when the Chief Devil in Charge (Satan himself) is lying and instigating and making a bad situation worse. We must continue to stay prayed up. Bishop preached from Acts 2 yesterday "How are We Going to Handle This?" He talked about putting our Faith in the promises of God and not the problem. I'm consistently grateful for the timing and relevance of his regular teachings, now more than ever!

Sunday 6/7 @ 6:20 AM (19th anniversary of Mom's death)

I'm up and at it today, as I was before and during Tee's hospitalization. My big brother-cousin, Merv, passed last week on June 1. That was certainly a huge loss for our family, leaving a deep hole in my heart. Why Merv, God? I'd been praying for everyone's strength. Merv was a professional writer, author, and television producer. We were working on some projects together, including my book. He told me that no one could write my story better than me, and encouraged me to write it and he would review it.

Today is the 19th anniversary of my mom's death. Yesterday marked one month for Tee being home. It's all so bittersweet.

What a difference one month can make! Tee has gained 10 pounds. He's looking and feeling healthier and stronger. He's doing everything but cooking and driving, although he's been threatening to do both. He's probably still a few weeks away from driving, as he needs to be able to maintain better control of his dominant right side.

I'm just pleased he's more and more like my old Boopy, Praise God! He's very motivated and does most of his exercises regularly. He's becoming less dependent and soon won't need his aide, Chris, who is actually more like a friend and overseer right now more than anything. Chris' biggest job is motivating this big kid and keeping him focused on the task at hand, which most times means making sure Tee stays safe and out of the bushes. Yes, out of the bushes…Tee was trying to trim the bushes with bad balance and one good arm. It's no surprise that he toppled over;

it's a blessing he wasn't injured by the hedge clippers. Imagine my shock hearing all this commotion beneath my bedroom window where I was working and looking out to see Chris panicking and scrambling to help "Sir" (his affectionate and respectful name for Tee) up.

I was amused and angered at the same time—laughing while scolding him like a mischievous child getting into trouble as soon as you turn your back. Never a dull moment around here! That's why most days, I let Chris do the "parenting" for Tee, so I can relax and focus on my work.

This COVID-19 pandemic is still very much alive along with the civil unrest due to inherent racism in America! We're constantly praying for both. Tee has been discharged from home PT and he's now working on home OT. He'll be transitioning to outpatient PT in a few weeks. He'll also be getting his EMG to determine if there's any truth to the suggested nerve damage in his right upper arm from lying in the prone position for so long. My PT friends warn me that this is a common occurrence among COVID-19 patients on a ventilator for long periods of time. For many, that position can be the only one that allows them to breathe freely. An unfortunate Catch-22 situation, indeed.

Tuesday 6/8 @ 8:46 AM

Yesterday, I enjoyed a well needed mental health day. Boy, did it feel good! I took Tee to get his COVID-19 retest and COVID-19 antibody test at JH-HCGH, back where this all started almost three months ago. I was able to get my own antibody testing done as well.

It felt great using the hospital's main entrance, instead of the ER, to get to the lab. Another wonderful feeling was running into our "adopted uncle" Dr. Nyanjom in the parking lot. How's that for timing? Seeing him chatting with Tee alive, well and whole again gave me such an emotional high I could barely contain myself!

Thankfully, Tee's retest came back negative and his antibodies were very high. Mine were very low, clearly labeling him as the sicker person.

There is also data now that suggests that antibodies dwindle over time, so we are still proceeding with much caution!

We attended Merv's beautiful virtual homegoing service. When I think about how much he encouraged me to write this book and how much planning he was already putting into it, I feel a sense of nauseating sadness that I know would only partially be resolved by me completing and publishing this book.

Saturday 6/13 @ 8:15 AM

This ended up being a decent week, as I worked swiftly and productively through my numerous tasks. Tee received over $600 in DoorDash and other food and restaurant gift cards. We've had a lot of carryout and delivery over the last few weeks and it's beginning to show on our waistlines. Tee has been pleased with his new weight, but I'm definitely not digging mine.

Tee is doing GREAT, as this was the BREAKOUT WEEK for him. He was discharged from in home OT and he'll be starting outpatient PT at a local MedStar Health location next week. He still needs to get that EMG I mentioned earlier.

His spirits are good and he's getting back to normal. He had a one-man DJ party cranking in the basement and he's back to trying to do his outside tasks with Chris' help. He even defiantly and proudly drove us to a local Popeyes a few nights ago in his big truck, LOL. He was so thrilled. I couldn't burst his bubble, so I just went along with it, part of me cheered for him inside. I was just so happy to have him healthy and whole again, and driving for the first time in 3 months. We finally scheduled the maintenance company to get our pool opened up and operating for the summer. His OT said it should be good therapy for him. I agreed to open it, as long as he doesn't try to take on too much, like with trimming the hedges. Swimming could be a nice treat for both of us and a nice opportunity to get a little R & R since we're not doing much of anything else this year in the way of recreation.

I am working on my book, which excites me. I was beginning to feel a bit smothered with all that's happened over the last few months. Writing is a nice outlet for me.

I heard some great advice this morning from my old buddy, Dr. Phil. It resonated with me as he said, "Surround yourself with people who have your best interest at heart." God are you using my friend to tell me something? Tee swears Dr. Phil and I are having an affair, because I tune in to him all the time and I revere him. I keep assuring Tee I'm not into old, bald white men, but he imparts a lot of wisdom. Even though he's speaking to numerous viewers, I feel like he's speaking directly to me. I tell Tee—he too, could learn something from Dr. Phil, imagine that.

Tuesday 6/16 @ 1:04 PM

Productive week, lots of wheels in motion. I've been having on-going meetings with my editor to discuss my book. She gives me tasks and I have deadlines to meet. I have a lot of content to be organized and sent over to the team. There's always something to do. I have tons of texts and journal entries and progress notes that I need to transcribe and organize. Tee has volunteered to help, which is GREAT. It keeps him involved. It also saves us money from having to hire too many people, and time-sharing documents back and forth since he's right here.

We've had a lot of early interest in our story thus far and the day is still very young. The interest level, coupled with well-written content and the current pandemic climate, should warrant a bestseller status, God willing! We're shooting for a release by the winter of 2020-2021, ideally.

Sunday 6/21 @ 8:09 PM

We enjoyed a nice, quiet weekend. The relaxation was welcomed after a tiring, hectic workweek. Tee started outpatient PT Friday; he'll be going twice a week, most likely on Mondays and Thursdays. We met his new

PT, Elise, and she performed an assessment. She appeared deeply knowledgeable, thorough and caring, so that was a good thing. I always pray for the best providers and services and God always sends us the best. I am rarely disappointed!

Saturday was a beautiful day. We opened the pool. Our future son-in-law, Marcus, came over and helped the old man set up the yard stuff before it began pouring.

Wednesday 6/24 @ 6:28 AM

We're going to conduct our first live social media interview with the Washington Informer magazine this week. Very excited about that! Gotta carve out time in this already too-full schedule of mine. During a typical week, I work at my 9 to 5, do a little real estate on the side, and look after Tee and G'mom. Tee's only job these days is to do his PT and get well while tackling smaller-scale household tasks and assisting me with this book. He's doing an excellent job! I just have to keep an eye on him, so he remains balanced and calm, and not try to take on too much, too soon!

Sunday 6/28 @ 11:49 AM

Yesterday was good. I completed some administrative work, household tasks and prayer call prep. We did our Saturday weekly "TC family and friends" prayer call at 4:10 PM. The number of participants has dwindled some during these summer months, but it's pretty steady. Everyone needs prayer right about now as never before! People always tell us how refreshing our prayer call is and how they look forward to it, so we'll keep it going until God instructs us otherwise.

Lots of people are back out in the public, despite the ongoing pandemic. Tee and I stay busy keeping to ourselves; handling phone calls, Zoom conferencing, taking car rides, going on day trips, swimming in the pool, grilling, eating carryout, etc. No need for outside interactions

—not yet. We just won't take that chance since we don't know where other folks have been or who they've been around. Better safe than sorry. We've had our once-in-a-lifetime COVID-19 encounter!

Our live interview with the Washington Informer went well. I sent out the link and posted it on our Facebook page for all to see. There will be more like that to come.

Friday 7/3 @ 1:40 PM (Independence Day Weekend)

The sun is shining brightly, it's very hot, and it's supposed to be like this through next Tuesday. Once again, we'll be chilling, eating, drinking, enjoying the pool and being merry together this weekend. I'm planning to sleep in and read a nice book, one of my favorite pastimes. I'm going to move the prayer call to Monday because it looks like a lot of folks will be unavailable due to the holiday.

Sunday 7/5 @ 11:00 AM

Yesterday, we got in the pool together and just talked and enjoyed the weather and tranquility. It was awesome. It saddens me to think how much pain and turmoil Tee went through only a few months ago, and how he almost didn't make it…BUT GOD!

Bishop just preached a mighty sermon called "Radical Religion" from Luke 10:30-37. He's very passionate and calling for us to do our part. I am surely praying for clarity on that.

Many fireworks have been canceled this weekend due to the pandemic. We safely watched a beautiful medley of nationwide fireworks on CNN. I also sent a letter to Dr. Sarkar, the ER doctor at JH whose proficiency and adeptness saved Tee's life at the beginning of his ordeal back on March 20. (See correspondence with Dr. Sarkar in Part I)

Wednesday 7/ 8 @ 12:50 PM

It's been a good week thus far, the usual busy. Tee got his EMG nerve test done and he does have confirmed nerve damage in his deltoid, a muscle that covers the shoulder and raises the arm away from the side. This is a result of the way he was lying in the prone position in the hospital for such long periods of time. We're believing by faith that this will be healed as well.

It's already July and Tee is due back to work mid-September. It looks like his firm will most likely be working virtually through the end of the year, which is great for Tee. It'll be quite a while before he can withstand an office environment, nor can he physically handle the demands of the commute. He'll most likely resume PT for the coming months as well. We'll be working out those details as it gets closer. His boss and colleagues have been phenomenal with their level of support—especially Janet R, chief of HR. We send much love and appreciation to all of them for what they've done for us during this time!

Thursday 7/16 @ 5:18PM (two months post hospital release)

It's been an extremely long week. Tee had a lot of appointments. I will never do that many in one week again! What was I thinking? He gets tired, and the legwork and driving falls on me, then it makes me tired. He had an orthopedic surgeon appointment and PT appointment on Monday. Wednesday, he had a follow-up and pulmonary function test with Dr. Nyanjom. Thursday, he had a follow-up EKG and cardiology appointment.

He received good reports from all of them. The orthopedic surgeon sent him for an MRI of his shoulder to get more info on his potential deltoid muscle and nerve injury. Dr. Nyanjom was very pleased with Tee's breathing and lung exam. He had a normal EKG at that appointment, so the cardiologist discontinued the Metoprolol he was started on at JH for the A-fibrillation. Praise God! He has to continue to follow up with everything to ensure there are no long-term consequences since there are still a lot of unknowns with COVID-19. We are truly grateful for these reports. This was a good week! TGBTG!

In Essence

Tee recently received a cortisone shot to assist with the swelling and discomfort from his deltoid muscle and nerve damage. He is continuing his semiweekly outpatient PT. He had experienced ongoing periods of ICU-related PTSD at home, which affected his sleep habits for weeks, due to the constant awakenings in the ICU. He has begun to sustain more of a normal sleep pattern with the aid of medication and implementation of better sleep habits (for example, no television or electronics before or during bedtime, no daytime naps, etc.).

He is also continuing to be checked on by his JH Pain Management and Rehabilitation Team (PM&R) and his Post-Acute COVID-19 Team (PACT). PACT includes Rehabilitation Psychology due to the cognitive effects and impacts of COVID-19. His sleep has improved, his spirits are good, he has gained back most of his weight, and he is looking and feeling more normal each day.

Tee is still experiencing some short-term memory issues, which are being addressed by the Rehab Psych team. From what they tell us, this seems to be fairly typical for someone highly affected by a viral illness. All his providers are pleased with his recovery thus far, and they feel like he will make a total recovery within a year.

COVID-19 quickly attacks and ravishes the body; it may take months, sometimes years, to recover from these effects. We are eternally grateful to God for sparing our lives and making Tee whole again. We are like the lyrics of the song by the legendary Winans, *"Millions didn't make it, but I was one of the ones who did"*. We are faithful that God will continue to heal him and make him brand new from the inside out. We are committed to sharing our story so that others know just how important it is to protect yourself from this devastating, life-changing disease.

As Bishop Thomas recently preached, "*There are some things we can't explain, but we cannot deny the goodness of God in our lives.*" Amen! We also want you to know that we are so glad we serve a God of second chances. To God Be the Amazing Glory!

Chapter 9

My Life-Altering Experience, as Told by Tee

My wife, Marcy, has done an amazing job telling our story up until this point, however I am glad that I have lived to be able to tell our story from my perspective, too.

ER visit:

Throughout the week, I developed a cough and a fever that would not break, so on Monday March 16, 2020, Marcy and I went to Patient First Urgent Care (PT-First) in Columbia, Maryland, to get tested for COVID-19. PT-First was unable to give us a COVID-19 test, but we both came back negative for influenza, strep and RSV. They sent us to Johns Hopkins Howard County General Hospital (JH-HCGH) for COVID-19 testing.

When I got my positive results on March 17, I was upset and frustrated. All I could think of is "How and where did I catch this disease?" Both Marcy and I move around a lot and we both work with the public. All types of thoughts ran through my head regarding whether I got this at church, work, or elsewhere. Meanwhile, Marcy and I decided to just stay quarantined and wait out the 14 days together.

Marcy spoke with my pulmonologist, Dr. Nyanjom, and my primary care physician, and they prescribed me some cough medicine mid-week to suppress the cough and allow me to sleep. Dr. Nyanjom told me to keep an eye on the cough and if it persisted to bring me to the ER for a lung CT scan and for further observation. We were reluctant to go back to the ER unnecessarily because of our unpleasant experience on Monday with COVID-19 testing.

My fever leveled out over the week, but unfortunately, my cough worsened, and it eventually became uncontrollable. I was very weak, lethargic, and seemingly short of breath (in hindsight). On Friday morning, March 20, Marcy reached back out to Dr. Nyanjom (my pulmonologist), but they didn't connect until late afternoon. He instructed her to bring me to the hospital immediately for a lung CT scan and he made arrangements for the nurses in the ER to expect our arrival. Marcy had given me some cough medicine with codeine earlier in the day, so I was a bit drowsy when she let me know that we were going to the hospital. I slept the entire ride and we arrived at the hospital in less than an hour.

When we arrived, I was still very drowsy, but I was amazed that the nurse was there waiting for us at the entrance. When I opened the door she asked, "Are you Mr. Clark? We have been waiting for you." She quickly rolled me into the ER and told Marcy that she could not come in due to her positive diagnosis. From there, my memory is vague, but the last thing I remember is that the doctor told me that my lungs were failing and that they would need to emergency intubate me. Although I was drowsy, hearing the doctor tell me that made my hair stand up. I started to panic and wondered what they were going to do to me, so I called my wife who was waiting for me and put the doctor on the phone.

Waking up after 28 days on the ventilator

When I woke up in the ICU, I was extremely tired, had a sore throat and was very thirsty. I arose to a medley of doctors and nurses hovering over me, one of them gingerly asking a whole slew of questions (first and last name, date of birth, did I know where I was, etc.). I passed their test with flying colors, answering all the questions correctly, even though I didn't really know *why* I was there and *how long* it had been. I couldn't tell you if the irritation in my voice was more because of the questioning or all the little bells and alarms going off constantly from those ICU machines.

After I answered the questions, all but one or two personnel went back to their normal duties. I informed the doctor at my bedside that I needed to go to the bathroom. I attempted to get up. At that moment, I realized I couldn't move. My entire body had experienced atrophy from being on the ventilator for 28 days and was immobilized. I immediately panicked and asked, "What's wrong with me?"

My blood pressure shot up and more alarms started. The other personnel rushed back over to me and asked me to calm down. The head physician assured me that everything would be OK. He immediately began to explain that my muscles were dormant, but that everyone would be working with me to restore my physical condition. I was extremely upset and nervous with the mere fact that I was paralyzed—at that moment, it didn't matter for how long. I wondered what my life would be like if they could not restore me. I tried to stay positive, but this new feeble condition was way too new and too scary to me, especially given my athletic background. It was hard to imagine not being able to walk again.

I vividly remember one of the ICU nurses named Jenny being very attentive to me. I asked her for some water to quench my unbearable thirst and was told I could not have any liquids because my throat muscles were too weak. Jenny did everything else to comfort me and even gave me some flavored ice that helped sooth my throat a bit. The cherry-flavored ice chips were so good, I kept asking for more. Finally, after three cups they cut me off for the day for fear of aspiration.

After several days in the ICU, I noticed I had grown a large beard. Jenny volunteered to cut it for me. I thought that was such a nice gesture and gave her the OK. I was very nervous, not just because I wasn't sure if she knew what she was doing, but also because I'm very meticulous about my appearance.

The next time I spoke with Marcy, I asked her to bring up my clippers, but JH would not allow any outside items to be delivered. Jenny said she had some electric clippers and would use those. The following day, Jenny came in early and proceeded to trim my facial hair. The whole time she kept telling me how glad the entire ICU staff was to see my recovery and that she was honored to help with the trimming of my facial hair.

After about 15 minutes, Jenny finished and gave me a mirror. I thanked her and told her I felt 20 years younger. She was ecstatic and only then did she confess that it was the first time she had shaved a man's face. After looking in the mirror again, I thought to myself, "Yes, I can tell!" I laughed to myself but thanked Jenny sincerely. I was grateful for her willingness!

My throat was still very sore, and my voice was barely above a whisper, but I tried to speak with Marcy via Zoom anyway. I became very emotional after seeing and hearing her for the first time in 28 days. I asked her why she wasn't there with me and when was she coming to visit me. She sadly informed me that because of COVID-19, JH has shut down to all visitors.

I told her I was paralyzed. She tried to reassure me that I would get better over time, but I didn't believe her. Instead, during our entire conversation, I kept wondering how I would be able to provide for her. At that moment, I felt helpless and became overwhelmed with thoughts racing in my head about what the future would look like if this condition never corrected as everyone said it would.

To combat this helplessness, I decided to put on my Big Boy Hat and began giving Marcy instructions on what I needed done at the house. I asked her to get in touch with my brother-in-law and ask him to come over and reset the water RO/DI unit. I asked her to contact our next-door neighbor to get the name and number of the contractor who cuts their grass. I also told her to call the pool guy to come to the house and open up the pool from its season's rest.

Marcy started laughing at me barking all these instructions like a whispering drill sergeant. "There you go," she said. "You're not even out of the ICU and you're already bossing me around!"

Unbeknownst to me, Marcy had already proficiently and graciously taken care of those items and more. She scolded me to focus on getting better and not to worry about the house anymore. I love how we always have each other's back. So, especially now, I had no recourse but to concede and just rest and heal.

Discharged from the ICU

On Friday, April 24, 2020, I was discharged from the ICU and moved to an intermediary step-down COVID-19 unit floor in another wing. It was a very exciting day and several of the doctors/nurses and aides all lined the hallway and cheered me on as they rolled me out of the ICU.

Apparently, I was their sickest and longest COVID-19 patient to survive in the ICU. They even played my favorite song ("Eye of the Tiger" from "Rocky") and the entire team clapped and cheered me on. I was so moved that I could not hold back the tears.

I'm extremely thankful for that team in the ICU. I was told before my departure from the ICU that when I arrived in the COVID-19 unit, I would be given three hours of physical therapy (PT), occupational therapy (OT) and speech language and pathology (SLP) daily. They let me rest over the weekend and my intense therapy sessions began first thing Monday morning.

Around 7:00 AM, I was awakened by a nurse serving my breakfast. I was really hungry and anxiously awaited what was prepared for me. I opened the tray and saw a beautiful fruit tray, some apple sauce and more ice chips. Initially, I wondered why there was no protein on the plate and my nurse told me I was on a restricted diet. At the time, I didn't realize what that meant, but the fruit tray was so good, I pretty much forgot about the missing protein.

My appetite was fierce since I hadn't eaten any solid foods for over 30 days. Upon being given my menu for dinner, I found wonderful choices available to me. I noticed the first choice under "Favorites" was a fruit tray assortment and a salad. I figured I'd had enough fruit and wanted something more substantial. The meat offerings included Salisbury steak, chicken, salmon and turkey. My inner self screamed, "Hola-Lu-Ya!" as I immediately ordered turkey with gravy and mixed vegetables.

Although my smell and taste buds were gone, I could feel my mouth salivating just thinking about my dinner request. The nurse took my order and stated, "Great, I'll get that order right away."

About an hour later, my food arrived on a beautiful silver platter. I was so excited for this first official meal with substance. When the nurse lifted the lid off the platter, my eyes darn near popped out of my head. What I saw was nothing like what I expected. There was a large round mound of pureed food staring at me. I asked the nurse in sheer disbelief, "What the heck is this?"

She replied in her sweet and calming voice, "This is your turkey dinner." She then reminded me I was on a restricted diet. I didn't realize "restricted" meant mush. I totally lost my appetite after seeing a heap of brown, beige lumpy stuff with a little hint of green.

The nurse went on to point out to me, "This is the turkey and here are the peas. Over here is the stuffing and gravy (all mushed together)."

I rationalized how hungry I was and decided to try it in spite of its looks. I took a few bites and quickly realized that it was far from the turkey and gravy my momma used to cook! It was also hard to actually eat since I still had a feeding tube running through my nose. Placing each bite in my mouth proved quite difficult. My fork kept hitting the tube, causing the food to fall. After a few failed attempts of maneuvering around the feeding tube, I eventually gave up and asked for another fruit tray.

I called Marcy complaining heavily about the pureed food they subjected me to. She reasoned, "Babe, you can't have solid foods yet, so I'll need you to try and eat what they give you so you can get stronger."

I retorted, "Heck no, I can't eat this! I'll just eat fruit until I get out of here!"

The nurse returned several minutes later and asked if I was finished.

"Absolutely!" That answer slipped out almost before she finished her question.

She detected my sarcasm. "You didn't eat much. Did you not like the turkey?"

"I just wasn't expecting my turkey in that form."

She understood and graciously asked if she could get me something else.

"Yes, please. I would like some water and juice."

She told me she would bring me some thickened water and juice. Now, I didn't understand what thickened meant when used in the context of the liquids I requested, but when she brought me the cup, I soon found out.

Because I was so thirsty, I quickly took the cup, lifted it to my mouth and tilted my head back for a much-needed sip. Whoa! Surprisingly, no water came forth, so I looked inside the cup to make sure something was even in there. I did see some type of clear substance, but it wasn't liquid at all.

"*So, THIS is what she meant by thickened water or juice,*" I thought to myself. I was given a cup of one of each. I have never heard of such a thing; both looked like Jell-O.

The nurse once again told me that I was on a restricted diet, including liquids. All liquids had to be thickened to keep me from aspirating. The same applied to my food. Apparently, my throat muscles were not healed, and they wanted me to be safe.

I tried to take all this in stride and asked if I could at least get some flavored ice chips. I was told they only had plain ice chips in that ward so she would bring me what they had. I asked for three cups of it. She agreed and returned momentarily with three full cups of ice chips. She must have realized I wasn't a happy camper with the food and drink situation, so she didn't mind giving me extra ice in each cup.

I was so upset about all that was occurring, and my thirst was getting the better of me that I started scheming. I took one of the cups of ice and placed it out of view under my nightstand and only ate from the other two cups. Several hours later, after the nurse had cleared away my empty cups, I retrieved the hidden cup and the ice chips had melted. Ta-dah! I now had water. I know I was breaking the rules, but I needed to have some real water to feel like I was normal again. I repeated this defiant act repeatedly to get the water I craved.

I did, however, take only small sips to avoid aspirating. It got pretty tiring, going through this water-making process week after week, which made me all the more determined to do what I needed to do to get better and resume a normal diet at home with my wife. Marcy shook her head in disbelief at my persistence in breaking the rules when I told her this story. Yes, all for a small drink of water!

I started out with Tara as my PT. She was wonderful and very caring. She told me my condition was normal from being on the ventilator that long and that she would have me up and walking soon. I was skeptical, but optimistic.

During our first session, we practiced rolling over and rocking to assist me with standing. On my first attempt, I rocked four times and then tried to push up on the walker and stand with her assistance. Since I had no strength and muscle tone, she basically lifted me up.

Once standing, I began to smile, but immediately noticed I was having trouble breathing. I felt weak then fell back onto the bed. Tara tried to comfort me, seeing how nervous I got. She told me she knows that I'm feeling like I just ran a marathon.

"Exactly right," I responded.

Again, she reassured me my progress was normal and that we would continue to work on my stamina and the rebuilding of my muscles. Her comforting words made a huge difference in me giving it one more try, as opposed to me giving up.

That was a very strange and emotional time for me as I continued to wonder if I would ever be able to walk again. I was distraught, until Tara's reassurance allowed me to see that I was making progress. I became highly motivated and did everything they told me to do and more when I could. As a result, I was transferred four days later to the Inpatient Physical Therapy floor, which would be my next step towards home.

JH Inpatient PT the road to home

After several weeks of intense therapy (from Dr. Pruski's PM&R team including Tara, Emily, Melanie, etc.) I was able to get out of bed, with the assistance of a nurse, and move over to the chair. This was such a relief for me because I had developed a bedsore and sitting in the chair relieved some of the pain associated with the bedsore. From that point on, I refused to be confined to a bed.

Unfortunately, though, my muscle tone was still very weak so I could only move around with the assistance of a walker or nurse. That was very nerve-wracking having to constantly call a nurse to get me up to use the bathroom. On many occasions, they could not get to me in a timely fashion, especially in those early morning hours, so I reluctantly used the bedside urinal.

After weeks of intense therapy, I was given the green light for discharge. Yea! My discharge date was set for Wednesday May 6, 2020, a day after my fifth wedding anniversary. I was so excited! I tried to get out on or before the 5th, but there were still some tasks I had to complete in order to check all the required boxes for my release. I later found out that Marcy needed that extra time anyway for all the prepping she did to create the most awesome and unexpected surprise "Welcome Home" event I could ever have imagined.

Between the send-off inside JH and Marcy's spectacular welcome outside JH, which included many friends and loved ones, as well as the press, I was truly overcome with emotion.

Chapter 10

The Return Home and Ongoing Recovery, as Told by Tee

Discharged from Johns Hopkins

On Tuesday, May 5, 2020, the night before my discharge, I could hardly sleep. I was so excited about going home, back to my comfortable and loving dwelling. Although, I appreciated all that JH did for me, I couldn't wait to get out of there and back with my wife and family.

Wednesday morning, I called Marcy at 6:00 AM. I told her I wanted her to pick me up at 10:00 AM. She responded with, "Hold on, Tee. Johns Hopkins will be calling me soon with the time of your discharge."

Around 7:15 AM, Marcy called me back and told me I would be discharged at Noon. I told her I wanted her here at 11:55 AM. She could tell I was super anxious to get out of there and she wanted to oblige but little did I know she had a lot going on in preparation for my release.

Around 11:50 AM, the nurse came in and gave me all my discharge papers and a white sweatsuit to wear out of the hospital. She told me that she had been in touch with Marcy and that she was 10 minutes out. We packed up all my things and then another nurse came in with a wheelchair to roll me down to the main level.

That was the longest wheelchair ride ever. It seemed like I was going through a tunnel of mazes and back elevators. Because of COVID-19, the nurses had to be in full PPE gear and certain elevators and doors were quarantined off for my departure. In addition, I had to have a security escort. After about 15 minutes, we finally arrived at a secured door on the side of the hospital. The security guard asked me what type of vehicle Marcy would be driving. I told him to look for a gray SUV (my wife's car). The security guard went outside to look for the vehicle and unfortunately it was raining so he couldn't find her.

About five minutes later, the security guard returned explaining that there was no gray SUV out there. I immediately panicked, wondering where Marcy could be. One of the nurses took out her cellphone and called Marcy. All I could think of was that she wasn't there where I needed her to be and so they would need to take me back to my hospital room. Marcy didn't answer, so the security guard went out again to look for her. He came back several minutes later smiling and said, "I found her! She's in a silver Lexus."

I let out a huge sigh of relief. "Oh, she's driving my car."

As they rolled me out the secured doors and down the sidewalk, I was getting a little wet from the rain, and was anxious to get into the car. Marcy and my daughter, Kaelyn, helped me out of the wheelchair and into the back seat. She and Marcy were still standing outside. I thought, "*What are they doing? I'm ready to go!*"

As it turned out, my entire exit was being captured by a few videographers from local TV stations, including CBS Baltimore. Marcy gave a quick interview. Then there were several minutes of emotional hugging between Kaelyn and Marcy (all captured on video, as well).

I kept seriously thinking the whole time, "Please get me out of here, before these people change their minds and take me back!"

Finally, Marcy got into the car and we drove off, with Kaelyn and her beau, Marcus, following behind us in their car. As we turned the corner, I noticed Marcy was pulling into a nearby parking garage. "*Where are you going?*" I asked.

We were still on JH property and all I could think is that they were going to take me back. Marcy told me she had to meet someone in the garage to drop something off. After driving around in the garage for several minutes, I realized she was lost. Very agitated at this point, I kept asking where she was going. Finally, she stopped and asked someone how to get to Level 4.

Once on Level 4, we turned the corner and there stood a bunch of my family members in the rain shouting my name! They had a huge Welcome Home banner with my name and picture, and all I could do was cry. Apparently, family members from near and far wanted to see me. Wow, I was so touched. And to think Marcy coordinated all of that (with the assistance of my cousin Jack)! To say I was grateful to all of them is an understatement. Those special moments will live on in my memory forever.

After an emotional reunion, my family members loaded up my car with food, toilet paper, wipes, snacks, and a ton of miscellaneous items. I didn't know that Baltimore's Channel 13 WJZ News had followed us there to the garage. There, they did an interview with Marcy, Kaelyn and me, as they captured my welcome home rooftop parking garage celebration for the evening news.

Thirty minutes later, we finally departed for our destination: HOME. Kaelyn and Marcus followed us there as well. Marcy kept looking in the rearview mirror at me, asking me what I was thinking. I told her that I was thankful to be alive and that I was just taking in all the sights.

I had been in the hospital for 46 days and hadn't seen much of the outside world. Therefore, my view of the world had vastly changed in that time. For starters, I appreciated more of the smallest, and most commonplace things like a bus stop bench, a patch of grass along the street, etc. I now saw them as things that may give people solace along their day.

But all that mattered on that day was that it was time for some serious, well-needed rest in that quiet sanctuary of a bedroom in my own house. Yes, Tee was finally on his way HOME. Thank You, Jesus!

Free at last: I am back home 46 days later

Upon arriving home, Marcus and Kaelyn assisted me inside. When I opened the door, Kaelyn's dog, Dexter, greeted me with his tail wagging ferociously, "Dad, Dexter misses you too!" I was happy to see him as well, but my arm was still immobilized, so I could not pat him.

My next destination was to our first-floor in-law suite. Marcy had a hospital bed delivered to that bedroom so I wouldn't have to climb the stairs at all. It was perfect. Everything I needed was right there. Seeing that space made me even more overcome with gratitude for being out of that hospital atmosphere with those ICU machines dinging and beeping all hours of the day and night. It's hard to even imagine the mental anguish one experiences from the noise and distractions over that long of a period of time. Ironically, it seems counterproductive to getting well.

Those hospital thoughts were behind me now. New calming and positive thoughts of total elation took precedence in my comfortable surroundings. I was still very weak and unable to walk, so after a few days at home, I realized I would need additional assistance. Some of the most common things we take for granted, like bathing, going to the bathroom, and dressing, I was unable to accomplish on my own. My wife had to help me with everything and although she didn't complain, I knew it was putting a lot of strain on her. After she bathed me one evening, she hurt her back. At that point, we decided we would need to get an aide to assist me with my daily activities.

I was not too happy about having another person in our home—especially at a time like this with the threat of them transmitting the virus and with my state of health still being so vulnerable. Reluctantly, I agreed just so my wife could get some much-needed rest.

Marcy and I had some interesting conversations with contrasting ideas regarding the type of aide I would need. I told her I wanted a pretty and petite nurse, while she envisioned a heavyweight-warden-type unattractive aide who would keep me straight. Marcy said I didn't have to worry about the young pretty girl option. She just wasn't having that. When she asked if I would consider a male aide, I quickly blurted, "Hell no!"

However, after much discussion, we agreed to give it a shot. Fortunately, one of our contacts informed Marcy about a male nursing aide who was very close, reliable and came highly recommended. Marcy reached out to Chris from Oula Home Health Services and he agreed to work with us.

Home help is on the way

Chris arrived promptly on Saturday, May 9, 2020. Although he was initially shy, he finally got comfortable with us as well as us with him. Chris has some strong family values and is from Benin, Africa. We hit it off right away. Marcy showed him around the house and gave him a "To Do" list for my care.

Most importantly, I was on a strict diet and vitamin regimen and it was important that Chris keep me on schedule. He was very attentive and promptly distributed my medication daily. He also assisted me with getting up and escorting me to the bathroom. At first, this was very awkward for me to have another man taking me to the bathroom, removing my clothing and even wiping me when I was done. I had no choice but to humble myself and become totally dependent on him until my body got stronger.

When it came to getting my first shower, I was extremely uncomfortable with him washing me from head to toe. Chris was very professional and I'm sure he noticed how nervous I was, but he assured me that he's done this many times before, and that it would be OK. At that point, I just had to suck it up and understand that because of my condition, I would need constant assistance for a while until my body got stronger.

Chris turned out to be a true blessing and he even assisted me with cutting my hair. As soon as he mentioned one day that he used to cut students' hair while in college, I asked if he wouldn't mind cutting mine. "Sure, Sir" he said, and I sent him immediately upstairs to retrieve my clippers. He did a good job and I felt relieved.

In addition to hiring a personal aide to assist me with my daily activities, we also had to enlist some outpatient professionals for PT, OT, and SLP, and a nurse. After a few days at home, Nurse Maria from Bayada Home Health Care came by and conducted a medical assessment. She was extremely upbeat and highly energized. It was a bit scary to see someone with so much energy since I could not relate at the moment. I grew to really admire her and could not wait to see her weekly to hear the updates she had on my condition.

In addition to our nurse, my PT professional Mark, also from Bayada, started soon thereafter. As with Maria, he also started out with an assessment of my health to perform his assignment. Mark was very friendly and quickly told us that "I would be easy to restore." He knew this because he noticed how eager I was to get better, and that I was healthy prior to my recent hospitalization. He vowed to do everything in his power to help me. I was surprised to hear that given my weak condition, but it gave me some serious confidence.

The following week, Mark began his twice-a-week visits to start my PT. He initially showed me techniques on how to stand up and how to push-off my legs to stand up from the sofa and kitchen chair. I quickly showed signs of improvement so Mark challenged me to ditch the walker. I was nervous about the idea of not having the walker because I was afraid of falling. I decided to give it a shot and I folded up the walker and put it in the corner in the adjacent room. From that point on, I did not use the walker any longer, but at times I would need the assistance of Chris, or my grandmother's cane, since she wasn't using it anymore. I decided to keep the cane by my side as a safety measure. I was even thinking about adding some "bling" to it.

After several weeks of PT, Mark challenged me to go up/down the stairs. I started with the basement stairs and was able to get down with little assistance. Coming up was a different story, but I managed to get back to the main level. Mark stated, "You're doing very well!"

The following visit, Mark challenged me to walk outside up and down the hill. This would truly test my stamina and balance. I was psyched because I really started to be more confident with my walking and I not only walked down the hill, but I also walked down to the mailbox from the main house. This was a huge task because my driveway is very long and hilly. When I reached the end of the driveway, I noticed Mark was sweating and breathing heavily. I asked if he was OK and he laughed, stating, "You're in better shape than me."

I was proud of myself that day, and that gave me an enormous amount of confidence. After four weeks of intense PT, he stated that he was amazed at how fast I progressed, and he wished me well.

In early June, I was feeling confident with walking, so I decided to see if I could do some small yardwork. I got my hedge trimmers to trim the bushes. This was not a hard task and I felt sure I could handle trimming the bushes. However, Chris was nervous and said he would go with me. I figured, great, I'll have an extra hand. However, Chris had no intention of helping me, but rather watching me. So, I started to cut the bushes and got to the end of my task when I stepped on my shoestring and tumbled into the bushes.

When I looked up, my aide was in total panic "Sir, Sir, Sir, are you all-right?" The expression on his face was priceless and I could not stop laughing. Ironically, Mamma Bear (Marcy) just happened to be looking out the window when I tumbled and she quickly yelled at me, "You See! You're Doing Too Much!" This was a hilarious moment and I just could not stop laughing. I really thought Chris was going to have a heart attack. I stopped trimming the bushes; well, I was finished anyway, and we went back inside.

Also, in early June, I started OT with Melissa from Bayada. Melissa was great and she started giving me a bunch of exercises (pushups, butterflies, quads and light weightlifting). At first, I could not complete the multiple reps of these exercises, so we decided to scale back a bit. Unfortunately, my stamina was low, and my muscles were not cooperating.

At one point, Chris got down on the floor with me to do the exercises and I noticed he was having trouble too. He said, "Sir, Sir, that's too much! I'm having problems doing that many myself." I said "OK, Chris, but I need to push myself to try to get stronger." Melissa agreed and stated that the exercises are designed to be difficult, but the more I did them, the stronger I would get. I'm still doing some of those exercises and I'm still having problems completing the multiple reps. I was told that it could take up to a year to completely recover.

Transition to outpatient therapy/services

Although I have good health insurance, Bayada was authorized to provide me only five weeks of outpatient care. After five weeks, I said goodbye to Melissa, Mark and Maria, but I still was quite weak and needed additional PT. My wife did a lot of research and with the recommendation from my OT Melissa, Marcy reached out to MedStar, which agreed to accept me as a new patient.

Initially, they were a little skeptical since I was their first COVID-19 recovery patient. However, their office was already following the CDC guidelines with gloves, masks and social distancing, so they assigned me to one of their best physical therapists, Elise. Elise has been great, and I see her twice a week as she works on restoring my body. The PT that I get at MedStar is more intense than what I was getting at home. In fact, when I leave their facility, I usually go home and take a nap because I am worn out.

When Elise did the initial assessment, my strength levels were unbelievably low. She gave me a hand device and asked me to squeeze it to gauge my hand strength. By the look on her face, I knew I had failed that test. I was also having issues raising my right arm. I generally could get it up halfway, but it would immediately drop. I had no muscle tone in my right arm and hand at all. Elise stated that they would concentrate on strengthening my hand and arm and then focus on my legs for balance.

Clean bills of health

On June 8, almost three months from my initial positive COVID-19 diagnosis, I received a negative COVID-19 test and positive antibodies. My antibodies were off the charts, indicative of the severity of my viral load. My wife who suffered mildly from COVID-19 symptoms contrarily had very low antibodies. I was ecstatic. Although I had been cleared by Maria (my home nurse) as "resolved" since I hadn't had any symptoms in months, it was very liberating to know that this virus, which had almost claimed my life, had FINALLY cleared my system. Praise God!

A few weeks later, I had my first live visit with my pulmonologist, Dr. Nyanjom. He gave me a pulmonary function test and reviewed my recent chest X-ray and gave me a good bill of health, as well. He confirmed my negative COVID-19 test and he was elated. Dr. Nyanjom stated he wanted me to increase my PT activity to help build up my lungs and increase my heart rate and stamina. Unfortunately, the X-ray did show a small spot on my right lung that he said they would be watching. We're not sure if this was from me aspirating or something else related to COVID-19, but he would continue to monitor me and schedule a lung test within six months.

In the meantime, Elise (my PT) had some concerns about my weakness and pain in my neck/shoulder and my inability to lift my right arm. She wanted to make sure that I didn't have any signs of hypoxia or stroke because of my prolonged stay on the ventilator.

She referred me to my post-COVID-19 doctor at JH, Dr. Kim, and an orthopedic surgeon to get a diagnosis of my shoulder. Dr. Kim gave me a thorough evaluation and determined that I did not suffer a stroke or have any major signs of hypoxia. She recommended that I get an electromyography (EMG), which is a nerve conduction test, on my right arm. The orthopedic surgeons' X-rays ruled out any tissue or bone damage. I had to follow up with him to get a cortisone injection for the pain after I received the EMG results.

Johns Hopkins EMG test

After weeks of scheduling difficulties, we were finally able to get into JH for the test. This test is very expensive and requires a lengthy insurance process. I wasn't sure what to expect and was a bit nervous. When we arrived, we had to go through the updated JH protocol (*i.e.*, preregister, answer COVID-19 questions and temperature check).

Once I completed those items, I was sent up to the second floor to get the test. I met with the lab technician, who gave me an overview of the test. He started by saying, "Most people cannot stand this test. You're strong so I know you can handle it."

My nervous response to him was, "You shouldn't have told me that!"

My heart began to race as he described the procedure that I was about to endure. It was a two-step process. The first 30 minutes was with the technician and the last 30 minutes would be with the doctor.

Electromyography (EMG) measures muscle response or electrical activity in response to a nerve's stimulation of the muscle. The test is used to help detect neuromuscular abnormalities. During the test, one or more small needles (also called electrodes) are inserted through the skin into the muscle to evaluate the health condition of the muscles and the nerve cells that control them. These nerve cells are known as motor neurons. They transmit electrical signals that cause muscles to contract and relax.

This test was not pleasant. In fact, I felt like my skin was burning as the technician shocked several areas on my hand, arm and shoulder. It felt like someone was poking me with intense shots of electricity. Although each shock lasted for only a second, it was very painful. After he finished lighting me up for 30 minutes, he said I did well for the first test, but the second test, with the doctor, would be more intense. I said to myself, "Are you kidding me? This crap hurts and I could barely stand *this* test!"

Several minutes later, the doctor came in and described to me how he would be sticking me with multiple needles throughout my hand/arm and shoulder to test the response of my nerves. There was a lot of discomfort at the time the needle electrodes were inserted. They felt like shots (intramuscular injections), although nothing was injected during the EMG. The needles being inserted weren't bad, but when he pushed them into the nerve, wow! Now, *that* was intense, and my muscles felt sore for a few days afterward.

The EMG confirmed that there was nerve damage in the deltoid muscle in my right arm. This damage to the nerve was caused by being in the prone position while on the ventilator for 28 days. The consensus was that I did not have a stroke and the doctor told me that I was fortunate not to have any major cognitive issues, which is common in COVID-19 patients. However, I still have issues with fatigue, strength and balance.

The JH study has found that this injury was indeed a part of the COVID-19 healing process. Post-COVID-19 patients with these and other long-term lingering effects have now been named "long haulers." I was also told not to expect a quick recovery and that it could take up to one year or longer to completely restore my body.

Ongoing recovery and restoration

Currently, I have completed almost three and a half months of in-home and outpatient PT, but I am still struggling with strength, stamina and balance. Although there have been some major improvements, I'm still having issues with my right arm. I'm determined to get better, so I'll be extending my PT treatments as necessary and I continue to see the JH's post-COVID-19 team to ensure the successful continuation of my healing process.

Returning to work (telecommuting)

On September 8, I was given the green light to return to work remotely. I am glad to be able to be back to work after my six-month absence (my last working day was Friday, March 13, before my COVID-19 diagnosis on Tuesday, March 17). I am now focused on working remotely, trying to resume a "new normal" safe life, while continuing with my semiweekly PT visits and maintenance doctor visits.

57th birthday celebration

On Saturday, September 19, 2020 my wife hosted an outdoor drive-up, social distancing birthday celebration for me at our home, with catered cuisine from my favorite local soul food restaurant, Georgia Peach. Of course, we indulged in the family line dances and we even got one of my co-workers, Carey, to sing several songs, mesmerizing the crowd.

Everyone donned their masks and maintained a safe and healthy distance. I was shocked to see so many loved ones travel from near and far during this pandemic to celebrate my birthday and my miracle survival of COVID-19. We had friends and family members who traveled as far as three hours to be in attendance.

Afterward, we received a lot of compliments about the party. Everyone certainly had a great time. I was so grateful to see everyone and elated for everyone to see me healthy and whole, and able to celebrate another birthday! (See Appendix photos)

Johns Hopkins White Coat Ceremony

On December 18, 2020, I was recognized (virtually) by Johns Hopkins, and given an honorary Doctor's white coat during their traditional annual white coat ceremony for incoming medical students. I was able to share my story for these future physicians, and I let them know just how valuable their work is to patients and families like me and mine. It was a very emotional and rewarding opportunity to be able to give a detailed recap of my experiences during my hospitalization. My friends and family have affectionately named me "Dr. Tee". I tease my Hopkins physicians that I am now their colleague, and that we can hold future appointments in the employee lounge, now that I have my white coat. I get lots of smiles on that one. They are very excited and proud of my progress since I was previously dubbed "their sickest COVID-19 patient."(See Appendix photos)

Reflections

The song "Millions," by the widely acclaimed gospel group The Winans, which goes *"Millions didn't make it (but I was one of the ones who did)"* is now among my personal theme songs. Our hearts ache for those who didn't make it, and our prayers go out to the families of the now 470,000, and growing, deceased in the United States. I know my life has been spared for a reason and I am determined to share my experience with others.

First of all, it is my hope and prayer that as this pandemic lingers on, people will not get desensitized and numbed to the point where they let their guards down. In doing so, they can easily become an unnecessary COVID-19 victim. The terrible thing is once you have it, you just don't know if you'll be one of the unfortunate ones who don't make it.

Secondly, I cannot stress enough the importance of 1) wearing a mask, 2) constant handwashing and 3) social distancing and now 4) getting a vaccine when it becomes available. If we would have known then what we know now, perhaps this could have all been prevented! People often complain about the discomfort of wearing a mask, and my response is, *"If you think a mask is uncomfortable, imagine what a ventilation tube down your throat feels like!"*

Lastly, Marcy always tells me that it was God's grace, coupled with unified prayers and good health care resources, that led to my survival. She also tells me that she admires my determination and perseverance. While I wholeheartedly agree with all those things, I also feel like I am in a fierce game of life where COVID-19 is the silent lethal opponent. Just like my athletic days where I always played to win, this is no different.

I have a great life filled with many blessings and a beautiful, spirit-filled wife, whom only God could've sent to me. Mix in with that my wonderful children, extended family and numerous friends, and I know I have so much to live for. I'm determined not to let COVID-19 win!

Thank God for giving me a *Praying Wife* and allowing me to be a *Healed Husband*! To God Be the Amazing Glory!

Chapter 11

Sentiments of a Praying Wife

Sunday 5/10 @ 9:45 AM (Mother's Day)

Boopy's been home four and a half days and it's been wonderful! His homecoming celebration was Awesome, and everything went according to plan. I'll do my best to recap this emotional journey.

A summary of Tee's Homecoming Day and celebrations

Tee had a session with a speech-language and pathologist (SLP), and a few other discharge formalities this morning. He was eagerly anticipating my arrival at Noon, which ended up being closer to 12:30 PM due to the rain and a few unscheduled last stops on the way, including FASTSIGNS to pick up the car magnets. I had to pick up the customized car sign, "CV Tried to Take Us Out But Jesus Saves."

I was coordinating with four to five people while in route, to make this a memorable day for all. I had my personal videographer, two news reporters, the JH discharge nurses with Tee, and a group of family members secretly waiting for my arrival. The JH discharge nurses called me at Noon to learn my ETA and instructed me to call when I was 10 minutes out, and I did.

It was a chilly and rainy spring day, as I arrived at JH, followed by Kaelyn and her beau Marcus in their car. We pulled up just before Tee's anticipated exit at 12:15 PM and waited in our cars out of the rain. Soon, the guard signaled to us that they were about to bring him out. The moment we had all been waiting for—for what seemed to be an eternity—had finally arrived. The hospital doors opened, the guard stepped out and pointed toward us. Two nurses came out in a flash, dressed in full alien-looking protective gear, with Tee riding shotgun. They promptly wheeled him over to us

That moment was magical for us. Everyone moved fast with a goal of getting Tee out of the elements and into the car expeditiously, without even little conversation or contact. We quickly joined in to assist in getting him out of the wheelchair and into the car. Everything went so fast; those JH nurses were not playing!

Once Tee was secured inside the car, we quickly gave the nurses our sincere thanks. As they were walking away, the reality of Tee's return back to us caused me and Kaelyn to embrace in each other's arms, crying and shouting our most honorable "Thank You's" To God for safely bringing Tee back home to us. This encounter was all captured on our professional video and on the news stations' cameras. Every time I watch it, I get emotional all over again.

There was a lot going on around us and in our minds at that time. It all happened so fast. One thing I know we had in common was joy and gratefulness to be reunited with Tee after his near-death experience!

As we drove away from the pickup area, I sensed that Tee felt uneasy. I later found out that he was experiencing paranoia, thinking the JH nurses were going to reclaim him and take him back inside. Unbeknownst to me, I would further increase his anxiety as I drove around the JH campus to my next stop: the hospital parking garage on Orleans Street.

With Kaelyn and Marcus, and our grand dog Dexter (a 60-plus-pound boxer) following in their car, we finally made it to our destination. There, in the garage, family members anxiously awaited our arrival for a grand "Welcome Home" drive-by celebration, also captured on video. Those several moments, too, were exciting and emotional for everyone present.

Some family members had traveled for more than three hours (including our niece Sharee from New Jersey, accompanied by her grandmother-which reminded me of me and my G'mom) in that adverse weather on a workday, to participate in the celebration. After his 46-day tumultuous hospital stay, with a fantastic miraculous ending, no one complained about, nor focused on, their own sacrifice made to be there for Tee.

Although outside it was physically rainy and gloomy, in our hearts the sun was shining bright!

Back together again

The ride home was surreal. The day we had been praying for nonstop, for one and a half months, had arrived. I felt like my tires were riding on cloud nine driving my husband through town toward our house. We chatted intermittently, catching up and re-acclimating ourselves after our life-changing 46-day separation. Occasionally, I glanced over at Tee, as he quietly observed his surroundings outside the window. He gazed in awe at the beautiful springtime scenery that he missed out on for almost two months, as though it had been two years. A near-death experience can do that to a person.

I watched him with deep adoration and happiness. I felt a renewed dedication and commitment to this amazing man whose life had been changed without any advance warning, by a virus too strong for his body to handle, but not too strong for his will to conquer. Having both tested positive, we had all intention of weathering that COVID-19 storm together, only to be ripped apart without knowing if we would ever see each other alive again. Over the last 46 days we both had separately endured and had survived the biggest fights of our lives.

I looked at Tee, a handsome, vibrant and healthy 56-year-old before this ordeal, returned to me in under two months looking like he had aged at least 10 years. He was frail in his stature and weak in his voice, with the fear of the unknown flickering in his eyes. He sported a full head of hair, along with a somewhat scraggly beard, looking like a finely aged version of his deceased father. There were visible battle scars on the side of his neck where his lifesaving ports were placed.

Kaelyn and Marcus helped Tee out of the car and into the house after we pulled up into our garage. Tee's wonderful therapists had been practicing and preparing him to be able to climb the three stairs leading into the house during the last days before his discharge. To Tee's surprise, our church member and friend Donnell B had surprisingly installed hand railings on the stairs (as well as railings in the lower-level bathroom) to further assist in his return home. We were so grateful, and Tee was mentally and physically ready for the task.

Once we all settled inside, Marcus helped assemble Tee's new shower chair. Tee's walker was delivered shortly after our arrival. Kaelyn made up Tee's newly delivered hospital bed with his newly purchased comforter set, then set up his pill box for me. I was marveled by how much she had grown throughout this ordeal, and thankful that she and Marcus were there to assist.

Everything had fallen nicely into place as planned for Tee's big day! Finally, for that moment, I took a long, deep relaxing breath.

'I got you, Babe'

Without a doubt, the days ahead would require every ounce of my physical and emotional being—for a short while, anyway, until Tee could receive more therapy by the PT. God already knew what Tee would need when He equipped me at birth with great inner strength and the gift of a helpful heart, and then brought Tee and me together 10 years ago.

So, let the record show that Wednesday, May 6, 2020, after a grueling 46-day COVID-19 separation, Tee and Marcy (aka Martin and Gina, as the nicknames given to us by friends, due to our resemblance to the TV characters from the comedy sitcom, "*Martin*") were reunited, one day after their fifth wedding anniversary, with a huge life-changing experience behind them.

Or was that event really behind us? Clearly, whatever we just went through became a part of our challenged history, as well as our enlightened future, forcing us to embark on a new normal. What's normal anyway? We had no idea, but we were just forever grateful to God for giving us a second chance to continue together on this journey called life.

In hindsight, we realized that the homecoming celebration for Tee as he left JH could've very well been his homegoing services while being laid to eternal rest. We are simply ecstatic for our second chance at life, while at the same time tremendously saddened by the thousands of other COVID-19 patients not given that second chance.

In our house, we have a one-bedroom in-law suite with a full bath that is essentially a one-bedroom apartment. Since it's on the main level, we turned it into Tee's temporary bedroom. Who knew that we would be needing this room for him when we purchased this house? Just another thing for us to be grateful for!

Tee's first night home was good, no issues. We were both very tired and at great peace with our first night in the house together. No doubt, that accounted for the deep sleep that came over us both.

I became Tee's nurse for the first few days until his aide, Chris, started on Saturday. I sincerely welcomed Chris' tremendous help, as being a caregiver is *not* for the faint of heart.

Tee came home with still lots of needs. He could walk with the assistance of a walker, but he was still very winded and weak. He needed to rebuild his endurance. He also needed help with getting to and from the bathroom, on and off the toilet, showering, and getting dressed. In many ways, it was like having a little baby to care for. Well, he is my baby so "I got him" and everything that goes along with it!

Family and friends have all offered to help, and as much as I wish I could've taken them up on it, we just simply could not take any chance of having them in the house at that time. We worked it out between the two of us. Tee was determined to overcome what fate had dealt him, so he didn't stay in that helpless condition too long!

Sunday 5/10 @ 8:30 PM

Our first outing was to the Dairy Queen

Friday night, we took a ride out to the Dairy Queen to get some fresh air and a treat. It was cute seeing us having ice cream together. I enjoyed having my Boopy in tow.

Overall, I know Tee was overjoyed to be home, even though he got frustrated and annoyed at times from feeling weak and lethargic. I kept assuring him that was to be expected. Those were the times I showed him pictures from the ICU to remind him of just how far he had come. He would totally get it then. He's been hearing and seeing all of the stories about us in various news outlets and social media. Viewing those really puts all of it in perspective.

We had an excellent prayer call yesterday with 25-plus prayer warriors present. Tee offered his greetings and shared words from his heart. He was very emotional and enjoyed receiving all the love vibes from everyone!

There's been an outpouring of continuous love and support for us during this time from family, friends, co-workers, church members, etc., and we're just incredibly thankful and grateful.

Chapter 12

COVID-19 AND OUR NATION'S HEALTH CARE DISPARITIES

Our challenging, scary and then victorious experience with Tee in the hospital for 46 days with COVID-19, and especially with him being on a ventilator for 28 of those 46 days, is not just for us to marvel at. No, our story is for every African American, or person of color, in the USA —whether suffering through the most minor toothache, stomach pain or fever that takes them to their doctor's office or faced with the most serious acute illness or near-death incident landing them in the ER, ICU or burn unit. Our story is for the realization of, and the subsequent justified anger toward, the cold hard facts that racial bias within America's health care system makes recovery stories like ours the exception and not the norm.

Because of our story, we have an obligation to assure our fellow Black and brown brothers and sisters that our victory is how it *should* be when we come into any one of the 6,146 hospitals (total number as of the printing of this book) across America. Treatments within our Western medical system *should* be excellent and unbiased. By the same token, our prognoses *should* be hopeful and not bleak. From the urgent care centers, to the ERs, the ICUs, and down every hospice corridor, stories of survival like Tee's should be plentiful. Sadly, they're not.

Sadly, when dealing with our health care system in America, members of the Black and brown communities cannot escape the inequalities and disparities experienced in other facets of our society. Did you think health care would be exempt simply because of the highly educated and board-certified personnel involved? Or because of its centuries-long dedicated practice of serving the masses day in and day out? (Nowadays, that's about 36 million patients per year in US hospitals alone.) Or how about the Hippocratic oath, historically taken by physicians to uphold specific ethical standards?

Keeping personal beliefs and emotions out of it, I was curious and wanted to examine a little closer this enormous trillion-dollar industry that, thanks to COVID-19, has consumed most of my physical and emotional energy, as well as some of my hard-earned dollars. What I found is that to a great extent, while American citizens pay equally into this medical and pharmaceutical system, this system does not produce equal results for my people. Why is that? Why so many disparities based on race and ethnicity?

It seems the more I sought *answers* to that very question, the more *questions* arose, instead. Like, why are Black people 1.3 times more likely to be obese or overweight than other groups of people? Why are Black women 50% more likely to be obese than White women? Why do Black men suffer from heart disease, heart attacks and high blood pressure at a greater rate than their non-Black counterparts?

Before we can answer any of these questions, or many others like them, I believe we must first *acknowledge* these truths—after all, the truth *is* in the numbers. According to the Robert Wood Johnson Foundation, the CDC, World Health Organization WHO, Brookings Institution, and other federal health-related agencies, confirm this dismal state of health conditions our people are in at this point. In a series of recent polls conducted by NPR, the Harvard T.H. Chan School of Public Health, and the Robert Wood Johnson Foundation, it was concluded that at least half of all households in the four largest U.S. cities—New York (53%), Los Angeles (56%), Chicago (50%), and Houston (63%)[1]—are suffering tremendously from myriad of financial problems, including not being able to

[1]**The Impact of Coronavirus On Households Across America.** September 2020. https://www.rwjf.org/en/library/research/2020/09/the-impact-of-coronavirus-on-households-across-america.html

afford medical care. In other words, the people who need the care the most are not getting it, or are getting it at a much lower quality. Of course, this is not just exclusive to COVID-19-related issues, but with all types of health care on an ongoing basis—from treatments for illnesses of a varying degree to elective procedures.

This disproportionate hardship, where our health and finances are concerned, keeps us at the mercy of Congress. We need them to pass healthcare legislation that would allocate the financial assistance so desperately needed to not only maintain individuals' health, but to actually save thousands of lives. It's not happening, though. Congress seems reluctant to do the right thing. From my limited perspective, it's not willing to allocate the millions, or billions, of dollars needed, so that's where we stand. My people continue to suffer.

Tee and I are extremely fortunate in that we have excellent medical insurance. Without it, I can't even begin to imagine what we'd be facing right now in terms of the cost of Tee's care, as well as the quality. I think of the millions who don't have even the most basic coverages to carry them through illnesses, accidents, diseases or the typical maladies of aging.

It's even less likely those same individuals are carrying long-term-care coverage that may be needed in times like these. Thank God, our long-term-care policy is serving us throughout Tee's rehabilitation, allowing him the proper time and resources for his body to be made whole again.

But aside from the physical aspect, there's the mental health to be considered in all this. The PTSD Tee has been suffering is nothing to sneeze at. There's still a long road ahead of us to learn and discover just how much all this has affected him mentally.

How will we know when there's no way of telling how far down the road the mental anguish, anxiety or depression will last, or to what degree? The mind is so complex and delicate, yet so strong. That strength can allow it to overcome matters or cling to trauma for years or decades. There is absolutely a disproportionate fair and adequate mental treatment in our society.

Bottom line, studies have proven that more sustained efforts need to be made from all parties involved to reduce health disparities. Health care providers need to be better educated and trained to treat Black patients. Members of our black and brown communities would benefit greatly to recognize the need for equipping ourselves properly with information and services. While not everyone can afford certain health insurance or assisted living facilities, everyone *can* afford to read up on state-funded services or programs that may suit their needs.

My heart goes out to those suffering through catastrophic health events without proper coverages and care. Especially when inequalities that we've already come to accept as the norm are being made worse by events like COVID-19. We must stop this madness! Now more than ever, we must expect our personal values and treatment preferences to be regarded as highly as our white counterparts. Only then can we chip away at this mountain of healthcare disparities.

Part III

Good Resources

Tee and I have shared many important factors surrounding our COVID-19 experience and the significance of God's grace and mercy coupled with a great support system, and good healthcare. All of which allowed us to become TRIUMPHANT over COVID-19. We also discussed the ramifications of this disease on the African American community and the treatment disparities amongst us. In this chapter, I'm shifting gears and in doing so will put on three hats of expertise: My 20+ years as a Pharmaceutical Rep, my 10+ years as a licensed Life and Health Insurance Agent, and my current experience as a Realtor. Together, they give me the wisdom to provide me, and now you, with some winning attributes for success.

My goal is to offer insight on how we can set ourselves up in advance for victory over life's unforeseen circumstances so that we can WIN, no matter what happens around us! It is my belief that my life's circumstances and my personal experiences both good, bad, or indifferent have laid a GREAT foundation for this chapter. While my professional credentials (resume), knowledge, and experiences may qualify me to guide others on what *to* do to win, my life's experiences and mistakes (both seen and made) along the way have further armed me with the knowledge to help guide others with what *not* to do, to win. Both are equally important!

While COVID-19 was the most recent health catastrophe to practically obliterate the African American community, it is not the first. However, prayerfully, with the correct resources, we can help it to be one of the last. It is important that we learn to maximize our resources for success so that we can win against these monstrosities which have the ability to decimate our community.

There are many other diseases which are predominant in the African American community including, but not limited to, diabetes, high cholesterol, high blood pressure (this is known as metabolic syndrome, often referred to as Syndrome X), prostate cancer, etc. Many of these diseases are attributed to our lifestyle (including poor eating habits, lack of exercise, and genetics). To further complicate matters, we are often uninformed or misguided about our healthcare options and relevant resources.

Doing Better

Maya Angelou once said, "Do the best you can until you know better, then when you know better do better." My modern day "Marcy-ism" simple translation of this is, "If We knew Better, We would Do Better." As I provide insight to help us to do better moving forward, we are set up to be victorious. I cannot stress how important it is for us to have our "Houses in Order" and that everyone is aware of their options for getting healthcare coverage regardless of their financial status. I cannot emphasize this enough. We must have a healthcare plan in place to ensure that we can access a physician for wellness and sick visits.

Health plans can be secured through various measures including but not limited to our employers, through state and federally funded programs (*i.e.*, Medicare/Medicaid) for those who qualify, and privately funded or self-pay programs such as the Healthcare exchange. In 2010, President Obama enacted the Affordable Care Act, often called Obamacare. Its main goal was to make insurance more available to more people. Despite the controversy, surrounding it in recent years, these plans are still available. These plans often make healthcare available and affordable to those who wouldn't otherwise be able to obtain medical coverage, including EXCLUDING PRE-EXISTING CONDITIONS. Additionally, some of these plans offer subsidized premiums for better affordability to those who may qualify.

I want to make sure everyone knows the importance of finding a good local trusted primary care physician that they see regularly for preventative services, and whom they can call when they get sick. It is imperative that you have relationships with trusted providers. Do you remember back in the Spring when we had to have a physician's permission to get a COVID-19 test? How many people got caught up in this death trap because they didn't have a relationship with a physician they could call on when they got sick? They tragically never made it to the ER, or got turned away when they got there. Remember how Tee's pulmonologist, Dr. Nyanjom, called and made arrangements for us to go to the ER, and how the nurse met us at the curb when we arrived? Tee had an emergency intubation because he was in lung failure within an hour of getting there. Do you know how different this could've gone if we didn't have that relationship with his Doctor??

Also, it is imperative that we get our mammograms, colonoscopies, and other recommended and routine preventative screenings. This is important because early detection is often the key to surviving many potentially fatal diseases like breast and prostate cancers, which highly impact the African American community.

Winning Tools

In addition to having all of the health and medical resources that we've discussed; it is also important that we must have our insurances (both living and death benefits) intact. Your Living benefits are long term care, chronic illness and disability related benefits. These are benefits that you need if you were to become disabled or incapacitated and unable to work or care for yourself. Your death benefits are your life insurance related benefits that protect your family and replace your income or cover your burial-related expenses when you die. People get sick, and people die, and we want to ensure that we are covered in life and in death.

Personally, I have seen perfectly healthy young family members have major life changing events, and even die. I learned at an early age that young people get sick and live, young people die, and old people live long. The common denominator is they all need money to live, and someone to help them. By the time I was 25 years old, I was wise beyond my years because of things that I had witnessed.

At eight-years-old, I had witnessed my mother's life become changed forevermore after a major debilitating stroke at the young age of just 32. I saw a young (adopted) aunt's life be changed from a disabling heart condition in her 30's, forcing her to delay a promising career, and a sister who passed away too soon from breast cancer at 37 years old.

Since then, I've been responsible for overseeing the care of various family members, including my grandmother who is 95 years old. Of course, as pointed out in previous chapters, I was and still am responsible for overseeing and coordinating my husband's healthcare and recovery efforts.

If something were to happen to you today and you could no longer work (temporarily or indefinitely), you need to ensure that you have a plan in place to cover your income. You need to have resources to ensure proper help if you become unable to care for yourself. Some of these resources include insurance plans with living benefits (aka Index or Variable Universal Life plans), that you can access during a chronic or critical illness, long term care plans, etc.

We don't want to wait until we get sick to try to scramble up resources or leave these burdens to our family members. Similarly, when you die, who will take care of your funeral and burial expenses? Do you have funds or a final expense plan, or will this financial burden be left to your family? It's so important to plan ahead. I'll say the same about ensuring that you have your legal documents, including your wills, power of attorneys, advanced medical directives, and ALL life insurances (including burial or final expense policies) in place before you need them.

Rewards for planning

When my husband Tee and I got married a few years ago, we did some mutual financial preparation and planning to ensure we would both be protected in life or death. In doing so, I made sure that he got a long-term care plan to match my benefits. I should say that he adamantly opposed getting this plan initially, but I convinced him of its importance, especially since he had just finished taking care of his (now deceased) father, who could've benefitted from a similar plan.

At the time, I was more focused on making sure that Tee would have care options for when we got older, (a lesson learned from being a caregiver at an early age). We were thinking that this would be something that he wouldn't use for another 20+ years, since he was healthy and in his early 50's when he got this plan. Who could've ever imagined that he would get deathly ill in less than a week from COVID-19, and need to use these resources at 56 years old?? When Tee came home from the hospital he couldn't walk, he needed complete care like a baby, and no other family members were allowed to visit because of his vulnerability. His long term care plan (in addition to his health insurance) afforded us the option to ensure that he got good in home professional nursing help. I truly believe that his continuity of care from when he returned home from the hospital, helped to give him an additional jump start in his healing and recuperation process. I attribute this to God's Grace (as always), but also to good resources and planning!

I cannot begin to express how much peace of mind it gave me/us to know that I/we could focus on my husband's recovery, knowing that we had the resources needed to ensure that he would get the best medical care in and out of the hospital, because of the plans that we put in place before we needed them. His medical condition and all of the abrupt changes were very stressful at times for both of us in different ways. Thank God we didn't have to worry about money or resources. To God Be The Glory For That in itself!

I am a HUGE advocate of planning ahead and getting your house in order by utilizing insurances and other Risk protection/management strategies…Insurance is one of those things that you pray that you don't need to use anytime soon, However You're So Grateful to God for Having it if/when you need it!

Getting Ahead (let your house work for you)

Family, it's imperative that we break generational curses and find alternative ways to get out of our financial ruts and get ahead in this life. Many of our people are struggling to make ends meet, while some of us have made more money than our parents have made, and more than we've ever dreamed of making. Nevertheless, we squander these good fortunes on material things because we were never taught the importance of saving and investing. One of the best ways to get started with investing is simply by owning your own home.

Generally speaking, a house is an appreciating asset that will continue to pay for itself over time. It is the easiest way to establish passive income by simply purchasing in the right area for the right price. It is not uncommon to see houses appreciate well over $50-$100k easily, within one to two years, sometimes more in a good market. In five to 10 years, you can have a potential six-figure nest egg by simply making a good purchase decision. There are so many ways to purchase homes these days with little or no money down. Your first house doesn't have to be a mini-mansion. It just needs to be something of value in a decent area, that you can parlay into a future investment. We must have a place to live, so why not make sure you are investing in yourself with a house of your own? If you're paying over $600/month for rent, you could be paying a mortgage. Stop paying someone else's mortgage and contributing to their wealth accumulation plan. Use your money to build your own wealth!

If you've been smart and or fortunate enough to already own your own home, consider re-investing some of your equity into another property and let someone else pay your mortgage, and duplicate the process. Other cultures have been doing this for years, and now it's our turn!

Quick story, when I was looking to downsize my then 90-year-old grandmother from her life-long home a few years ago, we quickly found out that most assisted living facilities (ALF's) were cash pay only, STARTING at $3-$5k per month. I kept seeing these beautiful new ALF's which seemed like they were emerging on every corner, and I couldn't figure out how people in her age group could afford these places. After speaking to the admissions director, she told me that many of them were paying their way with the equity from the sale of their homes, as well as using their Long-Term Care Plan funds. I was marveled by this finding, although it made perfect sense. Someone who has a house that they've owned for several years could be sitting on a gold mine, and many long-term care plans can easily pay $5-$10k+ per month depending on how the plan is structured. This made me further value the importance of real estate and long-term care plans, and solidified my fondness of both as necessary investment vehicles. Again, now that we know about these tools, we have to position ourselves to use them.

Go big and stress less

Many of you who know me know that I've always been a hustler who likes to multi-task (Yes, 10 jobs mon, a self-pro-claimed Jamaican: the Pharma Rep, the Realtor, the Insurance Lady, now the Author). I once heard Jay Zee or Russell Simmons say, "If you're not rich you don't have time to sleep." I've heard other successful people say, We'll have plenty of time to sleep when we die." There have been different variations of these types of sayings from successful entrepreneurs over the years. The "Marcy-ism" translation, is simply: "Get up and do something," or "Get your lazy tail up and make some money." Refer to whichever one motivates you the most.

While my thoughts and sentiments are not to be confused with the love of money, (as we're reminded ever so often, to put God first), but more with the options and resources that come with having money. Options and resources give you better neighborhoods, less crime, more access to better services, better healthcare, better quality of life, and LESS STRESS! Less stress can afford you more mental clarity, inner peace, overall happiness, vitality and longevity!! People often say that money doesn't make you happy and that is very true if you don't have inner joy independent of money. Personally, I tell everyone that I know that I've been with and without money, and I'm a lot happier with it! This doesn't mean we should all have millionaire ambitions, but we do need to strive to be COMFORTABLE and make sure we have our current and future NEEDS covered for ourselves and our families, Are you with me?

Plentiful Resources (Make Dat Money Honey)

If you're with me, then read on...We have more resources in current times than any previous generation, to increase our earning potential. The older folks call this "easy money." With the invention of the Internet, and use of a phone and computer, we can do business anywhere in the world any time of day. Have you called your cable, phone or utility company lately? Have you called your company's IT help desk and encountered someone on the other end with a foreign accent? There's a fat chance this person is working from their home office thousands of miles away. They are leveraging their technology beyond their geographical limits to make money! We can do the same, we can get simple jobs from customer service to the most complex IT job, the opportunities are endless if we're open to them.

Additionally, the virtual world has leveled the playing field, we can advance ourselves behind a keyboard without any fears or limitations. We can now get degrees and online certifications from the comfort of our home. It's time to leverage these resources so that we can stack our cheddar (save, pay off bills, increase our credit scores) and BE Financially FREE! Another Marcy-ism: "Poor is a mindset that we cannot afford!" Let's start thriving and not just surviving.

The silver lining that the COVID-19 pandemic cloud has created is a new acceptable virtual realm that we never had before. It is the new way of doing business. People are maintaining their employment and exploring new business opportunities in their PJ's. Ask me how I know? I've benefitted from many of these tools and I'm continuously discovering how to further utilize these tools to advance. I encourage you do to the same!

Family, God speaks to us in John 3:1-2 about being prosperous and in good health. While it is His will that we remain healthy and whole, we have to utilize the resources He's given us to do so. Remember "Faith without works is dead" (James 2:14-26). I hope this chapter has planted seeds for you to begin to employ some of those resources, so that we can Win!

Finally, once again, I believe this COVID-19 experience has happened to us for so many reasons, and the more I write, the more excited I am to share this story and corresponding information with you. Finally, our United States Vice President Kamala Harris, in her victory speech acknowledged the fact that she will be the first Black women VP, but certainly not the last. I feel the same way about book writing and leveraging my experiences to help others. While this is my first book, it is certainly not the last. I feel I have one more, possibly several more, books being birthed within me.

The flood gates are open, my cup is overflowing, and I have a lot to share. It looks like my purpose is becoming clearer with each keystroke. We will just have to see where God leads me. In the meantime, let's stay in touch virtually and spiritually. Visit my website to see how we can forge ahead together!

Take action

It is my personal commitment to help others who are in need. It is my pleasure to help to refer you to some of the best resources (as previously discussed) for "Getting Your House in Order."

Now that you know better, let's start doing better.

LET'S TAKE ACTION!

Blessings for a healthy & prosperous life!
Praying with and for you,
Marcy & Tee Clark
PrayingWifeHelps.com

Barometer Check (Please Answer Honestly, No One is Looking)

1.	Do you have medical insurance?	Yes ☐	No ☐
2.	Do you have a personal physician?	Yes ☐	No ☐
3.	Have you visited your physician within the last year	Yes ☐	No ☐
4.	Do you have life insurance?	Yes ☐	No ☐
5.	Do you have a final expense and burial policy?	Yes ☐	No ☐
6.	Do you have a retirement plan (*i.e.*, 401k, IUL)?	Yes ☐	No ☐
7.	Do you have at least six months of savings?	Yes ☐	No ☐
8.	Do you have long-term care plan insurance?	Yes ☐	No ☐
9.	Do you own your own home?	Yes ☐	No ☐
10.	Do you own any investment properties?	Yes ☐	No ☐
11.	Are you satisfied with your current financial situation?	Yes ☐	No ☐
12.	Do you have good credit?	Yes ☐	No ☐
13.	Are you interested in earning additional income?	Yes ☐	No ☐

If you answered **"No"** to three or more questions (#1-11), or **"Yes"** to #13, we can help!

For information on these resources please visit:

www.PrayingWifeHelps.com

Part IV

Chronological Account of Tee's Journey via Text Correspondence

This section contains group and individual text correspondence with family members and prayer warriors. These conversations took place from March 21, 2020, during those first few hospital days, through May 12, 2020, when Tee was released from the hospital. To protect the privacy of others, only *my* portion of the conversations from those text messages (with the exception of a conversation between me and Darrell) is being shared.

Text Correspondence

My text messages to family members and prayer warriors.

Saturday 3/21 @ 7:00 AM

Just spoke to the nurse, ICU Doc was just going in when I called. He's heavily sedated, breathing with assistance and his fever is down to 101. We're in God's hands, Thanks for your continued prayers! 🙏 💕 🙏 😷 💕

I just had to give consent for Tee to be transferred to Hopkins Main. They said that they have a central COVID-19 treatment unit and prayerfully he'll get the best treatment there.

Saturday 3/21 @ 1:50 PM

Hopkins nurses called a little while ago, Tee was about 15 minutes out then, he should be there now...

My good sister friend and nurse Marisa was on the line with me. They were proactively preparing for his aggressive treatment upon arrival....

We feel confident that he's in good hands...Keep those prayers going family!

Saturday 3/21 @ 3:15 PM

Tee has safely arrived at Hopkins Praise God, he's been admitted to their ICU, he should be able to benefit from all of their Great treatment and world renown professional care. I am Faithful that he is in the best place for the best medical care. Please continue to keep us uplifted. I will continue to send regular updates

Sunday 3/22 @ 6:15 AM

Good Morning: Please pass this update along, Thx...

Just spoke to the nurse, Tee is holding his own. He has NO fever and he's requiring less oxygen. He is pain free, comfy and resting....

Prayer works family, Please Keep those prayers coming!! 

Sunday 3/22 @ Noon

He still has a long way to go, but we thank God for baby steps. Please keep us in your prayers!

Sunday 3/22 @ 5:00 PM

Bishop Thomas just called! I'm so full right now...GOD IS AMAZING!! He spoke a good word and rendered a mighty prayer and left his cell phone number, I greatly appreciated it, and the timing was perfect!

I have seen Lazarus be raised from the dead a few different times...I know He's able!!

Monday 3/23 @ 4:59 AM

Tee is the same from yesterday, had a slight fever overnight, getting Tylenol, prayerfully it will break soon. Still requiring less oxygen. I'll get another update this afternoon.

Please keep the prayer chain going, Thx

Monday 3/23 @ 1:04 PM

Just spoke to a Nurse who reminded me of a female Tee (very friendly and bubbly, she was very interested in him as a person, since they haven't met any family members)

He's still about the same (requiring less oxygen), heavily sedated and resting. He's getting aggressive meds and treatments so his lungs can heal, NO FEVER! 👍 🙏 ❤

She also reminded me that he is in the best place in the world, and that they do very well with bringing a lot of sick people back. I told her Thanks, and that we've already claimed his healing!

Monday 3/23 @ 6:10 PM

Just spoke to the nurse. No real changes from earlier. He's still holding his own and resting. Today was a pretty good day. I definitely feel my Help coming! (*Psalms 121*-my favorite scripture)

I probably won't have any more updates until the morning. I'll be in touch if there's any noteworthy news tonight. Please continue to keep us uplifted family, Thanks 👍 🙏 ❤

Tuesday 3/24 @ 6:44 AM

Good Morning: I started my day with scripture and a musical reminder from Hezekiah that *Power Belongs to God.* https://g.co/kgs/yL5wrA [2]. There's nothing too hard for God.

I spoke to Tee's nurse this morning and she actually put me on speakerphone in his room. Although Tee is heavily sedated, I spoke to him as if he could hear me.

We prayed, I gave words of encouragement, I told him that he has a magnitude of Prayer Warriors pulling for him (including Bishop Thomas). I told him I didn't know why we were chosen for this virus, but God has something major in store for us, and we have a huge story to tell when this is over!! I let him know that we're rebuking COVID-19 in the name of Jesus, and that we are claiming his healing...And I miss him so much and I can't wait for him to come home!

He had a good night, NO Fever, and the breathing machine is doing its job, so he can continue to rest his lungs for his healing. 👍👏

[2] **Hezekiah Walker.** The Power Belongs to God. 1999. https://g.co/kgs/yL5wrA

I will give another update later on. Prayer works Family, Let's keep it going!

<u>Tuesday 3/24 @ 9:00 AM</u>

I just received this from our church, (New Psalmist) after my recent conversation with Bishop. Guess who they're referring to?

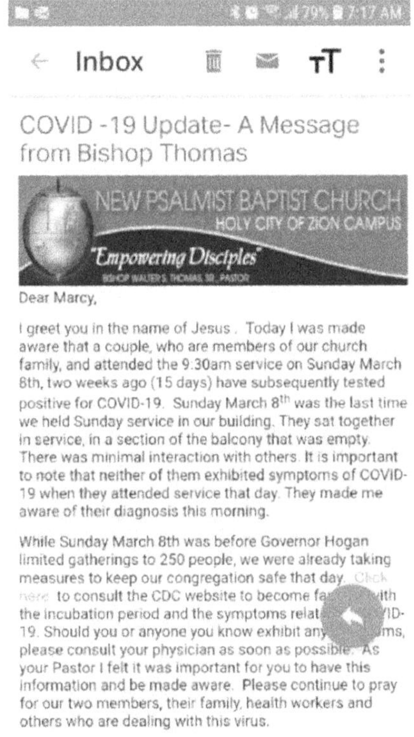

Inbox

COVID -19 Update- A Message from Bishop Thomas

NEW PSALMIST BAPTIST CHURCH
HOLY CITY OF ZION CAMPUS
"Empowering Disciples"
BISHOP WALTER S. THOMAS, SR., PASTOR

Dear Marcy,

I greet you in the name of Jesus . Today I was made aware that a couple, who are members of our church family, and attended the 9:30am service on Sunday March 8th, two weeks ago (15 days) have subsequently tested positive for COVID-19. Sunday March 8th was the last time we held Sunday service in our building. They sat together in service, in a section of the balcony that was empty. There was minimal interaction with others. It is important to note that neither of them exhibited symptoms of COVID-19 when they attended service that day. They made me aware of their diagnosis this morning.

While Sunday March 8th was before Governor Hogan limited gatherings to 250 people, we were already taking measures to keep our congregation safe that day. Click here to consult the CDC website to become fa[illegible]with the incubation period and the symptoms relat[illegible]ID-19. Should you or anyone you know exhibit any[illegible]ms, please consult your physician as soon as possible. As your Pastor I felt it was important for you to have this information and be made aware. Please continue to pray for our two members, their family, health workers and others who are dealing with this virus.

Email message sent to church members regarding our recent diagnosis

The irony here, we were in a row by ourselves, but I remember vividly the lady behind us coughing, and we looked at each other and gave the Ugh! I'll have to see if Tee remembers this when he gets well.

(Response to question on text chat, do we know where or how we got COVID-19?)

Only God knows! Both of us are all over, all the time.... But it surely makes you wonder...

Hence the importance of social distancing. This is why I wanted to share our story with so many people. There are still a lot of people in denial and doing dumb stuff. Please be safe!!

Marcy: (sidebar with siblings, discussion about previous pre- COVID-19 cautionary encounters)

Yes, we felt like that before COVID-19!!

(Note to sister)-I remember years ago, when you told the man who was coughing on the plane, that he needed to take a cough suppressant.

He needed you to tell him that he shouldn't be traveling on an airplane with a cough!

Yup, everybody's freaking out over hand sanitizers and wipes and stuff now. You know I've been had my stash. I'm trying to figure out what were they doing before??

Continued text discussion with siblings (I can always count on them to make me laugh when things seem unlaughable)

This will be our New get up w goggles, mask and all!!

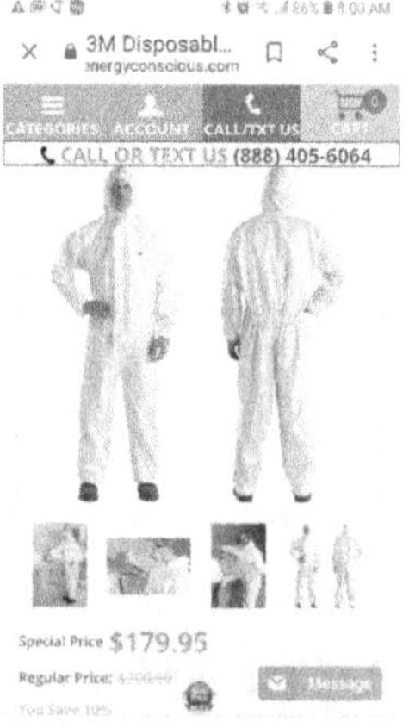

(Sent from a family member) Hey cute couple, can't wait to see you all looking healthy and happy like this again:

<u>Tuesday 3/24 @ 3:00 PM</u>

Kaelyn and I just spoke to his Doctor. No real new updates. His fever is still down and he's holding his own. They are going to be working to decrease his meds, Oxygen, sedation in the coming days.

We were reminded that he's made some small steps, but he still has a way to go, and that we have to be patient while his body SLOWLY heals.

This was a reminder of how important our prayers are, and how crucial it is to continue them.

Thanks everyone for your continued love support and prayers. We're claiming victory in the Name of Jesus. Let's keep it going!🙏🏽🙌🏽❤️

Please join in tonight if you can…

I want to try to arrange something like this with our prayer chain soon!

<u>Wednesday 3/25 @ 6:15 AM</u>

No real changes overnight. Still NO fever, breathing Ok on the machine. He's holding his own, still heavily sedated, lungs need to rest and heal, this will take time! I've been reminded that this is A LONG Marathon AND NOT A SPRINT. We'll need to remain prayerful and patient. Time for AM scripture and song. I'm being led to *Psalm 91* and *121*. Hezekiah reminds me that Jesus is My Help!

"Why Should I Worry, why should I fret? Look at all the ways he's made, and every promise kept...I look to the hills from which cometh my help, I Feel my Help Coming From the Lord." https://youtu.be/GiHZVB1fNRI [3]. Let's remain prayerful Family! KEEP sending them out and up!

**Family and Friends of Marcy and Tee (Anthony) Clark group prayer call this Saturday 3/28 @ 4:00 PM. I'll send all the call information in a separate text soon!

Side Note: Beginning of Saturday weekly prayer call.

Wednesday 3/25 @ 12:11 PM

Tee is doing good so far this Am, NO Fever and they've been able to decrease his Oxygen levels on the machine again (less is best).

We need this trend to continue so he can continue to wean down and off the breathing machine!

God is Great and he's hearing our prayers family...As my dad would say "Let's Roll"! Keep em coming!

[3] **Hezekiah Walker**. Help coming from the Lord. 2XXX. https://youtu.be/GiHZVB1fNRI

Wednesday 3/25 @ 2:00 PM

A few helpful strategies to deal with COVID-19:

We should be more than halfway through the virus at this point. I've remained pretty healthy by relying on prayer, and good common-sense practices incl staying isolated, using a mask and gloves at all times

Getting rest, eating veggies, and non-sugary fruits (*i.e.*, bananas), decreased stress, Coconut oil, Multi Vitamins-to increase my immune system, decreased sugar intake-I love sweets but sugar feeds white blood cells which promotes infection

Exercise- lots of walking around the house, gargling daily with hot water salt, vinegar, pepper — old trick for sore throat. Green tea also helps to heal the throat

Daily Flonase nasal spray, regular nasal saline mist — keeps the sinuses clear and clean, lots of colds, viruses start and manifest in the nose!

Hot Decaf tea with lemon and honey, Aunt Barb's banging healthy chicken soup w veggies

Refrain from negativity including Social media, news, and surround myself with positive thoughts, scriptures, affirmations and people (virtually). Life lessons!

Hope this helps! Thanks for your Continued prayers!

Marcy-Praying Avatar Emoji

"Yes, this is me, can't you tell? It's hilarious, eyes, hair, arms and all"

Thursday 3/26 @ 7:00 AM

Good Morning, I'm really missing Tee today! Some days will be harder than others, but my AM scripture reminded me (Joshua 1:5,9) that God will be with me and that He'll Never Leave or Forsake Me. Be strong and Of Good Courage, God is with me wherever I go: Tee is still holding his own, his breathing tube needed to be switched out for maintenance, so his oxygen levels needed to be increased while he re-stabilizes. We pray that he'll readjust and start requiring less oxygen again soon.

There will be ups and downs, during this process. Hence the importance of being vigilant in our continued prayers. Let's Go Family, keep them rolling out and up. God is waiting to hear from you today!

Thanks for all! 🙏 😇 💖

Private text from Big Brother Darrell

Good morning, via our conversation yesterday. We both agree that God is in control. Sis let me add, that I was Blessed by your faith as well AS humbled by your acceptance of what God has allowed. I encourage you to stay strong in your faith, while remaining prayerful. Be steadfast, knowing that the trying of your faith bringeth patience. I celebrate with you and our brother Tee, Victory through our Faith. In Jesus name. Luv u all.

Marcy

Yes, big bro, I appreciated the conversation and being able to share my spiritual insight with you!!

This experience is far beyond human comprehension, but we'll understand it better by and by (sometimes you got to go way back to old First Baptist-FBC days). Love you much!

Thursday 3/26 @ 2:38 PM

I know we're all especially missing Tee today, it's been almost a week now since we've seen or heard from him. I keep telling myself he's on a mini vacation, but he'll be back soon. It's really true because his body is truly resting and healing right now.

The good news is...We are going into the second week of the virus, and it should be on its way out soon, so prayerfully Tee can really begin to heal as this rids his system.

Just spoke to his nurse, he's still holding his own. They repositioned him to help aid his breathing so that he can regain his momentum back and start requiring less oxygen again. This really helped him previously, so let us continue to pray that we can get back on track soon!

Keep praying, God hears us, and I believe that Tee feels it! 

Thursday, 3/26 @ 9:56 PM

I just spoke to Tee quickly through the nurse's speaker phone. I gave him words of encouragement and told him that everybody was praying and pulling for him, and we can't wait for him to come home! I also told him how much love and support we've had in his absence.

He's still holding his own, His blood pressure is good, low fever and they're hoping to start being able to lower his oxygen requirements again soon.

Let's continue to uplift him in prayer and watch God do his thing! Thx for all. Love you all. Good Night.

Friday 3/27 @ 5:55 AM

The same nurse was nice enough to let me speak through speakerphone again this morning. I said a mighty prayer for his continued healing and for the minds and hands who are treating him, and she appreciated it!

Remember Tee is still heavily sedated but I'm praying that he's hearing me speak, and that he's feeling the power of our prayers!

Well, I just got affirmation on this. I just called right back to ask the nurse something else, and she was still in his room and put me on speaker a second time and I spoke to him again. She told me that he began to cough twice when he heard my voice!! I could just scream; I know GOD'S hand is working on us from the inside out!!

No real updates from last night. His blood pressure is good, low fever, his oxygen levels have been fluctuating slightly based on his position. It's a work in progress... remember this is a step by step, marathon, not a short sprint. We're praying that he'll stabilize again shortly and start breathing more on his own and requiring less oxygen as his lungs continue to heal!

Family, God needs time to work this out and show himself mighty... God is hearing us, Tee is feeling us!

We will continue to keep Tee in our hearts, thoughts and prayers, keep it going family...

Send them out and up!! Thanks in advance for the victory!!

Text from Big Bro Darrell

God's got him. 

Tee definitely heard your voice and knows how loved he is. Prayers up!!

Marcy: For sure, right in the palm of his hands!

Friday 3/27 @ 9:32 PM

I spoke to Bishop Thomas again today, it was right on time, today was not an easy day. Today marks 1 week for Tee in the hospital and on the ventilator.

Tee's nurse says he's still sedated, resting comfortably, good vitals, no fever, Oxygen levels decreased some from earlier.

Looking forward to tomorrow's prayer call at 4:00 PM. I will send out the details in the morning. Let's keep the prayers going. Love you all, good night

Saturday 3/28 @ 7:55 AM

No major updates overnight. Still NO fever, vitals are good, Oxygen requirements still fluctuating at times as expected, ongoing efforts towards stabilization. He's still heavily sedated so his lungs can rest and heal.

I'm looking forward to connecting with everyone later...We're going to pray that boy right back on his feet, TODAY!!

I'll send the conference call invitation out in a few hours, as soon as I get it finalized, I promise!

Family, keep lifting them up

Group text Saturday 3/28 @ 11:00 AM

1st Saturday Prayer call invitation

Saturday 3/28 @ 7:00 PM - (After first prayer call)

Marcy: Thanks everyone who attended. Wasn't that awesome?? How about Bishop's surprise guest appearance? It was very powerful, a mini church service...We were all Blessed. "We're coming out, and we want the world to know, we got to let it show" 🙏 ❤

Sunday 3/29 @ 6:28 AM

Good Morning, I fell asleep last night shortly after our powerful prayer service. Thanks everyone who participated... "WERE COMING OUT"!!

- Just spoke to his nurse, Tee is still holding his own, good vitals, NO fever. His oxygen levels had been high, they've since been decreased, and they're constantly repositioning him.
- They're going to see how he does, and prayerfully decrease his O2 (oxygen) levels some more today.
- I'll reach back out this afternoon. Let's keep up the positive momentum. God is a healer, He's got this!!

Sunday 3/29 @ 6:01 PM

View from car window.
First "drive by" visit to Johns Hopkins.

My quarantine has been lifted but I'm still laying low and hoping to get retested next week!

I decided to make a special trip today...

Greetings from outside of Johns Hopkins. I can't go in of course, but God told me to bring my prayers as close to Tee as I could get, so here I am.

Prayers are working family; Tee is doing WELL today. His Oxygen has been decreased, his meds are being decreased, NO FEVER, and they are trying to lower his sedation in hopes of waking him up soon.

Family God is Pleased with our Praise, and Tee is feeling our spirit!!

We've got to keep our momentum going... because we know when Praises go up blessings come down!!

The Best is Yet to Come!!

(Response to family text) Marcy

Yep, That's right. That's another reason why I went up there so I can see where I'll be picking him up from soon.

Sunday 3/29 @ 9:20 PM

Last update for tonight, Kaelyn and I just called in and his nurse let us talk to him through speakerphone which is always nice!

Tee's condition is basically the same as earlier...low grade fever, decreased meds and oxygen requirements. Still heavily sedated and resting. Prayerfully, we'll start seeing more reductions in oxygen requirements and sedation soon!

Thanks for all your continued prayers, please keep them coming!

Monday 3/30 @ 6:03 AM

Good Morning, this is the day that the Lord has made we will Rejoice and be glad in it *(Psalms 118:25)*

I just spoke to Tee's nurse. She also put me on speaker phone, and as always, I gave him words of love and encouragement and a prayer.

He knows that everybody is routing and praying for him, and eagerly anticipating his recovery!

No fever, he's still heavily sedated but has opened his eyes a little. His oxygen requirements have been a little high overnight, but they fluctuate, so we'll remain prayerful that he's able to reduce throughout the day.

I had this thought last night:

1. Get behind me Devil
2. No room for stress nor strife.
3. God's got my #1 Dude, My Boopy For Life!

I'll send an update later on today. Please keep those prayer lines open, keep uplifting my Boopy.

Monday 3/30 @ 9:00 AM

I was asked to be part of a 1 Million Lord's Prayer text to slow and stop the coronavirus. The idea is you pray then pass the message on to 8 other people. Let me know if you can't, so we don't break the prayer blessing. It took me 30 secs to do it!

> Father God in the mighty name of Jesus! I pray, speak and declare healing all over the land! We are standing and trusting in your promises! By your stripes we are healed! Touch the minds and hearts of our leaders! I humbly ask that your will be done! I pray a special blessing over the ones that are reading this prayer and passing it on to others! I declare and decree Victory in Jesus! Amen! Glory be to God!

Now pass it on please!

Monday 3/30 @ 1:58 PM

I just spoke to his nurse. Tee has No fever; his oxygen levels are still fluctuating. They're working diligently to get him stabilized...Prayerfully this is just a bump on the road to recovery.

Devil you're a liar, and a coward, because you know that we're believing in Faith for Tee's recovery. I rebuke you in the name of Jesus and I'm standing on the promises of God! Like the woman in the Bible in Luke 40:48. I'm believing by Faith in your continued healing powers! I'm watching patiently as you turn this situation around.

All hands-on deck for collective prayer efforts. Please continue to pray for the world and for our Tee/Anthony...Lift him up. And this too shall pass! 🖤😷 🙏

This is Satan trying to plant a seed of fear and doubt... I knew he would be trying to come for us after that prayer!! REBUKE, REBUKE, REBUKE!

Monday 3/30 @ 6:00 PM

Just spoke to Tee's Doc, he reassured me that there will be periods like this, it goes with the territory!

He reiterated to me the same thing that I've been telling you all, that this is a marathon and not a short sprint, and he said that time is our best friend (Healing in due time).

He also told me that Tee's recent chest X-ray has shown a slight improvement in his lungs. We Thank God for every little step!

Let's keep sending up our good prayers for signs of improvement and healing... 🖤😷 🙏

(Response to text) Marcy

That's going to be me when we come out of this. We have a lady who runs two laps around our church every Sunday, and me and Tee laugh our tails off, that's going to be me when this is over!!

Praise dance

Group text TC Update Tuesday 3/31 @ 5:55 AM

Good Morning. Tee was the same overnight, no real changes still holding his own....

I'm claiming brighter days ahead as I was reminded by the songstress:

"Sometimes I have to encourage myself, and sometimes I have to speak victory during the test." Be encouraged! [4]

Family, please remain diligent in our prayers! He's brought us too far to leave us now!

Tuesday 3/31 @ 8:07 AM

Divine Intervention this morning...This Message is for the real believers!!

I received this text from my sister Jackie this morning.

> (Remember Jackie was the one that I recently mentioned on the prayer call who was diagnosed early with breast cancer in enough time to be able to go through it and be fully restored)

We have to start being specific now. God has been granting our prayers to protect him and heal him, now we must ask God to awaken him and restore him to his natural state and make him to breathe on his own.

[4] **Donald Lawrence** & The Tri-City Singers. Encourage Yourself. 2009. https://youtu.be/JbEaftzaFWA

(Response to Jackie) Marcy

OMG!!

I wrote in my journal/notes yesterday a.m. that it was time to pray Aloud specifically for the restoration of Tee's lungs and removal of the ventilator by 4/6 *(See my attached writing)* and I printed out a bunch of scriptures about being specific in prayer. Although I profess this daily to God, I had not professed these specific prayers openly with a date to you all.

God used Jackie this morning as a vessel to remind me how important it was to share this prayer openly! **ISNT THIS POWERFUL??**

Please see my notes from yesterday (below) and the attached SPECIFIC prayers:

Not sure if you can read this...It says 3/30:

Specific Request for restoration of lungs and removal from ventilator by 4/6, and it lists 3 relevant scriptures including:

1. Philippians 4:6-Be anxious for Nothing
2. I Theses 5:17-Pray without Ceasing
3. John 14:13-14- Whatever you ask in my name this I will do that the father may be glorified in the son if you ask anything in my name, I will do it.

Please read the scriptures and join us in specific prayers with Faith and power for Tee's miraculous healing and that he be removed from the Ventilator by 4/6. Watch God move, HE knows we're waiting and watching in anticipation!!

FYI...I prayed a similar prayer for my Godmother Polly to be removed from the Ventilator prior to leaving for Aruba for my wedding in 5/2015 because I did not want to be away from her for two weeks without being able to speak to her. This was another one of the Miracles that God showed me. I remember the day they called me, and I heard her voice for the first time in months! GOD will do this family if we just believe!!

Thanks in advance for your prayers. I know this is Deep, but I already know, seen and experienced his healing powers first-hand!!

God's got this! 🙏 🙏 🙏 🙏 ✝

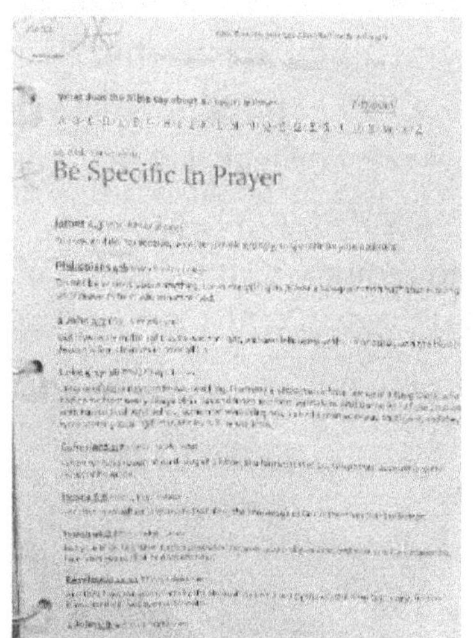

Be Specific In Prayer

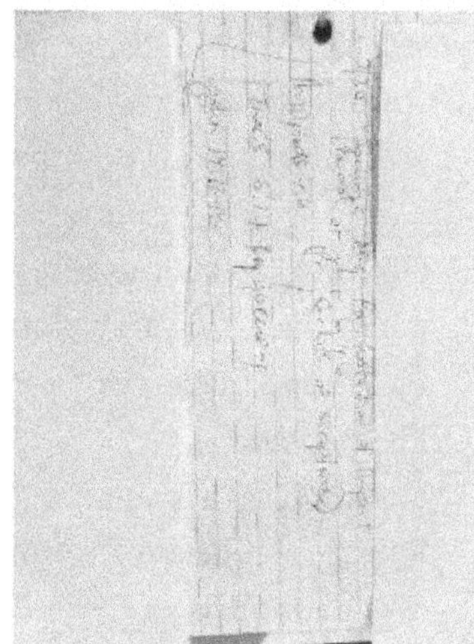

Earlier Journal notes, reiterating "Be Specific In Prayer."

Text sidebar from family: I received word that Philly legend DJ Jazzy Jeff had been hospitalized with alleged pneumonia/ COVID-19

God's got this! 🙏 🙏 🙏 🙏 ✝

He made it too. Praise God!

Marcy

Unfortunately, COVID-19 does not discriminate. Prayers for Jazzy!

May he also come through this with a story to tell about the power of God's healing!!

Private text-(Big Brother Darrell)

"As I watch this virus, make its presence known around the world. I am becoming more and more aware of God's desire, to get the world's attention. Never before in our lives, has the world been placed on notice all at the same time. To look at it a Lil further, it's attacking sport figures, actors, people of all color and walks of life. Had it only attacked white people, black people wouldn't have pay it any mind. The same goes, had it attacked blacks only. But because it's attacking us all and causing everyone to sit still at the same time. It's become evident, that God, is demanding all of our attention. "If my people, who are called by My Name, would humble themselves and turn from their wicked ways. Then shall I hear from Heaven and heal their land."

Marcy

EXACTLY!! You and I discussed this last week.

And I'll add that we will keep going through similar things if we don't get the lesson!!

Group text Tuesday 3/31 @ 6:05 PM

Tee's still the same, no major changes, still holding his own. Prayerfully getting stronger and healing from the inside out.

I did call in and me and Bud (son) spoke to him on speaker phone, and as always, we sent our love, well wishes and prayers for his continued healing.

Thanks for your continued prayers and positive sentiments, Let's keep them flowing family!!❤❤🙏🙏

Wednesday 4/1 @ 5:51 AM

(Today is Buds 34th birthday, Happy birthday Son!)

Good Morning. Tee had a good night. No fever. His sedation was lowered, and his breathing has been synchronous, and he also blinked his eyes! We Thank God for every little step towards Victory! This is a COVID-19 testimony from a friend of a friend.

I wanted to share the story of a Virginia man who was also recently affected by COVID-19, whose restoration can ONLY be that of a Miracle. Family GOD is able if we just believe. If HE can do it for this family, HE can do it for us! We claim Tee's healing @ 4/6 (two and a half weeks from his initial hospitalization).

We Thank God in advance for the miracle He's unfolding before us!

We claim Tee's victory like Titou's, as shown during this news coverage. https://fox42kptm.com/news/nation-world/coronavirus-recovery-nothing-short-of-a-miracle.

We pray that he will wake up restored with new lungs and not having any idea what he's been through, IN THE NAME OF JESUS!

(Thanks for sharing this blessing this AM Mommisond: The latest on Titou's recovery.)

Private text from Big Brother Darrell

Good morning. It's a Blessing to see that slowly but surely Tee is showing progress. It's important that we continue to stand strong in our Faith and not doubt. Sis, when my grandmother was sick 10yrs b4 she passed her situation looked hopeless. Even the Doctors were doubtful of her recovery. She too was on a respirator. Her kidneys collapsed. Her lungs shut down. Her heart began to enlarge because it was over working. I remember sharing with my Aunt Shirley and my Uncle Sam, that God told me, that she would be healed. These two were the Spiritual warriors of the family. Yet neither believed that she would recover. Yet I did. I never doubted God, though my Faith was challenged by what I was seeing. (A dying woman). On March 30, God gave me a poem. Basically, telling me to trust Him beyond what I was seeing. And that she would be healed. On April 30, while in my bathroom praying, Sally knocked on the door and said the phone. I said, "who is it I'm praying". Again, she said the phone. Again, I asked "who is it?" She said your Grandmother. Words can't describe the joy I felt when I picked up that phone and my grandmother said, "hey baby." Two weeks later she came home, needing no medical equipment or medical assistance. So, I know for a fact, that God is a Man of His word.

(Response to Darrell) Marcy

Darrell... Thanks for sharing the details of your testimony. Like I said to you and on the prayer call...This is not my first rodeo, and I know first-hand that God is able!!

I've seen Him raise Lazarus from the dead... I've seen them count my mom out a few times before she died and bring her back, same with my Godmother, and a few others!

His hand is all in this... He's strengthening the faith of the Believers and cultivating the Faith of the non-believers through this experience personally through Me and Tee and globally!!

Keep the Faith And continue to make your prayers known unto Him!

Marcy

Tee was a miracle himself in 2015 when he was hospitalized over four days with severe pneumonia. He was very serious at that time, came through with flying colors and had no idea what he had been through.

It wasn't until his follow-up doctor visit that the doctor showed him his chest x-ray and told him how close he was to the gates of heaven. I remind him of that every time we face an obstacle, and this is going to be the same with all of you guys as our Witnesses!!

Marcy

Here's one for you...Brother's not sure if you'll remember this:

Our mom was hospitalized at Haverford Hospital about 8 months before she actually died, and they were saying that she was "touch-and-go" I remember those words vividly...

Mommy snapped right back a few days later, and when she heard that we were crying she was laughing at me specifically...She was silly and couldn't imagine what we were crying for! I now know that was my preparation for what was to come, and we were able to have closure when she actually closed her eyes.

Number 2: My God Mother, Polly was intubated for months after her severe car accident in January 2015 with her siblings when she was ejected from the van.

I would go up regularly and stay and check on her. I begin praying for her, specifically in April that she would be delivered from the ventilator before I left to go to Aruba for 2 weeks (for our wedding and honeymoon), because I was afraid of leaving her without being able to talk to her or her being able to communicate.

I remember like Darrell does when and where I was and how I received the phone call.

Darrell was on the john when his Grand Mother called him, and I was at the hair salon when Aunt Wee Wee (Polly's sister) called and put her on the phone. I just cried, and Polly asked, "Why are you crying?"

Aunt Polly had no idea what she and others around her had been through! She ended up surviving that ordeal and living another four years thereafter! How's that for first-hand experiences? I could go on, but that's how and why I know God's infinite power!

Thursday 4/2 @ 5:40 AM

"Family Tee is in trouble, just got a call from hospital...Prayers for a miracle right now!!! Heading there shortly!"

Group texts upon arrival at Johns Hopkins Thursday 4/2 @ 7:30 AM

I'm at the hospital with the family praying that they will let us in...

Tee's still with us, holding on...Please keep sending up your prayers, we need a miracle!! God IS Able!!

Thursday 4/2/20 @ 1:01 PM

I spoke with Mike (P.A.).

- TC Oxygen levels are really low, almost on Max ventilator support@ 95%.
- Prone on his stomach
- Deep sedation
- On Paralytic
- Trying to decrease fluids
- Praying for improvement to stabilize Oxygen levels and start decreasing ventilator support
- Serious/Critical condition

Thursday 4/2 @ 5:00 PM

We did get to see him. He is responding to the medication that they gave him to treat his emergency earlier today, Praise God!

We were extremely grateful to be able to see him, touch him, pray for him in person!

I'm on my way home now, it's been a long and exhausting day... Thank you all for your continued prayers, I appreciate this more than you'll ever know.

I'll send an update later, thanks, love you all!

Thursday 4/2 @ 11:21 PM

I just spoke to Tee's nurse and he is stable and holding on. His ventilator settings were decreased a little.

Continued prayers for him to get back on track towards healing. Thanks again for all of your super prayers earlier today, during such a tough time.

From Kaelyn

"Thank you again for everything...I believe in my heart he heard us today ...love you."

Kaelyn says she believes Dad heard us, and I completely agree. I believe that both God and Tee feel and hears our prayers!

Family, please continue to pray this beautiful man of ours back to health. We love you all and thank you so much for All of your efforts. Prayer works!!

Side Note: Yes Daughter, we later learned that Tee thought you worked at Johns Hopkins, and he was trying to figure out why you wouldn't rub his feet. In hindsight, this is hilarious that Dad heard your conversations with the ICU Staff.

Friday 4/3 @ 6:05 AM

Please see attached flyer for our second prayer call Saturday 4/4 @ 4:00 PM. The call info is on the flyer. Again, No Social Media posts!

TC update

I just spoke to his Nurse. There were no real changes overnight, he's still maintaining. He has a low-grade fever (tends to get these sometimes esp. overnight). His ventilator settings are fluctuating some, but he's stable. Praise God!

Right now, it's crucial for him to remain stable so he can resume healing!

2nd Saturday Prayer call invitation

The nurse did tell us yesterday that 2-3 weeks is the average time for the ventilator, (tonight will be 2 weeks for Tee). They've seen people need them longer, and they've seen and heard of people coming off the ventilators! I sent out a recent success story about it.

<u>**Friday 4/3 @ 2:38 PM**</u>

I just spoke to the nurse; I'll give you a small update. I will send out a formal update after I speak to the doctor hopefully in the next hour or so if there's more: Tee has a slight fever...

His Oxygen levels are better right now, and his vitals are good. Thank God for Baby Steps! I Feel My help coming- *Psalm 121* 🙏❤🙏

<u>**Group text Friday 4/3 @ 6:47 PM**</u>

<u>**A new obstacle in our midst-time for more unified prayers!**</u>

Hey guys it's praying time again. My baby is having another complication, not quite as scary as yesterday but its serious...

Right now, he's developed atrial fibrillation which is an irregular and rapid heartbeat. They gave him medication, and it has slowed it down, but they are concerned!!

I would like to do a prayer call tonight at 7:15 PM using the same prayer information that's on the invitation for tomorrow:

Please call in if you can. Please mute your phones immediately!! THANKS!!

Group text 4/4 @ 5:25 AM

Thanks everybody for getting on the Spontaneous prayer call at a moment's notice last night. I just want to make sure that we continue to be diligent with our prayers, especially during this time, but also moving forward.

I believe there's power in numbers and if we continue to send up our prayers in abundance, we will be victorious. I know that God is pleased with our prayers and I'm STILL believing in His healing powers for Tee.

I just spoke to Tee's nurse and he is still stable. No fever and His heart rate has normalized again. Praise GOD! 🙏❤🙏

I believe that Johns Hopkins good works coupled with our prayers has and will continue to get him through these hard times! I'm also confident that Tee is fighting back (That's right get em Boop! 🥊

Family God hears us, and Tee feels us, let's keep the prayers going up!!

He's Able-Oh Yes, He is! https://youtu.be/a2Fl9QLm9VI [5]

Group text Saturday 4/4 @ 1:00 PM

We had a wonderful Noon prayer with Tee and his immediate family through speakerphone. We showered him with love, prayers and words of encouragement. We continue to believe that he is feeling and hearing our prayers!

TC update

I just spoke to his doctor and he's still stable and holding his own. She reminded me that he has overcome some major obstacles over the last 48 hours, and how he can't afford any more setbacks.

Let us continue to be mindful of the fragileness of his condition, while using it as a springboard to escalate our prayers! AND ultimately remembering that God is in control!

[5]**Kirk Franklin & The Family.** He's Able. December 16, 2008. https://youtu.be/a2Fl9QLm9VI

I'm committed to praying him through this if we have to do a call every day! I'm going to be doing a 24-hour Nationwide Christian based Fast starting on This Good Friday 4/10 @ 12:00 AM until Saturday 4/11 @ 12:00 AM. We will be fasting and praying for God to Release the coronavirus which has affected us personally and has plagued our nation and many parts of the world! It is time for us to unite as the Body of Christ to Rebuke this DEVIL in the name of Jesus!

I'll speak to this briefly on the call, if you're interested in joining me please let me know by text, and I will forward the details to you over the next few days.

Thanks again for your continued prayers, I look forward to us connecting today @ 4:00 PM for our Prayer call. We have a few new people joining us, it's going to be Awesome:

Please be sure to mute your phones. I don't want to have to fuss anybody out today, we've been doing this long enough now, you all know the deal!

Here are miraculous results of our prayers so far:

In a 48-hour period Tee had escaped death three times (4/1-108 degree temp Cytokine Syndrome Storm, 4/2-critically low oxygen levels, and 4/3-irregular heart beat- Atrial fibrillation). Each time prayers went up and out, as the Hopkins team responded with immediate interventions. As we prayed Tee responded, Death was Not an Option! TGBTAG!!

God had brought us through several close encounters the last few weeks, and we were determined to stay unified in prayer as the journey continued. The more we prayed the more Tee responded, our momentum was at an all-time high, we were watching a Real-life biblical miracle unfold right before our eyes. We were all hunkered down and sheltered in place because of the COVID-19 shut down, and God had our full attention. We all watched curiously and optimistically to see what God would reveal next!

Group text Saturday 4/4 @ 3:00 PM

I've been encouraging everyone to wear gloves and a mask in public...The idea is to cover your nose and mouth...If you can't find one make one (get creative like we used to) and use a bandana scarf and a rubber band or something similar, but Please protect yourselves family!! This is serious and COVID-19 doesn't discriminate based on age, color, religion, etc.

Many have and will continue to be affected/infected, especially if we don't protect ourselves!

Please stay home if you can, protect yourself if you must go out in public! Stay Safe and Healthy, my heart can't take going this again!

Maybe I'll see if the Pro seamstresses in the family (Mom Boonie/Sis. Jackie) can design some and put them on Amazon or eBay! TC AM update coming soon.

Marcy's private text message response

Yes, I even added making sure that you clean off your phones daily. with alcohol. Our Phones are a major source of germs!!

Yes, I'm so annoyed by the amount of people who are still not taking this seriously!! Please be safe.

https://www.aol.com/article/finance/2020/04/02/public-health-experts-americans-should-be-wearing-masks-in-public-amid-corona virus/23968563/ [6]

[6] **Public health experts Americans should be wearing masks in public amid coronavirus.** April 2, 2020. https://www.aol.com/article/finance/2020/04/02/public-health-experts-americans-should-be-wearing-masks-in-public-amid-coronavirus/23968563/

Correct:

Wear a Mask Covering Your Nose and Mouth!

Incorrect:

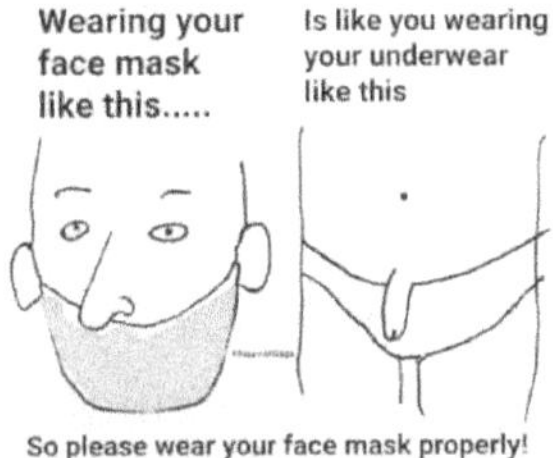

Is this how you wear your underwear? SMH, we need a public service announcement about how to properly wear your mask!

Group Text message Saturday 4/4 @ 6:00 PM (After the second prayer call)

Just believe and receive it God will perform it today. Hey, Hey!!

Thanks to everybody who continues to jump on the prayer calls. We have definitely been bonded and United during this time through these calls! To God be the Glory (TGBTG!)

God is pleased. Let's keep it going!

Group text Palm Sunday 4/5 @ 6:29 AM

Good Morning Family, It's Palm Sunday, the Sunday before the Resurrection which represents the Miracle arising of Jesus Christ after the crucifixion on Good Friday.

Today we are looking for a miracle for Tee. Here's an oldie but Bestie throwback from The Clark Sisters-I'm Looking For A Miracle" ...Twinkie and her sisters remind us that:

"I'm Looking For A Miracle, Expect the Impossible, I Feel the Intangible, I See The Invisible...The Sky is the Limit to What I can Have...."

"I Expect a miracle every day, God will Make A Way Out of No Way... Just believe and receive it God will perform it today, Hey Hey!!!"

TC update

Tee is holding steady, NO fever overnight...He's stable but Still Needs Your Explosive Prayers for a Miraculous healing!

Family, Let's remain prayerful and faithful that God is going to see him through this...Lets Expect Our Miracle!

This is from my nephew Todd in LA, he has never met Tee before... his description of Tee is bone-chilling, and ironically his description is just what Tee looks like right now with hair and facial stubble. "I wanted to share on the last prayer call, but I figured I'd let you know that when I first heard about his condition, I went into prayer that night and I saw Tee in the hospital laying on his back with no Ventilators, breathing on his own and it felt as though he was OK. Mind you, I've never seen Tee before in my life but this man that I saw was the exact picture of what you sent in the group message. The only difference was that he had stubble, like a shadow of a beard on him but everything else was the same. That's how I knew that he would be OK. We'll keep praying and pushing him to full restoration!!!"

Sunday 4/5 @ 2:25 PM group text TC update

Well, our favorite Nurse Julie answers the phone singing "I have good news for you" ...I spoke to her first, then the doctor called me back shortly and reiterated the same information:

- Tee's doing good right now...He was rotated on his back again and tolerated it well. His vitals are good, NO Fever, and the Nitrate med/ machine he was given previously to keep his Airways open (after his Oxygen levels dropped on Thursday morning.) has been Removed!
- He's still on the Ventilator and highly sedated (for now) but these are all positives, and baby steps forward!

Family Remember these are all baby steps, but Good news is Good News, right??!! Let's thank God for every little step... BTW, is it me or does it seem like he does better after our prayer calls??

Funny, I had a vision today to create a graph chart of his progress. I'll share the visual later with you but imagine a straight horizontal line which represents where he is today stable, then a huge upward line like this currently stable____/ (this line would be off the chart meaning healing/healed, Victory!!

Perhaps God was showing me something here...I'll take it! These are the best kinds of messages. Prayerfully there will be more, sooner than later!!Omg, I have so much to say today. I apologize for the long messages ... One of my friends suggested seeing if I could get some music playing in his room. Our favorite nurse Julie is working on getting him some Christian gospel music playing on Pandora in his room right now, so thank you (Monica A aka Mon) for that suggestion, looks like it may work! I want to make sure his mind, body and his spirit are covered from all angles.

Also, I did a drive-by prayer today with Tee. I just sat on the corner of the building where his room is and read scripture and prayed for a few minutes this morning. The crazy thing is... it's the same exact spot that I was in when I did my first drive-by last week, and I didn't know exactly where his room was then, but I know now, after our emergency visit a few days ago. Thank God for his Divine intervention that he would lead me to the right spot last week. Amen!

Family, God is pleased, and he is hearing our prayers and Tee is responding. You'll have my conference call number for the prayer calls. Save it in your contacts because we may need to make some periodic check-ins during the week. It doesn't have to be anything formal or long, just United prayer and Praise. Oh Lord, I feel my help coming! 👍 🙏 ❤️

Group text Sunday 4/5 @ 10:20 PM

No Real Updates from earlier Tee's still stable, sedated, NO fever and holding his own! Thanks for all of the continued love, support and prayers. Let's continue to pray him back on his feet, and watch God do His thing this week! Much Love 🙌 ❤️🙏

Group text Monday 4/6 @ 6:03 AM

TC update

Tee had a good night, he's still stable with NO Fever. Praise God!

Remember this is the week of miracles in the Bible, and we are continuing to pray for Tee's healing as we are approaching Easter, the GREATEST Miracle in Christianity.

If God can raise Jesus from the dead in 3 days, surely, HE can Restore and Heal Tee!! I'm looking forward to sharing some praise reports this week because I'm believing by Faith that this is going to be his breakout week, where we start to see the physical manifestation of his healing.

Family, please stay Faithful and Prayerful on this journey with us. I'm hoping more of you will join me on the 24-hour Good Friday fast...

There's power in numbers, and we are praying for the Destruction of the demonic force that's associated with the coronavirus!!

I'll send out the information tomorrow to any interested parties. I'm feeling led to have a prayer call tonight at 6:30 PM, nothing formal just Good ole Prayer, Praise. I will send out the reminder again with the call number this afternoon.

Everybody is talking about how these calls are so uplifting to them, I can't begin to tell you what it does to and for me!!

(Tears of Joy) I feel so Blessed to be able to connect with all of you regularly with so much love, during such a tough time, and I'm truly grateful for your continued love and support! We we'll get through this together with prayer and Faith!

Please Continue to Pray without ceasing!

Group text Monday 4/6 @ 2:05 PM

Tee is still stable and on the Ventilator with high sedation, holding his own...He is still on high oxygen levels from the Ventilator and they are looking to try to decrease oxygen settings later and reduce his sedation to see how he does.

We're claiming the Victory!

**Meantime he has NO fever, and he had a normal heart Echo Sonogram that shows that he didn't have any residual damage after his A fib issue on Friday, Praise God! **

My constant prayer has been to restore his lungs and to preserve his other Organs (*i.e.*, heart and brain, etc.).

The Doctor reminded me that he is definitely taking baby steps in the right direction, but he is still very sick. As much as I hate to be reminded of that, it propels me to push harder and higher in prayer!!

So, we will have our prayer call today at 6:30pm, and we will begin our fast on Friday at midnight. I will send details for those of you who expressed interest tomorrow. I hope that the rest of you will join us!

Meantime, please continue to send up your explosive prayers!!

We have some specific things to pray for on the call, and I'm also asking a few of you to share some recent Miracle testimonials that you've experienced personally or witnessed, since this is what we're praying for Tee.

Group text Tuesday 4/7 @ 5:31 AM

Happy 21st birthday Kai (Moogie Poo) Daughter Niece! Me and Uncle Tee Love you!!

Thanks again for joining me last night for our fourth prayer call last night. It was Awesome! We reinforced the power of Prayer, had a few testimonies of recent miracles (thanks Aunt Bunny and sister Jackie for sharing). We heard "I'm looking for a miracle" by the legendary Clark Sisters. We asked God for specific Restoration Preservation healing for Tee, and we closed with a positive song... "Hold on change is coming" by The Sounds of Blackness

P.S. Well do our regularly scheduled prayer call this Saturday @ 4:00 PM. We'll see if God leads me to do another call before then.

Group text Tuesday 4/7 @ 12:39 PM

TC update

I just spoke to Tee's Doctor and his nurse and he's doing well right now ...He's still stable, NO fever, good vital signs. They have been able to decrease some of his sedation medications, and his oxygen pressure settings (Peep) were lowered 3 points.

This trend needs to continue, and we need to pray for his own Oxygen levels to increase for him to be Ventilator free. This Friday is Good Friday and 3 weeks for Tee on the Ventilator. We need to continue with our Specific prayers for the Restoration of his lungs and the Preservation of his other vital organs as he continues to heal!

Family, God is pleased with our Faith and our steady communication with Him, and again Tee has physically responded to our prayers!

We have to keep up our momentum. We've come too far to turn back now! We are expecting A miracle this week.

Meantime I wanted to dedicate this song to my favorite Boopy. This is what I just told him when I spoke to him recently through speakerphone:

Hang in There Babe, You're Soon Coming Thru!

Sooner or later It will Turn in Your Favor,

It's Turning Around For You!!

****Side Note:** Steady Group Prayer Texts and coordination for upcoming Good Friday Fast for 4/11.

- Psalms 21
- Luke 8:40-47
- Psalms 92

Group text Wednesday 4/8 @ 5:36 AM

Good Morning, Tee had a good night, he remains stable, and it looks like his oxygen numbers have improved slightly. His sedation meds have also been slightly decreased. Let's be reminded that these are baby steps in the right direction, but he still remains very fragile, and we must continue to pray for his preservation and Full Restoration.

The nurse told me that he seems to be sensitive to talk, and his Blood Pressure fluctuates a little when people are in the room talking. I had to laugh to myself because I believe that's his way of telling them to shut up so he can rest, and it confirms that he can hear us!

He is seemingly making small but steady strides. We need to keep our momentum. I'm going to do a prayer call tonight @ 6:30 PM. Please join in as always if you can. I will resend the call information later today (It's still the same from the last four calls, should be stored in your contacts).

Also, I'm attaching the YouTube link below for the 24 hours Fast that I'll be participating in this Good Friday.

Please listen and join me as we unite as the Body of Christ to pray and fast against this Demonic force which is plaguing our world and has affected us personally. Thanks in advance for your continued prayers and support.

#GoodFridayFasting and Praying

First Church Washington

Prayer call is tonight @ 6:30 PM, same number ABC ya!

Group text Wednesday 4/8 @ 11:16 AM

TC update

Yes God, Yes!!!

I just spoke to the Doctor and Tee is doing well! He remains on the right track and heading in the right direction! They are making very small and Mild adjustments to his sedation and his Ventilator settings, and he's been tolerating them well!

My conversations are starting to change with the doctors. They are acknowledging his progress, and they're much more optimistic.

I just told the doctor he can call me anytime with this kind of news.

I'm just so full right now. Baby steps....in the right direction. Thank God for that! TGBTG!!

Thanks family, we got to keep it going... God is hearing us, and Tee is responding!!! 💖😇 🙏

"We're expecting A Miracle everyday God can make a way out of no way. Just believe and receive it God will perform it today hey hey!!"

P.S. I know today is going to be a good day, I just got this phone call, and I was able to get Tee's grass cut LOL, it was looking like a little jungle out there. You all know how he is about his yard!!

I sent out a separate email (to everybody who expressed interest in the fast) with a flyer and the YouTube link. If you did not get it, and you're interested please text me.

Group text Wednesday 4/8 @ 6:20 PM

TC update

No real changes from earlier, still holding his own. Today was a good day, like I said earlier they slightly lowered his sedation and oxygen settings. He's been opening his eyes more.

I just spoke to his Pulmonologist Dr. Nyanjom from Columbia, and he said when he looks at his chart, he knows that Tee is a living miracle! I told him that we know too, and that we've been praying, and we will continue to pray for his miraculous recovery! AMEN...

Dr. Nyanjom is a Christian and very spiritual, and he has and continues to pray for us, and he has also mentored my spirit through some hard times. He's the one who helped saved his life during his pneumonia episode in 2015... and he called the ER so that they would know that Tee was coming in during this most recent episode!

Got to give God the praise for sending us a praying Christian doctor!!

Group text Wednesday 4/8 @ 9:59 PM

Tee had a good day. No new updates. He's sleeping comfy. Prayerfully we'll get some more good news soon.

Thanks for all, we had another awesome prayer call tonight (despite the Devil trying to delay or deter us). We heard great testimonies of Miracles. We know God is Able!

We closed out by thanking God for all that He's done and all that He will continue to do. "Thank You Lord for All You've Done For Me

We're praying for and Expecting a miracle! Love you all, Good Night

Side Note: Family Prayer Call lead by Pastor Brian Murray; Song- "Its Turning Around For Me" Vashawn Mitchell.

Group text Thursday 4/9 @ 6:05 AM

TC update

Good Morning: Many Of you have told me that you look forward to the morning updates, so here you go:

Tee had a good night. They decreased another one of his ventilator oxygen settings (there are a few different ones), we just know that lower is better for the ventilator, and we continue to pray that his own oxygen levels continue to increase.

Things are changing daily over there with Hopkins as they are working to accommodate patients and families using technology, but I learned that they are on the fence with Zooming patients who are unconscious for obvious patient privacy issues, so well have to revisit that.

Meantime, I did get one of my favorite Nurses to Zoom me into his room last night on a whim (when nobody was looking), lol. I saw him briefly and I saw our family pics on the wall...

He was actually laying on his stomach when we saw him last week to aide his breathing. Last night he was on his back and I saw his beautiful face, freckles and all. He looked pretty good, given all that he's been through...A lot better than last week, and as he heals, he'll return back to normal. I wasn't able to talk to him because we were having some technical difficulties, like I said the nurses were pulling some QWIK favors for me. Prayerfully he'll be conscious soon, and we'll be able to do a planned family Zoom like the call we did last week with the immediate family...

That's all for now, I'll keep you posted on any noteworthy updates during the day. We're praying and expecting a miracle, so I'm looking forward to some Praise Reports.

Family, please continue to be diligent in your prayers, we all need them. God hears us, Tee feels us!

And it's only OUR Faith and prayers coupled with HIS Grace, goodness and Mercy that's going to pull us through these tough times!!

Group text Thursday 4/9 @ 4:36 PM

TC update

Good News!! Praise Report!!

Tomorrow marks the third week for Tee on the ventilator. He has had two Really good days in a row, and they are slowly but surely decreasing his ventilator settings and lowering his sedation. His ventilator oxygen pressure has dropped another 4 pts... he's getting there slowly but surely! He just has to keep this momentum! Me, Kaelyn and Bud just spoke to him through speakerphone and the nurse said that he blinked his eyes and looked around when he heard our voices. ("Where you all at?") LOL

We are overjoyed and committed to continuing to pray him back on his feet.

This is just the beginning of a living Easter miracle. Thanks for your continued prayers! We are extremely grateful for baby steps!!

Family Keep The Faith and keep sending up the Good prayers, they are working!! We're up to at least 37 Fasting partners, Yes!! Thank you all for joining me. The devil doesn't stand a chance here...I'll be sending out that information by the morning. "The Best Is Yet to Come"

24-hour prayer line

Let's meet here tonight @ 12:00 AM and Friday @ 9:30 AM.

Watch God change things.

Thursday 4/9 @ 6:00 PM - Group text to prayer warriors (Good Friday Fasters)

OK this is the text distribution list for the Good Friday fasters!! Let me know if I've missed anybody, and if I need to add them to the list. I have officially created my first text distribution list; Tee will be so proud of me!

There are at least 40 people on here, so if you need to reply or text me please send it directly to me...Everybody does not want to hear your response, and I probably don't either...Just kidding! Seriously, we're going to kick off this Fast TONITE at midnight, It's 24 hours so it will be tonight until tomorrow night at 12:00 AM!

You have 6 hours to decide what you're giving up and to get going. Remember this does not have to be food, it should be any of your vices or anything that's a distraction to you (*i.e.*, sweets, carbs, TV, cigarettes, social media, etc.). I know it's short notice but I'm going to try to kick this off by joining the ongoing 24-hour prayer line at midnight. Please join in if you can.

Let's also plan to check in tomorrow at 9:30 AM, especially if you were unable to check in at midnight. The goal is to start off with prayer and to be on one Accord...

Be sure to view this link to get a better understanding of what we're doing. I will also resend the flyer as well to the group. Thanks again for joining me, I can't wait to see the results after we collectively fast to break the yolk of the devastating coronavirus!!

24-hour prayer line

Let's meet here tonight @ 12:00 AM and Friday @ 9:30 AM

Watch God change things!

Group text message Friday 4/10 @ 10:15 AM - Happy Good God Friday

TC update

Just spoke to Tee's nurse, He's good, still stable. His Blood Pressure is up slightly, and he has a slight fever. He's being medicated accordingly. I'm prayerful and Faithful that this will normalize, and hell resume his good progress TODAY!

Let's be reminded that Some of this is normal and to be expected especially as he becomes less sedated and more aware.

We are also in Spiritual Warfare as we've collectively United to defeat the Devil, so you know He's mad...We Rebuke him in the Name of Jesus and we put him under our feet (STOMP), because we've already claimed the Victory in Jesus!

Let's continue to Fast and Pray as we get closer to Gods promises to heal Tee and restore our World!

Family, Thanks again for the 43 of you who have joined me in the 24-hour Fast....I can't begin to express my gratitude for your support!

"There's power in the name of Jesus To Break Every Chain." https://youtu.be/_cAUnuH7Lik [7]

P.S. Please continue to pray specifically for the unification and healing of our world as we Rebuke the Demonic spirit of COVID-19.

Also please continue to pray specific prayers for Tee's Full Preservation and Restoration. Amen!

Marcy

Ok prayer warriors I have a couple of special prayer requests right now:

1. Please keep my best friend CW in prayer, she is COVID-19 positive and having a lot of issues. I'm about to call and pray with and for her. She is also on this prayer chain!

[7] **Tasha Cobbs.** Break Every Chain. January 31, 2015. https://youtu.be/_cAUnuH7Lik

2. I'm asking for a hedge of protection around my family and friends today.

I just spoke to the HealthCare Center in Delaware where my grandmother lives, and they are having to take internal precautions because they've already had 4 other COVID-19 positives in sister facilities. Grandma is 94 years old and she can't do COVID-19, so Please send up prayers for her facility that they remain safe and covered by the blood!

**I'm also feeling lead to have our own prayer call tonight at 6:10 pm same phone number.

Group text Saturday 4/11 @ 5:51 AM - GOD Morning (GM)

TC update

Tee's having a few challenges right now. His heart rate is up a little bit, blood pressure down a little slight fever; Thankfully his oxygenation is still good, and these levels have remained stable.

They say these kinds of episodes aren't uncommon for patients who've been in the ICU for a long time. They are managing him through this. His nurse assured me that they're doing all they can for him, and that he's been with them so long that he's very special to them, very heartwarming!

They all tell me the same. They are surrounded by his family pictures and they all know of the AWESOME guy that he is, and the love that surrounds him.

I remain Faithful that he will get through this, and be back on track, because I'm believing by Faith that he is healed.

*Also Remember that Satan is mad, he's got a lot of people who have walked away from him and his ways and who are really trusting God, and he's not feeling that. He is definitely trying to Rattle us to plant the seed of disbelief, but we're not having it because We know God is In Control!!

I prayed with him through speakerphone this morning and I read the scripture about the man who was healed (John 5:1-15) at the well, and told him that he was healed, and that God told him to take up his bed and walk. I spoke life over him and prayed for him. I reminded him that we're All here with him and told him that we've been praying and fasting for his healing and that he's coming out of this bigger and better with a story to tell!

I also told the nurse that we were Believing by Faith that he's healed, and for them to continue to do what they're doing because it was a miracle coming out of this, and something that they needed to see as well!!

Just continue to keep God first...let's continuously pray for the healing of this world, and for the Full preservation and Complete Restoration of Tee.

Here's another inspirational song about the miracle of the Easter Resurrection, as were reminded of Gods miraculous powers, Enjoy!

Oh, What Love - Vicki Winans: https://youtu.be/IuRifOzDjws [8]

Side Note: Weekly Saturday prayer call @ 4:10 PM.

Group text Saturday 4/11 @ 11:31 AM

Happy Birthday Godbrother Bo (Polly's baby boy)

TC update

Thanks for your prayers, looks like Tee has weathered this storm, his heart rate and blood pressure have normalized. His fever is very mild! Praise God! His oxygen levels are still stable. TGBTG!

Get behind us Devil!!STOMP

He does get anxious as I anticipated when he wakes up, which is a double-edged sword. Please continue to pray his strength physically, mentally emotionally, during this time as well. It has to be a lot for him, especially not being able to see or hear any of us regularly!

We continue to pray for Tee's FULL preservation and COMPLETE Restoration!!

I'll send any new updates as I get them today. I was having technical difficulties earlier, and a lot of you got duplicate messages, and some of

[8] **Vicki Winans.** Oh What Love. March 27, 2010. https://youtu.be/IuRifOzDjws

you didn't get them at all. My apologizes, I think I've been overworking Textra (text app) ...

You all have been Great with keeping me on my toes. If for some reason too much time goes by and you haven't heard from me, you all are texting me like what's up? I appreciate that.

Please continue to keep my buddy CW in your prayers while in the Hospital in the Philadelphia area seeking treatment for COVID-19. Please pray for a hedge of protection over Grandma's facility in Delaware, that they remain COVID-19 free. Thanks

Prayer call today @ 4:10 PM, ABC ya!

Group text Saturday 4/11 @ 2:00 PM

Please tune into the play Jesus from Sight and Sound on TBN now if you can it's Awesome!!

- SIGHT AND SOUND THEATER
- Streaming Free— "JESUS"
- Easter Weekend Only!
- Live Play Stage performance - "JESUS", filmed at Sight and Sound Theater - streaming exclusively on Channel TBN!
- https://youtu.be/OtqaYgcjiSo [9]

We are thrilled to announce that JESUS will be made available for FREE in celebration of Easter! For three days only, experience the greatest rescue story of all time as it comes to life right in your living room! Available Online: April 10-12 only!

While we may not be able to gather together for Easter this year, may you still experience the joy of celebrating the ONE who came to save us all. Please share.

---

[9]**Jesus.** Sight & Sound Theater. TBN. https://youtu.be/OtqaYgcjiSo

Group text Saturday 4/11 @ 6:00 PM

Thanks to everybody who reminded me that The Clark Sisters movie is coming on tonight at 8pm on Lifetime. I had my recorder set this morning! I wish we could have had a watch party...Enjoy!

Hope to have a TC update within the hour...Ttys

Group Text Saturday 4/11 @ 8:52 PM

TC update

Tee is stable, no changes from earlier. They're giving him a diuretic tonight to decrease his fluids in hopes of increasing his respiratory status.

Tomorrow is Easter, we're still praying for and Expecting Our Miracle ... "Just believe and receive it God will perform it today hey!"

Please continue to keep Tee and Camille uplifted in your prayers of course, Thanks!

Everybody have a good night and Enjoy The Clark Sisters movie if you're watching it, and see why I love their music so much... (Dem girls can Sang)

Mama Mattie kicks butt and throws shoes like an old-school mama. Good Night, Talk To You Soon!

Group Text Sunday 4/13 @ 7:00 AM

I feel Really good this morning. My spirit tells me that Today is going to be a good day!!

Be sure to tune into virtual church services for your spiritual food. Feel free to join me @ New Psalmist Now 7:15 AM, 9:30 AM and 12:00 PM. See you there!

https://youtu.be/LYUu_9lSjoA [10]

[10]**Bishop Walter S. Thomas.** Senior Pastor. New Psalmist Baptist Church. Easter Sunday Virtual Worship 2020. https://youtu.be/LYUu_9lSjoA

Bishop is getting it in, he is preaching "You can't keep a good man down". It's almost over if you can catch it at 9:30 AM or 12:00 PM or on or on You Tube!

Side Note: Easter Sunday Miracle, TURNING POINT!

My girl is displaying my Exact sentiments!

Group text Miracle Easter Sunday 4/12 @ 11:43 AM

TC update

!!!Family this is the best Praise Report that I've had so far for you all...

I woke up with a surge in my spirit and God spoke to me and told me today was going to be a good day, as I text out to you all this morning...

I just spoke with Tee's doctor and she told me that he was doing very well and heading in the right direction.

They are going to be trialing him over the next 24-hours to see if he can breathe on his own without the machine. Once he shows that he can sustain himself, they will Extubate him (Remove him from the ventilator!)!!

I cannot explain how it felt to receive this news. After crying and thanking God for 10 or 15 minutes, I tried to make a few calls, and now I'm trying to get this text, but I just can't explain the feeling right now!! I'm just so Full and SOOO Grateful to God!

Family we cannot stop praying. We have to continually pray without ceasing to see this miracle come full circle! And once it comes full circle, we need to continue to be Faithful and Prayerful for the Healing!

I want to write more but I can't right now, just so full with tears of joy and praise

They say a picture is worth a thousand words. I guess I'll just have to show you how I'm feeling! **This photo symbolizes our praise for the good news, ironically the guy on the end resembles Tee, Get It Yall!**

Group text Easter Miracle Sunday 4/12 @ 5:58 PM

They are still weaning Tee down on his sedation, and down on the Ventilator settings. He's getting very anxious as he becomes more conscious, and they're having to give him meds to calm him down.

This is a double-edged sword. I know my husband well, and I warned them accordingly. Let's pray that all goes well and that there are no setbacks during this crucial time!

Thanks for your continued prayers, lets continue to pray for Tee's Full Preservation and Complete Restoration, and that he remains covered by the blood always, and especially as he prepares to wean off the Ventilator!

Continued prayers for Cousin Lawanda, Camille and Grandma's facility. Amen

"The Best Is Yet to Come"!!!

Group text Easter Miracle Sunday 4/12 @ 9:28 PM

Last update for today. Just spoke to Tee's nurse, he is resting comfy. They're aware of his anxiety when he's awake, and they're giving him something to calm him. I've also been praying for peace in his spirit.

His vitals are good, No fever, he's stable and on the right track. She told me that he keeps his eyes open when he's awake now ("I'm watching you all") ...

And she talks to him when she's working with him to relax him. I remain prayerful that he's in good hands and that God has not brought us this FAR to leave us now.

I continue to trust and pray that he will have a smooth weaning down and off the Ventilator soon! Thanks for your continued prayers, God is pleased, HE is listening, and Tee is responding!

Please keep our world, Tee, Cousin Lawanda, all facilities including Grandma in Delaware, Uncle Tony (Mom Boonies) bro, and anyone else who is going through right now and in need of a Blessing or Healing. In your prayers!

Good Night!

Group text Monday 4/13 @ 7:05 AM

Sorry I'm a little late, I've been on speaker phone for the last 45 mins praying and reading scripture with Tee in hopes of calming his spirit. Tee had a little bit of a rough night. He's getting very anxious as they are weaning down his sedation, he didn't tolerate it well, but he's stable again.

Please continue to keep him in your prayers during this time. He has come a long way and we sure can't afford to lose our momentum!

I read the entire Philippian's 4 and a few other encouraging scriptures to him. The good news is, he's more awake and aware, the nurse was working on him while I was on speaker. She told him to open his mouth and he did.

Again, it's a double-edged sword!

I'll be keeping my eyes on him and monitoring his progress as they add some additional anxiety meds to further relax him during this time. Please continue to keep him in your prayers as well as the others on our prayer list including: Healing for the World, Camille, Cousin Lawanda, Uncle Tony, all facilities including Grandma's in Delaware, etc.

Thanks, Ttys

Group text Monday 4/13 @ 9:32 AM

I'm going to do a brief 10 to 15-minute prayer call this morning at 11:10 AM, please join me if you are available, Thanks!

Same call number **Please mute out!

Group text Monday 4/13 @ 5:13 PM

TC update

Tee's having a pretty good day. It looks like he's stable and calming down. His meds are being adjusted accordingly. He had a good respiratory trial earlier today. We will see if/when its good enough for him to come off the Ventilator.

Kaelyn and I did a Zoom call with him this afternoon. I think he was happy to see us. His eyes were open and moving And I think he was trying to talk **(Hey)**

It was so heartwarming to see him. He looks so much better than the last few times I/we saw him. He has facial hair and a George Jefferson bush in the back. He'll be in the bathroom for several hours when he gets home, grooming himself.

Afterwards the Doctor told me that he did good on the bike today, and I laughed. I thought he had his patients mixed up, but apparently modern technology has this bike like mechanism for patients who have been in the ICU for a while. It keeps them from losing use of their lower extremities from being in the bed for so long. Thank God for that. Kudos to Hopkins!!

Kaelyn said, "Dads never done any exercise on a bike, wait till he hears about that." I was thinking the same, I haven't been able to get him on a bike in 10 years, even though every Summer we say we're going to get one.

Check it out:

SupineCycleAllowsPatientstoExerciseinICU

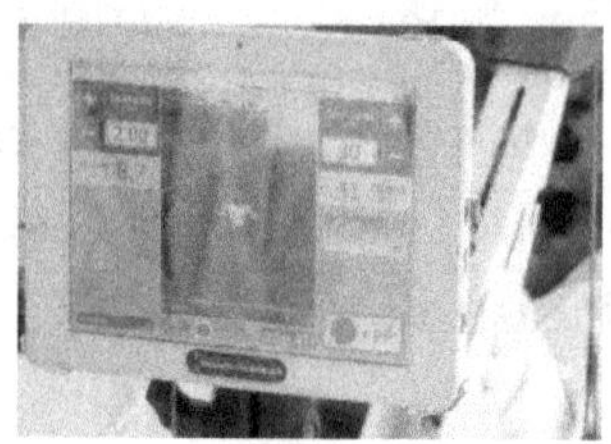

Portable device helps avoid physical decline.

https://physicians.dukehealth.org/articles/supine-cycle-allows-patients-exercise-icu [11]

Thanks to everybody who was able to jump on the morning prayer call with me I really appreciate it. Like I said these things keep me motivated /inspired as well!

We'll have the call today at 6:40 PM. It won't be long; this girl is tired. It's been a long day!

Same #, Please Mute Out, See you there.

Group text Tuesday 4/14 @ 6:03 AM

Good morning!

Tee had an uneventful night. He is on calming meds; his Blood Pressure and Heart Rate are stable. Praise God!

We'll continue to pray for his Full Preservation and Complete Restoration. I'm expecting some good news soon.

Ongoing prayers for World Healing, my best friend Camille, Mom Boonie and family, Cousin Lawanda and everyone who's hurting or experiencing some type of hardship during this time! Only God can bring us through this!

[11] **Amy M. Pastva.** Supine cycle allows patients exercise in ICU. 2020. https://dpt.duhs.duke.edu/research/faculty-research-spotlights/dr-amy-m-pastva-spotlight

Group text Tuesday 4/14 @ 1:25 PM

From Sis Brina: (Nephew) Si's card for Uncle Tee, please forward to the group:

Marcy:

Thanks Si, Uncle Tee definitely looks like this with facial hair, but he still has both ears.

TC update

I just spoke to Tee's Doctor, he said "He's Continually Improving."

Praise God!

Everything is stable, his respiratory trial went well on Monday, and they're going to continue to Decrease his sedation again, now that he is on anxiety meds to keep him calm, as he weans down.

Fam Were getting closer to the Finished Line! God willing Tee will continue to do well on his weaning and trials, and BE VENTILATOR FREE in the NEXT 24-48 hours!!!

An Angel sent this my way this morning, just as I needed it!

Group text Wednesday 4/15 @ 6:13 AM

Good morning!

Tee had a pretty uneventful night Again, Praise God. He is still on calming meds; his Blood Pressure and Heart Rate are stable. Oxygen remains good.

He is on the lowest ventilator setting now!!

They are just trying to balance and make sure he's comfortable as he's weaned down...

He's also been having a slight fever, they started him on an antibiotic to make sure he's not developing any secondary infection. This is why we have to pray for him to get off the ventilator Asap, so he can get strong enough to come home soon, and out of the germy hospital!

We'll continue to pray for his Full Preservation and Complete Restoration. I'm expecting some good news soon.

Ongoing prayers for: World Healing, my best friend Camille, Mom Boonie and family, Cousin Lawanda...Grandma's Facility in Delaware and all other facilities-remain COVID-19 Free. Lorraine Overton family (loss Uncle to COVID-19), Henderson and Spears family for loss of two family members and Maurice and family on loss of his wife from COVID-19. God Bless

Everyone who's hurting or experiencing some type of hardship during this time!

Group text Wednesday 4/15 @ 1:49 PM

TC update

Tee is still doing well. They are SLOWLY decreasing his meds and preparing him for relevant trials and assessments to ensure that he is in fact ready to come off of the ventilator. We must wait patiently, prayerfully and Faithfully, as he completes these tasks.

They have to make sure that he is ready, to avoid any futuristic setbacks once he comes off!

I know the anticipation is killing us all. It's the 4th Quarter, we're at the 5-yard marker at a football game and were on a commercial.

Ready, Break. Hold tight, keep praying, touchdown is coming soon. (Thx Kel for helping w this analogy)

GO Eagles!

Whoops, I forgot where I was!

Seriously, Good news is coming soon, we just don't know Exactly when and we can't rush the process. Meantime, we'll continue to pray for his Full Preservation and Complete Restoration.

Ongoing prayers for: World Healing, My best friend Camille- (Just released from the hospital) , Mom Boonie and family, Cousin Lawanda (Released from hospital still in need of our United prayers)...Grandma's Facility in Delaware and all other facilities-remain COVID-19 Free, Lorraine Overton family (loss Uncle to COVID-19), Henderson and Spears family for loss of two family members and The Maurice Clark and family on loss of his wife from COVID-19. God Bless

Everyone who's hurting or experiencing some type of hardship during this time!

Group text Good morning Thursday 4/16 @ 6:25 AM

TC update

Another peaceful night. Just spoke to Tee's nurse, He says he successfully tolerated the lower sedation overnight, and he's following more commands and becoming more alert and responsive, just as we prayed for on our prayer call last night. **TGBTG, HE'S ABLE!!**

He's heading in the right direction. We just have to continuously pray that he is able to check all the necessary boxes and tasks needed (physically and cognitively) to be successfully removed from the ventilator!!

Reminder that We must wait patiently, prayerfully and Faithfully, as he completes these tasks!

Good news is coming soon, we just don't know Exactly when, and we cannot rush the process!

Meantime, we'll continue to pray for his Full Preservation and Complete Restoration.

Group text Thursday 4/16 @ 12:01 PM

TC update

I just spoke to Tee's nurse she told me he is doing GREAT today. He is very responsive, squeezing hands.

Today may be the day for the ventilator to be removed. Waiting for the doctor to call me pray pray pray, Ttys!!

Side Note: Next check-in at 8:30 PM – 9:00 PM (Zoom/Ph Call)

Group text Thursday 4/16 @ 4:17 PM

TC update

So were still waiting...They said he's still a little lethargic and they don't think he's quite ready yet but were getting close.

Prayerfully tomorrow... (Tomorrow will be 4 weeks, Ugh!)

I'll keep you'll posted! Thanks for the continued prayers!

Group text Thursday 4/16 @ 10:00 PM

Sorry, I fell asleep. No new updates. He was resting comfortably when I called @ 9:30 PM.

We're remaining prayerful that his pain meds will continue to wear off to the point where they can Extubate Soon!

Let's see what tomorrow brings.

Group text Friday 4/17 @ 6:34 AM

TC update

I just spoke to his nurse she said, "He looks Good, better than last week when I saw him". I said yes, he's getting better each day.

I was thinking you last saw him before that Easter miracle kicked in! She said, "They are constantly lowering his sedation, he's following intermittent commands, and despite still being on the machine he is doing most of the work and taking his own Breaths". Praise God.!!

Tee appears to be physically ready for extubation but were still praying for him to wake up some more. He needs to reorient after being on medications for such a long time, so we continue to pray for his preservation and restoration, and that his system safely and timely rids the medication, for him to continue to increase his awareness!

Preparing for landing

Today's analogy for Tee's condition. He is just circling in the sky, Waiting for God to give him the cue for a Safe and Perfect landing. He will be landing soon, and we will all be on the sidelines cheering!

Reminder that We must wait patiently, prayerfully and Faithfully, as he continues to heal! I had to go to God myself on this...I was a bit frustrated yesterday! Tonight @ 7:30 PM will mark 28 days (4 weeks on the ventilator).

Good news is coming soon at any time! We just don't know Exactly when, and we cannot rush the process!

Meantime, we'll continue to pray for his Full Preservation and Complete Restoration.

As always, I'll keep you posted! Thanks for your ongoing prayers...God is pleased, Tee is responding!

God Bless Everyone who's hurting or experiencing some type of hardship during this time!

We Need all hands-on deck

Group text Friday 4/17 @ 12:13 PM

TC update

Hello, I just spoke to Tee's Doctor. He is very weak as to be expected after 4 weeks (28 days in ICU) on the ventilator. They are going to try to Successfully extubate today. WE NEED ALL hands-on deck that this is Successful, NO Complications!!

I'm going to open up the prayer lines at 12:25 PM in 10 minutes!! Please join me if you can. I will not be long! I have to jump on Zoom call for work @ 12:50 PM. No need to respond if you can't join us, just say a prayer wherever you are! Thanks

I will have a follow-up update this afternoon!! GOD IS ABLE!!

The flight has landed safely:

Group text Thursday 4/17 @ 2:33 PM

Text from Son Theirrien "Bud"

"Did you know they took my dad off the Ventilator an hour ago? I just called the hospital. He's conscious but very drowsy. Throat is too sore to talk but Kaelyn and I were able to talk to him"

Marcy

THEY TOLD ME; I WAS ON MY ZOOM call! I was planning to check in afterwards-AMEN!

Thanks for the United prayers. Once Again, God heard us, Tee Responded! After 28 LONG days, Tee is FINALLY VENTILATOR FREE

TGBTG!!

Nothing but God-NBG!!

John 8:36. SO, IF THE SON SETS YOU FREE YOU WILL BE FREE INDEED! Thanks, God, for Never Leaving Us or Forsaking Us, You Did Just what you said you would do, and for this Milestone, we are extremely grateful!! Ayyy Men....

Marcy Praise Emoji

Group text Saturday 4/18 @ 5:57 AM

TC update

I just spoke to his nurse and she said he made it safely through the night without any major issues. The first 12 to 24 hours are the most critical when they come off the Ventilator. His oxygen levels are fine, his heart rate is a little high, but they're going to Medicate him to normalize it. He is still very drowsy.

Prayerfully his HR will normalize shortly (it usually does with medication), and he'll start waking up more soon!

Please continue to pray Tee's strength (Physically, Emotionally, Spiritually, Mentally) and that he successfully continues to heal with No residual effects. Were continuously praying for his Complete Preservation and Full Restoration from head to toe!

Thanks for your ongoing prayers...God is pleased, Tee is responding!

SATURDAY PRAYER CALL @ 4:10 PM. We've had a Glorious week, and We have a lot to be Thankful/Prayerful for!!

Ongoing prayers for: World Healing, my best friend Camille- (Just released from the hospital), Mom Boonie and family (loss of brother from COVID-19 complications)

Cousin Lawanda (Released from hospital still in need of our United prayers) ...Grandma's Facility in Delaware and all other facilities-remain COVID-19 Free, Lorraine Overton family (loss Uncle to COVID-19), Henderson and Spears family for loss of two family members and The Maurice Clark and family on loss of his wife from COVID-19.

Sondra's friend Kittina (released from hospital previously and still battling complications from COVID-19). God Bless

Everyone who's hurting or experiencing some type of hardship during this time!

Group text Saturday 4/18 @ 2:50 PM

TC update

I spoke to his Doctor earlier and he says that his vitals and heart rate are good.

His heart rate normalized @ 9:30 AM with prayer and meds as usual. He is still getting some oxygen from a nasal tube; he is still very weak. He is slowly becoming less drowsy as his system eliminates all of the pain medicine that he's been on over the last month!

He needs to gain more strength to be able to breathe completely on his own without any Oxygen help. This is to be expected, given the amount of time that he was on his Ventilator.

As usual we will continue to pray him through this point as well! God has showed up MIGHTILY FOR US, and HE will continue to do so!

Saturday prayer conference call @ 4:10 PM. MEET YOU ON THE PRAYER LINE SOON!

Group text Sunday 4/19 @ 9:00 AM

Please Watch this Beautiful healing melody dedicated to Tee from Our friends, The Waters family:

"Tiara Jayla and Jordan Waters" on YouTube https://youtu.be/z9WIv Sr5bXY [12]

Thanks Waters family for creating such a beautiful tribute, I can't wait for Tee to see this! You all will have to come participate at our Homecoming celebration when we're able to do one.

TC update

Tee had a pretty calm night. He had a small fever of 101, it has now subsided to 99. Praise God! He's stable and doing well and his nurse said, "He's definitely with it". TGBTG!!!

We're hoping to connect with him today to hear his voice. I'm so excited, it's been 32 LONG DAYS since we've heard his voice! I'll keep you posted! Please continue to pray Tee's strength, and that he successfully continues to heal with No residual effects and were praying for his Complete Preservation and Full Restoration from head to toe!

Thanks for your ongoing prayers...God is pleased, Tee is responding!

PRAYER CALL Tonight @ 6:40 PM. Meet us there if you can! We have a few new people on our prayer list...

[12] **Tiara, Jayla and Jordan Waters.** His Presence is Here to Heal. April 19, 2020. https://youtu.be/z9WIvSr5bXY

Group text Monday 4/20 @ 1:38 PM

TC update

Tee had a good physical therapy session. He sat on the edge of the bed for 15 minutes. We were able to Zoom in with him afterwards, but by the time we got to him he was sleep. He tried to acknowledge us, but he was wiped out!

He's still very weak...But God is strong, and His strength is made perfect in our weakness!!

He's still getting high amounts of oxygen through his nose, so we have to pray that his own oxygen levels continue to increase so that they can decrease the settings and eventually discontinue the nasal tube. He still has a little bit of a fever, but his labs don't show any sign of infection.

He's waking up more, and a little more alert...they all say he's with it (Of course he is).

The Doctor told him that we have been rooting for him and that We're all in his corner and he smiled. He has family pictures on his wall, we were able to see them during one of our Zooms.

The Doctor asked him does he want to relay a message that he loves us, and he nodded his head Yes!!

The Doctor started to tell me how long his road to recovery would be, and I respectfully thanked him for his opinion. I told him that he's made it this far by Our Prayers and Faith and that we needed them to keep doing what they were doing, and We would keep doing what we were doing, and he agreed! Enough said, THE END!

So, prayer warriors you know what we got to do... because when the Praises go up, the blessings come down...So let's keep it moving. Please Continue to lift up your prayers and keep Tee uplifted. We're praying for Tee's Complete Preservation and Full Restoration in the name of Jesus!

Group text Tuesday 4/21 @ 6:09 PM

Get your tissues ready, this is a tearjerker:

The nurse told me that he's been a lot more pleasant since his call this morning with me and his kids. I think today was his most alert day so far and he woke up angry trying to figure out what was going on, and where we were, because he knows we would have been there, so I think he got a boost when he saw and heard us earlier!

I was able to Zoom with Tee for a brief, but heart filled moment a few minutes ago. I dropped off his glasses and his cell phone to him earlier, so when I saw him on Zoom, he had his glasses on, and he looked really cute. LOL...

When I called the nurse said we were just talking about you. He was trying to figure out his cell phone password. I guess he thought I knew that too...Not!

He still talks very low, so I had to try to listen well, read his lips and have the nurse translate, but we did good. He told me he was thirsty, and he asked me to Come see him… Ugh, Heartbreaking!

I explained to him why I/we can't come. I told him that we would all be up there all the time if we could! I also told him what happened, how long he's been there and how far he's come. I told him that we came up there one time when we weren't sure if he was going to make it, but he's pulled through by Grace and Mercy.

I told him that a lot of people have died from COVID-19, but he's made it, and God hasn't bought him this far to leave him, and that **He's a living Miracle!**

I let him know that Everybody is praying for him all over, all the time. He said Amen...and He told me "We got this" … (one of our sayings). I actually told him that I too tested positive for COVID-19, but my symptoms were mild.

He's doing really well!! I'm so excited.

Prayer warriors, we prayed yesterday that his oxygen be restored and that he be able to come off the high-pressure oxygen, to a lower pressure oxygen, and soon off the nasal oxygen. Well...He transitioned to the lower pressure oxygen today, Praise God. I think he's going to come off the nasal oxygen soon!!

This has been a very gratifying, touching and emotional day!! I'm exhausted, but SOO GRATEFUL yall!!

TC strong, Go Boopy!

I'm telling you all, it's our United prayers, God is pleased, and Tee is responding... I will check in with him tonight before I go to bed, but I'm thinking he'll probably be asleep during my next check in, he's been pretty up all day today, and his eyes were getting heavy at the end of our conversation!

So, if I don't send an update tonight, NO news is good news and well resume in the morning.

Family, I want to keep our momentum going.

I'm going to shoot to do a prayer call Wednesday or Thursday evening. I will let you know tomorrow morning.

"Lord you've been Sooo, you've been so Faithful even though Sometimes I didn't do what you wanted me to do":

Enjoy this selection... https://youtu.be/C-SjcoynzLs [13]

P.S. I am praying for him to return home by 5/1, God willing! Please join me.

Group text Thursday 4/23 @ 5:56 AM

Great God morning!

TC update

Tee slept very peacefully last night. His heart rate is still a little high, so they were about to start him on the IV of the fast-acting medication that he's been responsive to. I'll be calling back in a few hours, and I'm sure he'll be normalized.

[13] **Eddie James & the Phoenix Mass Choir.** You've Been So Faithful. https://youtu.be/C-SjcoynzLs

Prayerfully this is just a small speed bump, and he'll be able to continue to push forward. He's gained so much momentum over the last week... We've come this far by faith!

Devil get under our feet...STOMP ya with a Momma-Mattie Moss Clark (the original MMC) shoe!

I have a full morning. I'll be checking in with him a few times throughout the day, and I'll be talking to the Doctors and nurses. We didn't get to connect with him yesterday, and I'm feeling a little disconnected, So We will Connect today, God willing!

I will send out an afternoon update as soon as I can. No worries, NO news is good news...Just keep the prayers going! God hears us and Tee responds!

Right now, we're praying for his heart rate to normalize, and that he continues to progress forward without any interruptions. We want him to continue to get stronger inside and out, so that he can graduate out of the ICU, and get closer towards coming home!

Our continuous daily prayers for Tee

Please continue to pray Tee's strength, and that he successfully continues to heal with No residual effects and were praying for his Full Preservation and Complete Restoration from head to toe!

We have a few new people on our prayer list...Our list is growing. We extend our prayers to everyone on and off the list:

Group text Thursday 4/23 @ 1:57 PM

TC update and praise report

Tee is doing Really well. We just had a quick Zoom with him, and he looks good. He was really happy to see us. I said Hey Boop, he said Hey baby…Ugh this is so hard!

I just wanted to reach through the screen and give him a big forehead kiss! Ok, alright I know...

I just spoke to his doctor, his Heart Rate normalized as expected, Praise God, and he's being introduced slowly back into solid foods. He can eat thick liquids and Jell-O types of things, NOW! He was getting Water Ice (that's what we call it in Philly LOL), I think they call it Italian ice everywhere else. I know he's really grateful to be able to quench his thirst. This is another huge milestone for him!

Group text Thursday 4/23 @ 9:27 PM

Today was another Great Day for us! Every day with Jesus is sweeter than the day before! God is Mind-blowing. This time last week we were praying for Tee to get off the ventilator. 6 days later he's eating, drinking, talking, and Standing...Yes!

Tee is enduring various daily therapies including strenuous physical therapy, and he's rolling like a champ. He stood up three more times today, for a little longer. He's getting stronger each day. He's slowly but surely resuming solid foods, and he drank some water today for the first time since he's been off the ventilator. Praise God! He'll continue with the various therapies to continue to strengthen him over the coming weeks to get him ready to come home.

Everything is stable, and bar NO surprises he should be transitioning out of the ICU soon. Each day is a pivotal step towards his long-term healing process. I'm feeling confident that the worst part is behind us, and the Best is yet to come!

I'm looking forward to him being able to reconnect with the family as he becomes more independent. The continued love and support from afar will be a huge contribution to his healing process.

Thank you, God for the Victory. We've come this far by faith and the latter will be greater! Thanks for your continued prayers and support.

Love you all!

Good Night!

Clark Sisters - Victory https://youtu.be/RPQEDJQTZrc [14]

[14] **The Clark Sisters**. Victory (Lyric Video). November 2019. https://youtu.be/RPQEDJQTZrc

Group text Friday 4/24 @ 6:34 AM

TC update

Tee was sleeping peacefully this morning when I called, he didn't go to sleep until late, because he had been sleeping all day after physical therapy.

They're trying to get him on a regular sleeping routine so he can be up during the day for his Therapies.

Well, Family...Today is already starting out victoriously. Tee was removed from the nasal oxygen @ 4:00 AM and BREATHING FULL ROOM AIR WITH OUT ANY ASSISTANCE - 1 week after coming off the ventilator. ain't GOD GOOD?? We're just so Hallelujah Grateful for his progress!!

We're going to keep praying and praising God as we watch Tee rebound and return back to us Bigger and Better. I feel some more victories coming...Praise Him!

As the Winans sang, "Millions Didn't Make It, But I was one of the Ones Who Did" (Thanks Sis Bri and Aunt Debbie T for dedicating this beautiful and relevant song)

Our continuous daily prayers for Tee:

Please continue to pray Tee's strength, and that he successfully continues to heal with NO residual effects and we're praying for his Full Preservation and Complete Restoration from head to toe!

We have a few new people on our prayer list...Our list is growing. We extend our prayers to everyone on and off the list.

Group text Friday 4/24 @ 3:34 PM

TEE IS LEAVING THE ICU THIS EVENING. WE'RE ECSTATIC!!

He'll be going to an intermediary care floor where he'll receive more care than a regular floor, but less care than an intensive care unit. Praise God!

His voice is still very low, and he's still weak and tires easily so he's not ready to talk on the phone yet, but he's getting closer each day. Kaelyn and I watched him graciously chug some water through a straw on Zoom earlier.

My heart is just Soo incredibly full and this reminded me how important it is to make sure that I ask for enough time to pray with him at least once a day, He Needs and wants it, Glory!!

Another GREAT day in this Modern-day Biblical miracle. Please keep the prayers going. God is pleased and Tee is responding. Well keep you posted. TGBTG!!

P.S. Please keep us in prayer through this transition as we will be communicating with A whole new set of rules and medical staff on the new unit.

ICU staff have become friends, I talk to them several times a day, and they have been PHENOMENAL! This new group has huge shoes to fill! They better bring their A game...

Group text Saturday 4/25 @ 11:17 AM-(first morning out of ICU, in the Intermediary Floor)

TC update

Tee is doing well; He's getting antsy and ready to get healed and moving. When I first called him, his voice was really low, and I could barely hear him.

Somehow, he managed to raise it when he started asking questions and telling me what to do...He wanted to know when they were coming in to do his New consults for the new floor...I figured its slow there since it's the weekend, and they're probably not starting anything fresh until Monday, and the nurse confirmed this.

You all, He's starting to boss me around again (some things never change, the sheriff is back!). He told me that I needed to find the guys who cut our neighbor's lawn and have them cut our grass and get on a contract lol (which you all know I did a few weeks ago for Tee's grass) LOL, and I hired landscapers to do a nice Spring cleanup next week!

He also told me to find the pool guys information and touch base with him so he could open the pool. Really boo??

I told him I wasn't thinking about NO pool right now, and we don't need the extra expense (and I was thinking who is going to be taking care of it?). We can revisit when we he gets home. I had to remind him that we're in the midst of a pandemic, and we're not doing a bunch of extra stuff right now!

I told him that his sister Vera told me that he was going to be in there thinking about all the stuff he needed to do around his house, and she hit the nail right on the head!

You all know Tee is Mr. Gadgets and our house is Fort Knox with all types of remote security systems and cameras that we can access from our phones. You know he's going to be on it, when he's able to get back on that phone and see them cameras... "**Marce**, they cut the grass too low, **Marce**, why did you move my truck"?

More importantly I read the Daily Word to him which was actually about The Story of Lazarus being raised from the dead John 11:44, and a good message about Releasing all that does not contribute to my highest good. It was a timely message, because I was able to tie that back into his restoration and not focusing on negativity that could hinder his progress. He started to fizzle out so I let him go, but he's definitely Still very sharp as you can see. Praise God!

Group text Great God Morning Sunday 4/26 @ 10:14 AM

From Cousin Dana:

"Sometimes God will let you get into a situation where there is no possible way out so that when He turns it around, everyone will know it was Him.

This just popped up in my Twitter feed. Just wanted to share this with you True Indeed!"

My response

Yes, I know this personally to be true. I've certainly been here before, this was a HUGE Reminder for me, but definitely relevant for some others who've never experienced his power firsthand.

This is what I refer to as a NOTHING BUT GOD (NBG) Blessing, when you know that it couldn't have happened any other way! Thanks so much for sharing!!

Group text Sunday 4/26 @ 6:57 PM

Today was without incident. Tee is physically doing well, but he was a little down, mainly I think because he was a little bored, and there wasn't much going on this weekend around there with his Rehab and Consults. They are all scheduled to resume Monday.

We had a nice heart-to-heart, and I reassured him that he would be fine, and that his situation is temporary...I told him that everything still functions, he just needs to rebuild or strengthen it since he hasn't used it in over a month. I also had to remind him that he's only been off the ventilator for 1 week and he's made great strides!

I think once he gets busy and feeling productive like he's reaching milestones, his spirits will improve. He did Tell Me that He's Truly Glad that He Made it!

As Tee recovers, I will probably only send out one to two updates per day...No worries though, no news is good news.

Well keep doing our prayer calls and standing up our Collective and United prayers.

Group text Monday 4/27 @ 5:48 AM

GREAT GOD MORNING!

Tee had a good night; he slept all night. He's getting very annoyed with the interrupted sleep in the hospital setting, so they tried to give him a break last night.

We spoke to him briefly last night @ 9ish. He was supposed to Zoom at 10:00 PM with his kids, but he fell asleep.

I'm going to strive to get Tee on a call soon, so he can witness firsthand how we've unified in prayer.

Our continuous daily prayers for Tee

Please continue to pray Tee's strength (Physically, Emotionally, Spiritually, Mentally) and that he successfully continues to heal with No residual effects. Were continuously praying for his Full Preservation and Complete Restoration from head to toe!

Specific prayers for the coming days

1. All of the above prayers for Tee:

A. Specifically, for his throat to continue to heal so that he can swallow- To safely reintroduce foods and drink so he can lose the feeding tube! AND resume talking at a normal level.

B. Improved Overall physical strength incl dexterity and ability to use his hands and limbs successfully

C. Overall strength to be able to sit up, stand, walk, with and without assistance!

Boopy Strong!

1. Healing for the world and Our prayer list

2. Marcy (MMC) to find and implement better group texting options

3. MMC continued strength to support my hubby during the next physical, emotional, spiritual part of his healing process!

** As I type this message, I know this is already done, and we Thank God in advance for the Victory. I look forward to sending out the Praise Reports!

I will say this...Tee looks Great, he's lost some weight, but he's still beautiful! I told him that he got 10 years back when he shaved off that Gray beard lol. He surely doesn't look like what he's been through, Praise God!

TGBT Amazing GLORY!! (TO GOD BE THE AMAZING GLORY)

We have a few new people on our prayer list...Our list is growing. We extend our prayers to everyone on and off the list:

After 4 days on the Intermediary step-down floor, Tee moved onward to In-patient physical therapy, his last stop towards home. Tee was super-motivated to come home but he was still extremely weak, and the therapists couldn't give a definitive timeline on when he would return, so we shot for a 5/15 release date initially, which would give him close to a month of in patient therapies. I made it clear to everyone including Tee that I needed him to resume a certain level of independence before he could come home. I wanted him to maximize his therapies while he was there, even if it took a bit longer and delayed his arrival. I knew we would both be frustrated if he came home bedridden.

Tee had overcome insurmountable odds; he was alive and doing well and working so hard to get back home. He would have 3-4 hours of intense therapies; we would talk on the phone in the AM and PM and he would talk to family members and Zoom whenever he wasn't sleeping. Everyone was so excited that he was alive and well. He was weeks from coming home and I knew that I had to put the pedal to the medal to ensure that he had everything he needed at home to resume a comfortable and healthy transition.

My days were long and productive, but this was a good "long". I knew that my Boopy would be on his way back to me soon. I wanted Tee home when he was truly physically ready, and he was determined to be out by 5/5, our fifth anniversary and he did everything in his power to do so. He was working hard on the inside to get here and I was working hard to get him here. Our efforts would soon pay off.

Group text Thursday 4/30 @ 6:03 PM

Hot off the press, His ETA is by 5/10! I'll know for sure by early next week!! Yes!!

<u>**Group text Friday 5/1 @ 7:41 PM**</u>

I almost skipped todays update, the first in over a month... Tee is GREAT, He's getting stronger and happier, in anticipation of coming home next week. TGBTG!! We're both exhausted and heading to bed soon. Thanks for your continued prayers.

I hope to have an exact release date for you by Monday...Most likely the middle to end of next week! Prayer call Saturday @ 4:10 PM, Ttys

Text messages from 5/2-5/4 were minimal as there were No noteworthy updates as we were both preparing for Tee's arrival within the next 10 days. We were both working diligently to check all necessary boxes. On Saturday 5/2 Tee notified me that there was a possibility that he would be released sooner on Wednesday, 5/6. He had also re-tested positive for COVID-19 recently, and we were unsure if this would delay his release.

<u>**Group text Saturday 5/2 @ 1:05 PM**</u>

Hello Family, Tee is telling me that he may be released sooner on Wednesday 5/6. However, his recent COVID-19 re-test just came back positive so we have to confirm if this will delay his possible release date in anyway on Monday. It is my belief that he is most likely no longer contagious, but in fact still showing lingering traces of COVID-19 due to his high viral load. Again, I will confirm everything on Monday. Please pray that he is on track for his 5/6 release. I don't think he'll last much longer, he's pretty ready to go, understandably so after being gone for over a month! See you'll on the prayer call at 4:10pm.

More Answered prayers:

On Monday 5/4, JH confirmed Tee's release date for Wednesday 5/6, and I alerted the group that he would be returning back to us, 1 day after our 5th anniversary! I let them know that I would be very busy making final preparations for his return, and I needed them to co-ordinate with our cousin (Little Jack) for his Welcome Home celebration details, and they did!

Group text Tuesday 5/5 @ 6:37 AM (our fifth wedding anniversary)

First Dance Wedding picture-Aruba 5/5/15

TC update

Tee had a Great night medically; he's experiencing some pain in his shoulder (most likely from PT and lying in an uncomfortable hospital bed). I'll check on that today!

Were excited about him coming home tomorrow. He's been working super-hard in his therapies to reach his goals...He talked to some of his family last night, and everybody was excited to hear how strong his voice has gotten. He's back laughing and joking and feeling better and very optimistic about his temporary plight.

He's Extremely Grateful for God's Mercy and Grace over his life and He is/We are Extremely appreciative of all of your love and support during this time!

Group text Tuesday 5/5 - Marcy and Tee's 5th anniversary!

*****TC Homecoming UPDATE!!****

Today is 45 days @ Johns Hopkins. Family, Remember Our first prayer call in March when I told you'll that we were Coming out of this. Well, Gratefully Tee's Coming Out this Wednesday 5/6. It looks like I'll be picking him up around 12ish...

https://youtu.be/zbYcte4ZEgQ [15]

"I'm Coming Out"

Its scheduled to rain, so were planning to meet in the high-rise GARAGE directly across from the main entrance at for a safe social distancing celebration in our cars!

1800 Orleans St. Baltimore, MD.

I'll pick Tee up on the Wolfe Street side entrance then well head over there, so please plan to be in the garage by 12:00 PM!

Our cousin Lil Jack is spearheading this effort so please reach out to him if you have any specific questions, I hope you'll can make it!!

PLEASE pass this along to ensure that all of our prayer warriors get this message, Thx!! 1 possibly 2 news stations are planning to be there tomorrow!

[15]**Diana Ross.** I'm Coming Out. March 24, 2014. https://youtu.be/zbYcte4ZEgQ

Tee is finally home 46 days later!

Group Text Wednesday 5/6 @ 5:58 PM

TC update

Tee is home!

We had an amazing Homecoming celebration for him in the rain. Thanks Cousin Jack for spearheading this, you did an amazing job!!

Thanks, to my Niecy Sharee for surprising us and representing my side of the family all the way from Philly/New Jersey (in the rain, on a work day during the pandemic)!!

Tee was so surprised, and we were extremely emotional! It's a nasty dreary day in Baltimore but he said it's an ugly day but it's a good day. He ate his first home cooked meal in 46 days from his Aunt Barbara Ann, and his family hooked us up with supplies. We are So happy, grateful and loving life, Praise God!

We were featured on Baltimore's CBS News WJZ Channel 13 today, airing at 5:00 PM, 6:00 PM and 7:00 PM. Please tune in if you can, they did a phenomenal job on our story! Let me know if you get a chance to see it. If not, the station is supposed to be sending me a direct link. I was trying to get it out soon!

Please pass this text on to our friends and family:

This was the best fifth Anniversary present ever. TGBTG!!

Man hospitalized with coronavirus released one day after wedding anniversary.

"Love to you and Tee! I cried as I watched this video!"

https://baltimore.cbslocal.com/video/4541043-man-hospitalized-with-coronavirus-released-one-day-after-wedding-anniversary [16]

Marcy:

Johns Hopkins celebrates after COVID-19 patient recovers.

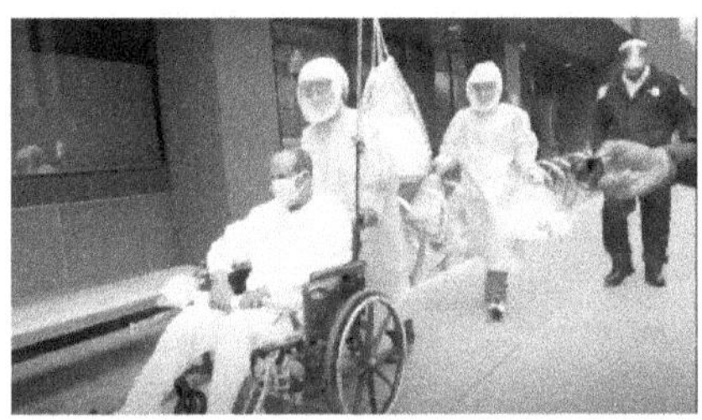

BALTIMORE, Md, (WBFF) – A man from Washington D. C. was released from Johns Hopkins Hospital in Baltimore on Wednesday after recovering from COVID-19. Marcy Myles-Clark, 47, and her husband Theirrien Clark, 56, a Sr. Manager @ a Law Firm in Washington D.C., both began to feel sick on March 14, 2020. They went to the Patient First in Columbia on March 16, 2020 because of recent symptoms and a persistent fever over 101 degrees.

http://foxbaltimore.com/news/local/johns-hopkins-celebrates-after-COVID-19-patient-recovers [17]

Group text Saturday 5/9 @ 12:28 PM

Happy Mother's Day!!

I totally forgot this beautiful day, given all of our excitement this week! We're all good, Tee is all settled in at home. Everything has worked out with all of his equipment and home supports. We have a good Aide, and Tee's starting his home therapies on Monday! Praise God for that!

---

[16]**Man hospitalized with coronavirus released one day after wedding anniversary**. Baltimore CBS 13WJZ. May 7, 2020. https://baltimore.cbslocal.com/video/4541043-man-hospitalized-with-coronavirus-released-one-day-after-wedding-anniversary

[17]**Johns Hopkins celebrates after COVID-19 patient recovers.** Baltimore Fox 45. May 7, 2020. http://foxbaltimore.com/news/local/johns-hopkins-celebrates-after-COVID-19-patient-recovers

Thanks Again to Donnell B for putting up the handrails in the bathroom. Donell also installed the handrails on the garage steps, a few weeks ago for us. Tee came inside with ease on his return home, using the railings. This has truly helped Tee maintain his independence in getting in and around the house and were forever Grateful to Donnell and his wife (my girl) Priscilla, you all are the best!!

He is glad to be home and I'm overjoyed that he's back...Were Reunited like Peaches n Herb.

He made me help shave off his George Jefferson hair and Bishop Thomas beard, so he's back looking like our Tee. He looks Great despite all he's been through; we just have to fatten him up and help him regain his strength and endurance!

Thanks for your continued prayers, like we've been saying God hears us and Tee is responding!! Let's keep them going Family!! We'll still be doing weekly prayer calls on Saturdays @ 4:10 PM! Prayer call tonight @ 4:10 PM.

Group text Tuesday 5/12 @ 2:29 PM Happy Birthday Mom Boonie!

Our continuous daily prayers for Tee

Please continue to pray Tee's strength (Physically, Emotionally, Spiritually, Mentally) and that he successfully continues to heal with No residual effects. Were continuously praying for his Complete Preservation and Full Restoration from head to toe!

"TC back home update"

Tee has been home 6 days today, were adjusting well and he's doing GREAT! He's getting stronger and more independent each day. He started Physical Therapy (PT) yesterday. His PT is a huge Latino dude (Mark) and his aide is a little African dude (Chris) *i.e.,* Gary Coleman (Arnold)...So he's got Arnold Schwarzenegger and Danny DeVito as new

Best friends (BFs). He likes them both which is totally hilarious since he was reluctant to have a male caregiver!

His PT told him that he was going to be easy to restore because he is extremely motivated and had been totally healthy prior to this experience! We were excited to hear this! He's been walking with a walker, but he is working on ditching it slowly but surely, per his PT. He's eating well and has placed orders with family for his favorite meals and desserts. You know he's still a fat boy at heart! Thanks for the food and supplies, family!

We're grooving, getting used to our new Temporary norm and just grateful for love, life, and second chances! Byrd, I let him hear the words to "Blessed and highly favored" by The Clark Sisters, and he liked it. I told him you dedicated that to him. We're still planning to do our weekly Prayer Call each Saturday @ 4:10 PM.

We may try to do a Zoom call soon so you all can see him, he's still beautiful! We have a few new people on our prayer list...Our list is growing. We extend our prayers to everyone on and off the list:

*We already know this is a done deal, and We give God the Glory in advance!

Ongoing prayers for world healing, and recovering from sickness…

Part V

Chronological Account of Tee's Journey Via Johns Hopkins' Progress Reports

This section contains progress reports I recorded as I received information from the medical staff at Johns Hopkins Hospital. These conversations took place from March 24, 2020, during those first few hospital days, through May 6, 2020, when Tee was released from the hospital.

This will show you the clinical progression of Tee's health from the beginning to the end of his hospitalization. This also clinically shows the manifestation of his miraculous healing.

Side Note: Please take note of the frequency of my communication with his caregivers. I firmly believe that family support equates to better care!

TEE'S PROGRESS REPORTS RECORDED BY ME AS RECEIVED FROM HOSPITAL PERSONNEL

Tuesday 3/24/20 @ 5:54 PM

I spoke with Nurse Jeffrey. (JH ICU 2nd floor A=Zayed #54)

- Lots of fluids
- 50% oxygen support

Wednesday 3/25 @ 11:45 AM

I spoke with Nurse Fatou.

- Afebrile (fever) 99-F
- Oxygen 40% support

Wednesday 3/25 @ 4:40 PM

I spoke with Dr. Hussein –and Tee is stable.

- Switching out old tube
- Oxygen up to 60%, Will gradually come back down; sedation will increase
- Off blood-pressure meds
- Kidney-good, Lungs-stable

- Afebrile @ 100F-hasn't spiked, still on Tylenol
- Experimental (Trump touting Antimalaria — Hydroxychloroquine), Tiliquinol-antibiotic
- Expecting clearance in 2 weeks

Side Note: So far, the longest COVID-19 patient they've had in the ICU was 10 days

Wednesday 3/25 @ 6:00 PM

I spoke with Nurse Jeff.

- No real change from earlier. Oxygen Still 60%.

Thursday 3/26 @ 6:22 AM

I spoke with Nurse Jeff.

- Need to prone again to increase oxygen
- Blood pressure down
- He's at 70% oxygen support
- Fever @ 100.5 (Low grade)

Thursday 3/26 @ 4:00 PM

I spoke with Jennifer F (PA).

- Breathing tube needed to be replaced because balloon burst
- I prayed with him this morning over the phone
- Looking to reduce ventilator 70-60%
- Temperature 100.8 (was 105 upon arrival last week)
- Blood pressure OK
- Sent blood for culture
- Total COVID-19 patients (20) currently

Thursday 3/26 @ 9:06 PM

I spoke with Nurse Fawn.

- Still prone
- Oxygen level at 70 — Just turned on his side
- Working to get him down to 50-60%
- Fever down to 38.1 C (100.5 F)

Friday 3/27 @ 5:36 AM

I spoke with Nurse Fawn.

- Had to go up on oxygen 80 now (was 70)
- Going to turn in 1 hour, prayerfully able to come back down on oxygen settings
- Goal is to get oxygen back down to 60 today
- Fever is down, he is still on high-dose Tylenol until the fever breaks (goal is 37c/98.6 F)
- **Fawn and Bethany let me speak to Tee on speaker phone

Friday 3/27 @ 10:50 AM

I spoke with Nurse Sherri.

- Oxygen down a little approx. 80%
- Down from 100%; had developed a fever overnight
- Still in prone position; constantly adjusting sedations
- Orals are up, IV sedation is down

Current Meds:

- Tylenol — fever ATC (around the clock)
- Methadone — Long-acting opioid (using to decrease sedation)
- Fentanyl
- Midazolam- (Benzodiazepine sedative)
- Pharmacist is rounding with doctors; there are lots of experimental uses
- Will stay prone — 2 days prayerfully able to reduce requirements
- Last blood gas (measurement of oxygen levels) was really good — looks like he should be able to start reducing oxygen support

Friday 3/27 @ 3:25 PM

I spoke with Nurse Sherri.

- Tee is sedated and paralyzed @ 9:00 AM (Vecuronium) Transient
- Still prone
- Synchronized with ventilator — oxygen 94-97%

Friday 3/27 @ 9:22 PM

I spoke with Nurses Peggy/Joy (teacher).

- Sedation
- Prone
- Good vitals
- No fever (36.7)
- Oxygen 70%

Saturday 3/28 @ 6:41 AM

I spoke with Nurses Peggy/Joy.

- Good vitals
- Favoring left side
- Oxygen low to mid 90s (93%)
- Kidneys and Liver Function Tests (LFT) is OK from midnight; drew labs again around 6:00 AM
- Still prone — still turning on each side
- No fever

Saturday 3/28 @ 3:08 PM

I spoke with Dr. Broderick.

- Oxygen was up to 100%; currently 80-90%
- Has had some fevers -38 C/100.4 F
- Reviewed current meds
- Kidneys normal; LFTs slightly elevated
- Still prone (on stomach); will flip him back in 24 hours

Sunday 3/29 @ 6:18 AM

I spoke with Nurse Joy.

- Oxygen levels down
- Tried to reposition @ 10:00 PM on right was oxygen up to 100%; currently back to 80%
- Vitals OK
- No fever

- Want to try turn him on his back; He doesn't do well on his right side
- Going to draw another gas

Sunday 3/29 @ 11:58 AM

I spoke with Dr. Broderick.

- No change — about to flip him on his back
- Still on 80% oxygen going to leave it high until after he gets flipped and stabilized
- Once he appears to be doing better, they'll decrease it
- OFF VECURONIUM paralytic (PRAISE GOD)

Sunday 3/29 @ 5:43 PM

I spoke with Nurse Caleb.

- Tee has been repositioned on his back
- Sedation is down
- Oxygen is down @ 70%
- No fever

Sunday 3/29 @ 9:12 PM

I spoke with Nurse Adina.

- Tee is on his back
- Oxygen saturation levels are down, ventilator settings 93-94% — may go down to 90%
- Next blood gas @ 9:45 PM

Monday 3/30 @ 5:45 AM

I spoke with Nurse Adina (37 = 98.6).

- 37.4 — normal temp
- Oxygen up to 96% machine. Next gas hopefully enough to drop
- Still sedated but he opened his eyes a little
- Still positioned on his back
- Specific prayer for restoration of lungs and removal of ventilator by 4/6/20
- Pray without Ceasing 1 Thessalonians 5:17
- John 14:13-14

Monday 3/30 @ 1:41 PM

I spoke with Nurse Kasum (one of my favorites in ICU).

- Tee is still positioned on his back
- Oxygen is up and down; he has changed sedation
- Oxygen saturation 93% - 73% — wavers back and forth
- Machine is on full support for oxygenation saturation
- Temp is 99
- Nurse needs to give Vecuronium again to sync him with the ventilator

March 3/30 @ 1:54 PM

I spoke with Nurse Kasum

- Sent blood cultures
- Negative cultures — finish last dose of antibiotics (Cefepime)
- Trying new antibiotic Zosyn

- Heart rate higher possibly because of fever
- Oxygen 91-94 (good)
- Blood pressure 130-160 (higher due to medicine)

Monday 3/30 @ 2:12 PM

I spoke with social worker and inquired about me being able to send some pictures/photos

Monday 3/30 @ 5:30 PM

I had a follow-up call with Dr. Broderick.

- Tee is on same settings this morning
- Used paralytic to calm him down to synchronize with ventilator
- High sedation to ensure he doesn't remember
- 38.2 (100.8) low-grade fever
- Recovery timetable unclear
- Dr. Broderick reinforced that this is a marathon and not a sprint
- Tee is still on his back, which should allow them to be able to change ventilator settings more frequently
- Hope to see change in 24 hours
- Another chest X-ray — lungs look a bit better
- I asked about immune antibiotics for clinical trial. No clinical trials currently enrolled
- No real experimental options in the works…
- **Hydroxychloroquine (Trump touting panacea). Historically used to treat malaria, to lower inflammation and decrease virus shedding times, Doesn't know if it's effective(seemingly not impressed)
- Goal is supportive care — ventilator to support oxygenation assists with pressure needed to keep lungs open

- TC is on volume-controlled ventilation
- Subtle changes made over time to get necessary support

His lungs are currently too infected and inflamed right now to breathe on his own, machine is keeping him comfortable"- (Ugh, I would hear this too many times, this reminds me of hospice)

Monday 3/30 @ 8:50 PM

I spoke with Nurse Kim.

- Tee is still sedated
- Low fever .38
- Oxygen 70%
- High-dose sedation shall help with anxiety
- He is still positioned on his back
- On Vecuronium

Tuesday 3/31 @ 5:42 AM

I spoke with Nurse Kim.

- Same overnight
- Heart rate down
- Fever better
- Stable

Note to self: Sometimes I have to encourage myself, Sometimes I have to Speak victory during the test.

Tuesday 3/31 @ 11:00 AM

I spoke with Nurse Kasum.

- Finished (slow acting) IV drip of (Vecuronium) paralytic; gave Bolus dose (quick hit, large dose)
- Tee has been trying to breathe over set rate
- Heart rate is up, and blood pressure is up (because of Vecuronium 38 C-No fever

Tuesday 3/31 @ 5:07 PM

I spoke with Nurse Kasum.

- Increased sedation
- Another dose paralytic @ Noon
- ^{0}38.2 ^{0}100 F-Temp
- Lungs still healing — want him to breathe with ventilator

Tuesday 3/31 @ 9:14 PM

I spoke with Nurse Danny.

- Added Propofol anesthetic ("The Michael Jackson killer med")
- He is synching with ventilator
- Going to try to decrease sedation
- Blood pressure on the low side
- Antibiotics
- Positioned on back
- Fever down now 38.3 (100.9) Was 38.5

Side Note: I emailed family pics to Nurse Kasum for Tee's room.

Wednesday 4/1 @ 5:46 AM

I spoke with Nurse Danny.

- Fever down 37.3C (99 F)
- Good night and sedation down
- Breathing with ventilator
- No blood pressure meds
- Eyes blinking

Wednesday 4/1 @ 11:50 AM

I spoke with Nurse Mallory.

- Meds everchanging daily
- New oral med to decrease sedation
- Ventilator pressure (Peep) down
- Sedation down
- Trying to decrease ventilator settings (about to draw blood gas)
- Oxygenation well
- Goal: Watch ventilator settings to see if/how much they can be decreased
- Opening eyes and blinking

Wednesday 4/1 @ 2:17 PM

I spoke with Dr. Shannon N (fellow ICU).

- Tee developed an infection (Cytokine Storm Syndrome)-I later found out that he had developed a 108-degree fever.
- Started on Vancomycin (broad-spectrum antibiotic)
- White count on rise

- Still requiring a lot of support
- Breathing is stable — (not really up or down)
- Trying to lower sedation
- Tee has fever overnight, running at 100^{0}.
- He was as high as 104^{0}
- Oxygen 94
- Blood pressure 150/64
- Temperature 99^{0}
- Heart rate 86
- Goal is to make him normal air 21%; TC 80%
- Overall condition stable (small improvements, not worst)

Wednesday 4/1 @ 9:34 PM

I spoke with Nurse Danny.

- Peep is down, saturation greater than 90%
- Off Propofol (sedation)
- Increase in Fentanyl
- Low fever 37.2C
- Vitals good, pretty well synced with ventilator
- Opening eyes and moving head — more awake

****Thursday 4/2 AM-Life threatening Oxygen drop which prompted the emergency family visit**

Thursday 4/2 @ 1:01 PM - (We were on the Hopkins campus awaiting permission from Administration to visit)

I spoke with Mike (P.A.).

- TC oxygen levels are really low, almost on max ventilator support @ 95%.
- Proned on his stomach
- Deep sedation
- On paralytic
- Trying to decrease fluids
- Praying for improvement to stabilize oxygen levels and start decreasing ventilator support
- Serious/critical condition

Thursday 4/2 @ 11:17 PM

I spoke with Nurse Sophia post-visit.

- Stable, repositioned
- Gave Dose of Lasix (For fluid removal)
- Small decrease in ventilator settings from 80% to 75%

Friday 4/3 @ 5:58 AM

I spoke to Sophia.

- No changes, still maintaining
- Keep tweaking ventilator settings
- Fever fluctuating; currently 38 C; if it rises, he'll get a cooling blanket

Note to self: Doctor Inquiry-How long to clear virus?

Friday 4/3 @ 2:16 PM

I spoke with Nurse Julie.

- Tee will stay prone, on full ventilator support

- Oxygen @ 80%
- Peep was 20, down to 18; ULTIMATE GOAL IS 5 FOR EXTUBATION
- Still paralyzed, a lot of sedation
- Fever 37.8 C (101 F), highest was 38.2 @ 11 AM

Friday 4/3 @ 5:09 PM

I spoke with Michael (P.A.).

- Same overall
- 80% oxygen
- Still requiring a lot of Peep
- Still trying to decrease fluids
- New cultures for infection
- Keep same ventilator settings overnight
- Trying to decrease oxygen
- Needs time and support through to get virus and inflammation down
- Liver enzymes normal, bilirubin is elevated
- White count elevated 20,000 — normal is 8,000

Friday 4/3 @ 6:36 PM

I spoke with Dr. Liz Carstens (medical resident).

- Atrial fib –irregular and rapid heart rate – 150-160
- Has been given IV Amiodarone; slowed down heart rate some
- Blood pressure – Stable
- Oxygen — stable
- Plan is to get Tee's heart rate down

Friday 4/3 @ 9:27 PM

I spoke with Nurse Sophia.

- Tee is holding his own, monitoring — Stable
- Heart Rate still elevated, Prayers to level Out

Saturday 4/4/20 @ 5:11 AM

I spoke with Nurse Sophia.

- Tee is stable
- Same sedation
- Turned once – tolerated well
- Tube feeds off — Lots of fluid
- Had issues with a line overnight; replaced tubing
- Heart rate normalized @ 95 (Normal 60-100); less than 60, greater than 100 is problematic
- Fever down, was 38 ($100F^0$); <100
- Oxygen same 80-97% — Peep 18 – pretty consistent

Saturday 4/4 @ 10:22 AM

I spoke with Nurse Julie.

- Still on drip
- Oxygen levels 70% (ventilator setting)' TC 93% oxygen saturation
- Requested doctor call-need to clarify if he has an infection and cause of atrial fib
- Spoke with Julie — prayer call with family @ Noon

Saturday 4/4 @ 1:10 PM

I spoke with Dr. Liz Carstens (medical resident).

- Heart rate normalized
- Oxygenation same 70% (a little lower)
- Tee's oxygen levels drop when he is turned on his back, still in prone position
- No infection; will continue to monitor — still on antibiotics
- Had to pause tube feedings because Tee's seemingly regurgitating
- May need to revisit alternative ways to give nutrition
- From 4/2/20 last chest X-ray –infiltration (fuzziness in lungs) looked worst, shows mild improvement on 3/30
- Blood gases minor improvement
- Fever trend seems to be down today; overall stable
- PM antibiotics consistently since 4/1

Saturday 4/4 @ 8:50 PM

I spoke with Andrea (new nurse).

- Inquired about ECMO machine

Side Note: Song on my heart: The Clark Sisters "I'm Looking for a Miracle"

Sunday 4/5 @ 5:51 AM

I spoke with Nurse Andrea.

- Oxygen and sedation lowered
- No fever

Sunday 4/5 @ 1:03 PM

I spoke with Julie.

Side Note: "The sky is the limit to what I can have, I expect a miracle every day. GOD can make a way out of no-way. Just believe and receive it. God can perform it today."

- Doctor inquired about ECMO
- Music in room

Per Julie

- Turned over on back; tolerated well
- No fever
- No real changes, vitals are good, normal heart rate, sedation is the same, still on paralytic
- Able to remove second machine to keep airways open (nitric oxide, from Thursday AM)
- Good progress – baby steps
- Julie said they consulted Cardiology about ECMO machine. Was told Tee wasn't a candidate because he was intubated more than 1 week. (why wasn't it sooner?)

Side Note: I was led to map out Tee's progress to date and I'm also prophesizing his healing as charted below, "Victory is mine sayeth the Lord"!

Tee's progress – Healed Victory!

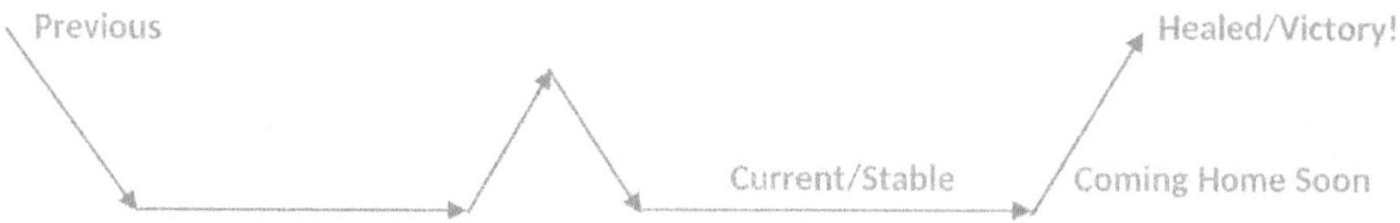

Sunday 4/5 @ 1:37 PM

I spoke with Dr. Hussein (resident).

- Same
- Oxygen saturation 97%
- Still a lot of support
- Making progress

My ECMO machine questions, and the doc's responses

Per Myrna

- Says they use ECMO when ventilator isn't successful; he was initially doing fine on the ventilator, worsened after seventh day
- Current protocol-to use ECMO prior to 7 days…
- Says they consulted with cardiologist last week (after his event on 4/2), and it was ruled out

I requested clarification from the current attending, Re use of ECMO Dr. W. Checklee:

- He reiterated it's a challenge to make sure he's oxygenating well.
- Reiteration of use of evidence-based medicine-proning, inhaled nitric oxide ventilator; His numbers are moving in right direction — still one of the sickest patients.
- Typically, ECMO is used within the first 7 days of treatment (outside of COVID-19 use).

He referred to NEJM trial, not a lot of evidence-based results in general with patients using ECMO; says ECMO doesn't come without complications (including infection) and right now he's doing well on the ventilator (70% vs 100%) and he's not convinced that it would make a difference given this stage.

Dr. Checklee says his therapies have been optimized for his body to recover.

Once he gets down to 50% oxygen, he'll be out of the danger zone, current peep is 18; normal is 5…

Side Note: I wasn't crazy about Tee not being considered for ECMO, but I had to trust God and Hopkins' judgement. I consulted with Dr. Nyanjom (Tee's personal pulmonologist who fully agreed with my stance). We decided to LET GO, LET GOD!

Sunday 4/5 @ 5:10 PM

I spoke with Nurse Julie.

- Same medical update as earlier 5:10 PM
- CB Andrea late check-in 8:30 PM – 9:00 PM

Sunday 4/5 @ 9:37 PM

I spoke with Nurse Andrea.

- Tee is doing better
- Oxygen back up to 70
- Still paralyzed
- No fever

Monday 4/6 @ 5:49 AM

- Same oxygen 70%
- No fever
- Probably going to make decisions about paralytic

Monday 4/6 @ 1:26 PM

I spoke with Dr. Hussein.

- Inquire normal numbers needed for oxygen withdrawal, vitals: fever and infection
- Was 100% – Peep 20 when doing bad; Peep is now 18
- Current: Still 70% oxygen; high pressure
- Removed paralytic
- Trying to lower pressure and oxygen settings
- No fever (99.3 F)
- Still on antibiotic to treat pneumonia
- Normal heart echo sonogram
- Numbers needed to come off ventilator (30%) – Peep 5-10 (normal range)
- Baby steps in right direction
- Still very sick

Monday 4/6 @ 1:39 PM

I spoke with Nurse Jeremy.

- Trying to lower sedation and ventilator settings
- Oxygen saturation numbers are holding up

Side Note: Midday update to family.

- Share miracles
- TC specific prayers for normal numbers

Monday 4/6 @ 5:23 PM

I spoke with Nurse Jeremy.

- Oxygen saturation was high
- Lower oxygen went down to 60% (from 70), Peep still 18
- Getting Lasix to reduce fluid volume
- Tee is back on tube feeds; small quantities; stopped previously because of regurgitation (goal is 45, at 20 currently-rate of tube feed flow)
- Off paralytic
- Lower Oxygen (FIO)Tube

Tuesday 4/7 @ 5:14 AM

I spoke with Nurse Kasum (I fell asleep and was unable to call back Monday PM).

- Tee doing great and is stable
- Call back to schedule Zoom with day shift
- First major sign of improvement

Tuesday 4/7 @ Noon

I spoke with Nurse Rose.

- Trying to decrease sedation, lowered Midazolam
- **Peep has dropped from 18 to 15 (down 3 pts)- normal is 5-10
- Blood pressure a little low
- Synced with ventilator
- Saturation 98%
- No fever
- I asked doctor about underlying anxiety

Tuesday 4/7 @ 12:06 PM

I spoke with Mike (PA).

- Slow progress on ventilator support (from 18-15)-3 point drop! (WOOHOO-this was reiterated from what the nurse told me earlier)
- Lower oxygen and Peep
- Finished antibiotic
- Reduced fluids
- Still think he may have pneumonia; constantly monitoring
- No fever since Friday, 4/3/20
- On Midazolam (Benzo) — anti anxiety, also has sedative benefits
- Blood gases have been stable – will decrease oxygen settings

Tuesday 4/7 @ 8:50 PM

I spoke with Nurse Kasum.

- No real changes in settings and medication
- Peep 16%
- Oxygen was 60% — now 50%
- No fever
- Blood pressure little high – moving around a lot.

Wednesday 4/8 @ 5:18 AM

I spoke with Nurse Kasum.

- His oxygenation is a little low; up to 50 – 60%
- Peep 16
- Blood pressure a little high; Clonidine able to improve and lower sedation

On Wednesday 4/8 @ 11:00 AM

I spoke with Dr. C Lambeth.

**Side Note: Conversations beginning to be more positive regarding his current state and projected outcomes.

- Minor adjustment to sedation
- Try to come down on Midazolam medication
- Strategy — once respiration status gets better – wean down slowly
- Tolerating changes very well
- **Lower ventilator support — in right direction toward, small but surely
- Oxygen @ 60% — Peep @ 14% (5-10 normal range); We're getting closer!
- For extubation –lower ventilator settings and lower sedation
- Last chest X-ray 3/2
- Monitoring bloodwork, vitals and ventilator settings

Wednesday 4/8 @ 5:44 PM

I spoke with Dr. R (resident) and Nurse Kayley (nurse).

- Tee is stable
- Slow steady changes
- Lower sedatives, eyes open (more awake)
- Peep still 14%
- Same — slow but steady
- Tolerated ventilator changes today
- Getting physical therapy (PT)
- Big goal — Lower sedatives and pain medications

Wednesday 4/8 @ 6:00 PM

I spoke with Nurse Megan.

- Bud and Kaelyn were on the phone call
- She said Tee opens his eyes and blinks to our voices
- Tee started with 14 (Peep) 10
- Michael (PA) lowered sedation
- Slow and steady, lowered ventilation
- Slow and steady improvement

Wednesday 4/8 @ 9:16 PM

I spoke with Nurse Kasum.

- Slowly dosing down on medications
- Oxygen 60%
- Peep 14
- Blood pressure up

Thursday 4/9 @ 5:42 AM

I spoke with Nurse JJ.

- Lowered (FIo2) oxygen 60-50%
- Bathed and turned
- No major changes; meds same dose
- A little agitated @ midnight; had to give Bolus sedative
- Next check-in 11:00 AM – 1:00 PM Inquire about anxiety meds as he decreases sedation (don't want him to start freaking out as he becomes more conscious)

Thursday 4/9 @ 11:37 AM

I spoke with Nurse Megan.

- Oxygen good
- Lower ventilator settings
- Lower sedation
- *Reminder to increase anxiety as lower sedation
- Tylenol ATC
- Low fever 99.7

Good Friday 4/10 @ 2:53 AM

I spoke with Nurse Haley.

- Weaning down ventilator and sedation to wake up
- Getting intermittent pain meds. He looks a little uncomfortable
- Vitals good
- Blood pressure a little high
- Fever 38C

Friday 4/10 @ 9:28 AM

- Blood pressure up; need to relax; add hypertensive
- Oxygen remains the same
- Mental status — Opens eyes and blinks
- Fever 38.4 C/101F- Tylenol
- Next check-in at Noon– 2:00 PM

Friday 4/10 @ 2:08 PM

I spoke with Jennifer F (PA).

- 50% oxygen
- Fever up –send up cultures to check for infection
- Need to change out lines currently in groin, right neck, switch to wrist and left side

Friday 4/10 @ 3:07 PM

- Peep is now (10) doesn't appear to have more lung secretions
- Chest X-ray, same not worse, will improve over time
- Fever 38.4 (101)

Friday 4/10 @ 8:19 PM

I spoke with Nurse Angie.

- Changed PICC lines (used for IV draws)
- Blood pressure little high
- Comfortable on sedation
- Still getting IV meds
- Fever 101.8 F — (Added Tylenol and Ibuprofen ATC)

- No antibiotics currently
- Resent cultures — takes 24-hours to confirm
- Oxygen levels 97% saturation, 50% oxygen level, Peep 10
- Still fairly highly sedated
- Monitoring blood pressure
- Next check in @ 5:00 AM

Saturday 4/11 @ 5:32 AM

Spoke to Nurse Angie.

- Heart rate up-A fib; blood pressure down- to be stabilized
- Fluids shifting; heart rate to be stabilized
- Fever 101.8
- Oxygenation good; no changes
- Lab work good
- Next check-in 9:00 AM – 11:00 AM

Saturday 4/11 @ 11:13 AM

I spoke with Nurse Brooke.

- Adjusted oxygen – just sent blood levels
- Wakes up, doesn't acknowledge commands
- No more atrial fibrillation (started @ 3:00 AM ended @ 6:30 AM)
- Blood pressure– normal
- Fentanyl Midazolam (sedation meds) they gave bolus of fentanyl to relax
- Slight fever 37.9 (99) — Was 39 C last night
- Doctor to confirm if new cultures needed
- 98% saturation, Peep 10, His oxygen concentration 40%

<u>**Saturday 4/11 @ 1:45 PM**</u>

I spoke with Dr. Lambert (resident).

- Trying to adjust sedation give less IV, give oral (through tube)
- Discussed anxiety concerns
- He's still on Fentanyl and Midazolam for sedation
- Recently added Clonazepam oral (for anxiety)
- Developed secondary infection; Started 2 antibiotics and took cultures, results in 24-48 hours
- Developed atrial fibrillation last night – back on medication
- Blood pressure high, Gave IV
- He's leveled out today
- Overall oxygen remains stable
- Weaned down some, Now requiring 40% oxygen! Remember <30% needed for extubation from ventilator
- Tee's oxygen saturation is NOW 97% — normal is 100% (these measures how much hemoglobin in the blood)
- Peep is 10
- FIo2 40% — normal 20% "Want to see this one down"
- RASK Score used to determine levels of sedation includes:
- Fever
- Infection
- Oxygen level
- Mental status
- Medication
- Overall progress

Saturday 4/11 @ 8:32 PM

I spoke with Nurse Emily.

- Stable/no changes
- Seemingly wakes up quicker
- Trying to remove fluid to increase lung status
- Vitals good
- Temp 38.2
- Blood pressure 152/76
- Heart rate 86 (<=100 normal)

EASTER Sunday 4/12 @ 6:21 AM

I spoke with Nurse Emily.

Side Note: I woke up this morning with a surge in my spirit, feeling like today was going to be a good day and I sent out a relevant text to the TC prayer warriors!

- Good and uneventful night
- A lot of fluid
- May wean down ventilator today
- No fever - 8:00 PM
- All vitals good/normal

Easter Sunday 4/12 @ 11:12 AM

I spoke with Dr. Judith.

- Stable overnight
- Decreased sedation
- Weaning down and off meds
- **Trying to get him ready for extubation!!

Side Note: The Best News In Weeks!!

Sunday 4/12 @ 5:35 PM

I spoke with Nurse Fred.

- Trying to wean him down
- Lower ventilator settings
- Lowered sedation
- Tee gets anxious once sedation is lowered
- Reminder to give appropriate meds to accommodate his underlying anxiety
- Gets Bolus when agitated
- 40% oxygen
- Peep 5 (Was 18-20 in his worst days, Normal is 5-10)

Sunday 4/12 @ 9:04 PM

I spoke with Nurses Jada/Emily.

- Trying to wean sedation down – still anxious
- On fentanyl + other sedatives
- Keeps eyes open
- Had 38.1c fever earlier (approximately. 100 degrees)
- Peep still 5
- No infection

Monday 4/13 @ 6:15 AM

I spoke with Nurse Emily.

- Stable now – Episodes of anxiety
- Didn't tolerate weaning down
- Peep 5

Monday 4/13 @ 10:22 AM

I spoke with Nurse Bianca.

- Bolus this morning — very hypertensive
- Lasix given to remove some edema
- Lower sedation, still on tube feeds
- Still on medication for atrial fibrillation
- Still getting meds and possible (antipsychotic — will depend on EKG)
- Trying to do pressure trial support
- Lowered sedation
- Hypertension under control (157/79)
- Has increased oral pain medications – prayerfully allow to decrease sedation

Monday 4/13 @ 2:02 PM

I spoke with Nurse Bianca.

- Lowered IV fentanyl, increased patch
- No updates on antipsychotic
- Started new sedative (Precedex)
- Goal is to lower Fentanyl to discontinue eventually

Monday 4/13 @ 2:30 PM

I spoke with Dr. Rogers (resident).

- Current status — good improving
- Discussed respiratory trials, extubation status
- Meds —anti anxiety twice daily

- Tee was on the physical therapy bike for the lower extremities (Supine Cycle) — did well
- Got more Lasix
- Current ventilator settings-oxygen 50%, Peep 10
- HR 90-100, BP normalized, oxygen saturation 93-96

Monday 4/13 @ 8:45 PM

I spoke with Nurse Mark.

- Heart rate keeps going up and down — BP from 180 to 170
- Keeping comfortable with fentanyl and meds
- Added 3mg Clonazepam
- Trying to find right balance

Tuesday 4/14 @ 5:28 AM

I spoke with Nurse Mark.

- Night was good; increased sedation
- Heart rate stable — only goes up when he's moved
- Blood pressure stable
- On amnio drip for atrial fibrillation
- Tee is more comfortable now Midday Doctor follow-up repeat trial extubation
- Next check-in 11:00 PM –Noon

Tuesday 4/14 @ 1:04 PM

I spoke with Nurse Jeremy.

- Lowered ventilator settings – tolerating well

Tuesday 4/14 @ 1:06 PM

I spoke with Dr. Rogers (resident).

- Doing well
- Still very sedated, trying to lower ventilator so he can control his own breathing
- Lasix to decrease fluid
- *Continually improving
- Respiratory trial went well Monday; just overly sedated; trying to come down on meds
- Possible extubation tomorrow. Once Clonazepam initiated (2x's daily oral) he began to settle down
- Vitals good
- After removal from ventilator, Tee will be downgraded to another floor
- Could be another couple of weeks for discharge, post-extubation

Tuesday 4/14 @ 5:09 PM

I spoke with Nurse Jeremy.

- Still get Bolus sedation
- Still lowering ventilator settings and reducing IV meds
- Tee responds best, helps to let him know what's going on beforehand

Side Note: This demonstrates a level of consciousness and awareness which is a Great sign!

Tuesday 4/14 @ 9:57 PM

I spoke with Nurse Mark.

- Vitals stable — temp was 37.7 was 38
- Off IV drip from heart rate
- Lowered fentanyl
- Lowered Lasix
- Tee is comfortable
- *Lowered ventilator settings to the lowest setting
- Peep 5
- Off Midazolam again

Wednesday 4/15 @ 4:00 AM

I spoke with Nurse Mark.

- Fever 38.1
- Increased fentanyl and Precedex, Started antibiotic
- Looked like he was breathing too hard when resting
- Going to try and slowly lower all, He becomes hypertensive when lowering sedation
- Trying to find right balance to keep him comfortable as he's weaning down
- Lowest ventilator settings
- Comfy and wean down
- Heart rate good, No atrial fibrillation
- Next check-in 11:00 AM – 1:00 PM
- Inquire about fever/infection extubation

Wednesday 4/15 @ 10:38 AM

I spoke with Dr. Lambert.

- On pressure support, taking his own breaths to get breathing muscles re-acclimated
- Remaining fluid from lungs to be dry
- Optimizing all to ensure no setbacks
- Continuing to lower sedation
- Re-sent cultures, no infections – treating empirically
- Still mild fevers
- Needs to do spontaneous breathing trial; if he responds appropriately, they can possibly remove him from the ventilator in 1-2 days
- Extubation/ventilator removal usually occurs early morning when all hands on deck
- Blood pressure a little high; may need to continue

Wednesday 4/15 @ 12:36 PM

I spoke with Nurse Tida.

- Goal is to lower sedation
- Still on lowest ventilator settings
- Tee is unresponsive on following commands; Prayerfully, he will become more responsive as they lower medication
- Fentanyl 225 mc/hr.
- Precedex — 0.7 for anxiety
- Clonazepam on 2mg

Wednesday 4/15 @ 5:13 PM

I spoke to Nurse Tida and Martha (resident doctor).

- She confirmed that they are decreasing his sedation. I'm still praying that he'll become more responsive as his meds are decreased

- BP is good
- He needs to be calmer and awake for extubation
- He has to check all boxes on their list, including lowered ventilator settings, increased responsiveness, ability to follow commands

Wednesday 4/15 approximately 9:00 PM

I spoke with Nurse Chris.

- Lowered sedation for him to wake up more
- Still on IV Lasix drip
- Vital signs stable, Not anxious

Thursday 4/16 @ 6:07 AM

I spoke with Nurse Chris.

- On lower sedation
- More responsive
- Low-grade temperature
- Vitals and heart rate good
- A little hypertensive

Thursday 4/16 @ 11:53 AM

I spoke with Nurse Rachel.

- Doing great today
- Plan to get tube out later this afternoon
- He's been given steroids to get ready for extubation
- I also spoke with Dr. Rogers. Weaning sedation
- Stopped antibiotics
- Trial extubation set for 2:00 PM

Thursday 4/16 @ 4:09 PM

I spoke with Nurse Rachel.

- Tee is doing great, but needs to wake up more for extubation
- All meds are down, off fentanyl
- Possible extubation tomorrow!

Thursday 4/16 @ 8:58 PM

I spoke with Nurse Mary-Lou.

- Tee is doing well
- Still sedated
- Not following commands

Friday 4/17 @ 5:45 AM

I spoke with Nurse Dee.

- Lowering sedation**Tee is taking his own breaths, and doing most of the work (vs. the ventilator doing all of the work as it has previously)
- Dee says, "He is much better than he was last week"
- He is following intermittent commands
- Next check-in 11:00 AM – 1:00 PM

Friday 4/17 @ 11:56 AM

I spoke with Dr. Ho.

- Lower ventilator settings
- He is very weak
- Going to try to extubate today!

Friday 4/17 @ 2:49 PM

Side Note: OH, HAPPY DAY! Good News, I was notified by Bud and Kaelyn that when they called to check on their dad, they found out he was successfully EXTUBATED 1.5 HOURS AGO!

- Tee is off ventilator without any issues
- Getting oxygen
- Throat is sore
- Awake/conscious/weak

Friday 4/17 @ 4:58 PM

I spoke with Nurse Jeremy.

- He confirmed that Tee was extubated around 1:30 PM
- No sedation
- Lasix
- On oxygen
- Still drowsy – and weak
- He needs to be monitored in ICU at least 24 hours and then downgraded to stepdown unit
- TODAY WAS A GOOD DAY-AMEN!

(Post-extubation)

- Next check-in 8:30 – 9:00 PM (Zoom call)

Friday 4/17 @ 8:37 PM

I spoke with Nurse Haley.

- Tee is doing well

- Tee needs to cough
- Will be kept in ICU for observation for a few days
- Zoom call @ 9:15 PM
- Note to self to inquire about anxiety medication

<u>**Saturday 4/18 @ 5:20 AM**</u>

I spoke with Nurse Haley.

- Good oxygen
- Heart rate a little high
- 1st 12 hours post-extubation have been good; they monitor them to make sure they don't need any additional supports
- Cannot give anything for anxiety because he's still lethargic; some anxiety medication also compromises breathing
- Nods that he's not in pain
- Next check-in 9:30 PM – 10:00 PM (Zoom call)

<u>**Saturday 4/18 @ 9:33 AM**</u>

I spoke with Nurse Raquelly.

- Doing well, still pretty sleepy
- Heart rate normalized w/ Amiodarone

<u>**Saturday 4/18 @ 11:09 AM**</u>

I spoke with Dr. Ho Kim.

- Vitals and heart rate good
- He's getting 30% oxygen on Hi Flow Nasal Cannula
- Still very weak — needs to gain more strength to breathe more on his own without oxygen
- Next check-in @ 1:30 – 3:30 PM

- Good day
- Sitting on side of bed
- Following commands
- Same amount of oxygen

Monday 4/20 @ 6:18 AM

I spoke with Nurse Haley.

- Tee had a slight fever, was 101.5 F, now 99 F
- Will send labs and blood cultures

Monday 4/20 @ 9:46 AM

I spoke with Nurse Vickie.

- Inquire/coordinate with physical therapist to see when Tee will be awake (best time to call)
- Note to doc to – inquire about retesting for COVID-19
- Says he's still on 30% oxygen, doing good, wouldn't be surprised if he went down to regular pressure oxygen
- 12:06 PM, Tee Zoomed with Bud and Kaelyn, he's still very groggy, sat up for 15 minutes during PT

Monday 4/20 @ 1:12 PM

I spoke with Dr. Ho.

- Tee is waking up more
- PT is scheduled, working on OT consult
- Still on hi-flow nasal; may be a few more days until he can transition to stepdown; release will be a few weeks or months out
- Tee message to wife-Love you very much

- Still some fever; white blood count up-sent for cultures; finished last round of antibiotics a few days ago
- BP good
- No protocol for retesting
- Goal to get out of ICU and step down
- 30% on Hi-Flow — been stable here.

Side Note: Prayers for lowering.

- He's been more interactive

Monday 4/20 @ 5:12 PM

I spoke with Nurse Vickie.

- Tee sleeping OK
- Physical therapy (PT) earlier, 30 minutes on bed bike
- Sat on the side of bed
- Next check-in at 8:30 PM (speakerphone)

Monday 4/20 @ 8:44 PM

I spoke with Nurse Dan.

- Steady
- Oxygenation good – may be able to switch
- Removed Foley catheter
- More awake — opening eyes spontaneously
- Little atrial fibrillation (in and out) — getting PO medication
- AM check-in at 5-5:30 AM
- On anxiety medication

Tuesday 4/21 @ 5:45 AM

- Pressure 99.1
- Heart rate good – more awake (still tired)
- Thirsty
- Cough getting stronger (good sign)
- Next check-in 9-11:00 AM

Tuesday 4/21 @ 10:33 AM

I spoke with Nurse Jenny.

- Tee is well
- Doing exercises with occupational therapist (OT)
- He asked (whispered) to see the news this morning
- Still weak
- *Jenny (Asian nurse-Tee and Kaelyn's favorite) shaved Tee today and took a selfie. Tee told her she did a great job shaving him. Jenny confessed this was her first time shaving someone.
- He's a little down/discouraged. He wants to communicate and do things (get up/move around)
- He's very stubborn

Side Note: This was Tee's first shave in 1.5 months, Thanks, Jenny. He/We appreciate you and we'll never forget you!

Tuesday 4/21 @ 11:23 AM

I spoke with Nurse Jean Marie.

- So happy to see his progress, will check on his glasses
- *OMG – at 11:10 AM, Marcy, Kaelyn and Bud had a Zoom call with Tee. He was sitting up, alert and trying to talk and move

- I spoke to clinical coordinator about dropping off his personal essentials

<u>Tuesday 4/21 @ 3:13 PM</u>

I spoke with Dr. Coleridge (resident).

- Doing well on oxygen
- Very weak
- Goals: Strong cough, nutrition, signs of delirium (common)
- Still on 30% oxygen
- Next 1-2-day goal off Hi-Flow, onto regular-flow nasal oxygen

<u>Tuesday 4/21 @ 4:54 PM</u>

I spoke with Nurse Jenny.

- Tee received glasses and cellphone that I dropped off earlier
- Another Zoom call scheduled
- Tee is doing well
- Switched to lower-pressure oxygen doing well
- Called Verizon Wireless to reset Tee's cellphone password
- Spoke to Hopkins research department (Paul Blair), will send info with contact information
- Agreed to enroll him in a 1-year research study, not for marketing, no compensation
- Can always opt out

<u>Tuesday 4/21 @ 8:59 PM</u>

I spoke with Nurse Jonathan.

- Giving medication for blood clots

- Tee on his way to sleep — Marcy and Kaelyn said good night
- Next check-in at 5:30 AM, inquired about Zoom call @ 10:00 AM – 11:00 AM

Wednesday 4/22 @ 5:26 AM

I spoke with Nurse Jonathan.

- Urinated a lot and got a bath
- Gag reflex a little weak
- Just swabbed with cold water
- "He's a very nice man"
- Next check-in @ 9:00 – 10:00 PM

Wednesday 4/22 @ 9:26 AM

I spoke with Nurse Peggy.

- Tee is sitting up and getting consultation from speech, language therapy
- He's getting tolerability and swallowing evaluation – trying ice chips
- Peggy was happy with his progress from the last time she had seen him (Praise God!)

Wednesday 4/22 @ 11:57 AM

I spoke with Dr. Coleridge.

- Tee is on the lowest nasal oxygen setting – HUGE STEP
- Working on weakness and restoration
- Eval by speech pathology — nervous to have him eat yet
- Biggest ICU challenge, still here because of mental status, a little confused

- Going to get tilt bed to allow his lungs to open more – to clear lungs and gain strength

Dr. Coleridge continued:

- Tee will remain in ICU for mental status help
- Speech will continue to work with him and re-evaluate
- He still needs to strengthen — gag reflex, swallowing, etc.
- No fever in 2.5 days

Wednesday 4/22 @ 5:50 PM

I spoke with Nurse Peggy.

- His heart rate is a little elevated — needs medication to calm him. I reminded her to tell doctor about his underlining anxiety
- Amiodarone
- Heart rate was 160, but down to 103 now

Wednesday 4/22 @ 9:30 PM

I spoke with Nurse Kathy.

- Heart rate is a little high
- Metoprolol takes a little long to kick in
- Blood pressure/oxygen stable
- Trying to stabilize
- Very tired because of the physical therapy (PT) and HR
- Next check-in 3:00 AM – 5:00 AM

Thursday 4/23 @ 5:04 AM

I spoke with Nurse Kathy.

- Tee is comfortable but heart rate is still high; HR is hovering in high-teens -140
- Started Amiodarone — IV peripherally
- Next check-in @ 8:30 PM to inquire about anxiety medication or supplement
- AM Zoom

Thursday 4/23 @ 8:23 AM

I spoke with Nurse Peggy.

- Peggy started on Amnio drip
- Heart rate 84
- Need to speak to attending physician

Side Note: On Thursday 4/23, I spoke with Tracy, the charge nurse, and explained my ongoing concerns with Tee's recurring anxiety and requested to be transferred to the attending physician.

Thursday 4/23 @ 12:37 PM

I spoke with Michael (PA).

- Successful speech therapy— starting with thicken diet/liquids
- (Post-intensive care) PIC Syndrome
- Has support clinic @ Johns Hopkins to help with transition
- Tee is being evaluated by psychologist
- Heart rate back down, no neck ports since 4/18
- Small IV in arm

- Has feeding tube and nasal canula — (on lowest dose)
- Possible to take off today
- Goals: heart rate controlled, Eating on his own, Rehabilitation
- Zoom call with Peggy @ 1:10 PM
- Next check-in 5:00 PM, then 8:30 PM

Thursday 4/23 @ 5:20 PM

I spoke with Nurse Peggy.

- Tee sipped some water
- Stood up 3 times
- Reminder of torn meniscus (left side/left knee)
- *Next check-in @ 8:15 PM
- Inquire about COVID-19 retest before going to stepdown unit

Thursday 4/23 @ 8:25 PM

I spoke with Nurse Angela (Angie).

- Tee was drinking water earlier
- Stood up 3 times

Friday 4/24 @ 5:40 AM

- Took a little bit for Tee to settle down and sleep
- All stable, including heart rate
- On room oxygen – now off nasal oxygen since @ 4:00 AM
- Trying to set Tee on a normal sleep schedule

Reminders for nurses and doctors: torn meniscus (left side/left knee)

- COVID-19 retest
- Inquire about iPad music
- Inquire psychologist consultation findings
- Next check-in @ 10/11:00 — see reminders

Friday 4/24 @ 9:27 AM

I spoke with Megan (Rehab Psychologist -my girl, still very helpful).

- Megan is planning on meeting with Tee today

Friday 4/24 @ 10:37 AM

I spoke with Nurse Jenny.

- Tee is leaving the ICU today (later today after 4:00 PM)
- Zoom call with Tee — Tee is getting a shave today by Jenny

Friday 4/24 @ 12:07 PM

I spoke with Dr. Coleridge.

- Mr. Clark has been progressing very well on room air
- Still weak
- Making measurable improvements
- Amiodarone can cause lower thyroid issues
- A fib late last night; (has been experiencing every 3-4 days)
- Put in for thyroid consultation from Endocrinologist
- Tee saw Roberto Salvatore a few years back — will follow up
- Any stress can cause A fib; can be a consistent problem

- Plan for Metoprolol PO – preventively — will give Amnio drip as needed (episodic)
- Long-term management if needed through Cardiology; BP is stable
- Normal heart rhythm to next stepdown level (with full monitoring) on Intermediate care unit
- *Reminder: torn meniscus
- Concerns about Anxiety — as delirium decreases
- Trying holistic protocol approach to re-acclimate
- Finish Amnio drip; (on Metoprolol PO and Amnio — preventively)

Friday 4/24 @ 4:31 PM

I spoke with Nurse Jenny.

- Tee had physical therapy and speech pathology therapy today
- Transferring out within an hour or so

(Discharged from ICU-35 days later)

Friday 4/24 @ 4:53 PM

I spoke with Megan (rehab psychologist).

- Tee was having a hard time praying–timing of earlier prayer perfect
- Very tired and overwhelmed with thirst and breathing on his own
- When tired, he gets more delirium
- Megan suggests non-pharma approaches initially for anxiety

Inpatient PT

Thursday 4/30 @ 9:30 AM

I spoke with Emily (OT).

- Physical therapy (PT) @ 2:30 PM with Tara
- Working on strength and endurance
- Discussed items needed for discharge, including: rolling walker, hospital bed, commode, railings (including garage, bathroom, etc.)
- Will most likely need 24/7 care — in home services (home care)
- **His projected release is now 5/7-10, PRAISE GOD!
- Tee is extremely motivated to get home sooner than later and he will prove this to anybody and everybody!

Side Note: We have an approximate release time frame after 41 LONG hospital days. We are so excited to finally see the light at the end of the tunnel. 5/5 is our fifth wedding anniversary, what a nice anniversary gift for us!

Thursday 4/30 @ 1:15 PM

I spoke with Adam Miller (social worker) to begin planning Tee's exit and return home.

- Inquire about rental/purchase of wheelchair
- Forward physician documents to be signed to Adam
- Supplies/equipment- will make docs order and request
- In-home services -insurance will provide 2-3 days week/home. PT/OT/Nurse
- Home care office will coordinate — can Reg HHA (probably 1-2 hours/week)
- May need to purchase (shower chair/commode)
- Inquire about wheelchair
- Will provide a list of agencies for aide
- Will have discharge confirmed by Friday PM

Thursday 4/30 @ 5:19 PM

I spoke with Noor (speech language pathology).

- Tee is on regular food
- Upgraded to nectar — less thicker fluids
- Concerned with some cognitive skills due to ICU delirium, *i.e.,* selective attention, alternating attention-multitasking, executive functions-complex thinking
- Can improve with various cognitive exercises
- Suggests ongoing speech therapy as well

Friday 5/1 @ 5:00 AM

I spoke with Linda (overnight nurse).

- Good night — No oxygen issues
- No other notes documented today. I spoke to Tee directly and continued to encourage him to stay the course. He's beginning to get very restless and frustrated as his exit date approaches.

Saturday 5/2 @ 5:28 AM

I spoke with Linda (overnight nurse).

Side Note: Linda is one of Tee's favorite nurses, he still remembers her, he says she came in on her day off the day that he left.

- He did well on 1 Liter of oxygen
- Stronger than day before
- Speak to doctor regarding COVID-19 results
- Oxygen CPAP
- Discharge date

Side Note: Tee was positive for COVID-19 less than a week before his planned discharge and almost 2.5 months since our original diagnosis on 3/17. He was very upset and worried that this may delay his discharge. Once again, we had to go to God in collective prayer!

Saturday 5/2 @ 11:47 AM

I spoke with Nurse Emma.

- Still mildly thick liquids
- Regular diet
- Had physical therapy (PT)
- Now speech language pathologist (SLP)
- **Still COVID-19-positive –will retest in a few weeks; should not affect discharge plans
- Dr. Raja called Tee and told him that he wasn't sure if this will affect his discharge plans for next week; he will call him to follow up
- Emma will page Dr. Raja for me

I spoke with Tara (physical therapist) PT

- Inquire about status
- Discharge plans possible Wednesday
- COVID-19 positive retest (should be OK) affect discharge
- Tee is getting better, breathing better
- Elbow, wrist and hand OK
- Right arm, right hand weak
- Right shoulder very weak (possible damage); will need further testing
- Will have home care coordinator coordinate details with Adam

Saturday 5/2/20 @ 6:30 PM

I spoke with Dr. Raja.

- Confirmed positive COVID-19 test Saturday morning. Unsure if this will affect release plans
- Need to confirm all on Monday, including plans, resourcing equipment, etc.

Sunday 5/3 @ 5:30 AM

I spoke with Nurse Preet.

- Tee had a good night — didn't need oxygen
- Refused CPAP — did not fit properly

Dr. Raja called Tee today 5/3/20 and said his recent positive COVID-19 test would NOT affect his release, still on track for next week, PRAISE GOD!

Sunday 5/3, approximately. 8:30 AM

I spoke with Nurse Emma.

- Breathing seems to be labored at times
- Doctor to confirm heart rate and pulmonary status

Sunday 5/3 @ 9:00 AM

I spoke with charge nurse.

- Vitals good
- Confirmed plans for discharge for Tuesday 5/6-YIPPEE!

Monday 5/4 @ 5:00 AM

I spoke with Nurse Hairong.

- No oxygen overnight — Oxygen levels @ 95% - 96%, constantly monitoring
- Tee slept good overnight
- Nurse check-in after 9:00 AM

Monday 5/4 @ 10:26 AM

I spoke with Melanie (PT) — Tee's buddy, aka the Drill Sergeant.

- "Many COVID-19 patients have a surge in mobility" Today Tee has reached his all-time high!

Side Note: This man is motivated to come home in 2 days, Ain't No Stopping Him Now!

- Tee does stand and walk alone and with assistance
- Tee will try steps on Tuesday (in preparation for getting into the garage when he gets home)

Monday 5/4 @ 1:25 PM

I spoke with Nurse Mindy.

- No COVID-19 retest
- Tee is doing extremely well; Wednesday release goal is no fever or symptoms (no need to quarantine — he's been asymptomatic for weeks)

Monday 5/4 @ 2:28 PM

I spoke with Dr. Patel.

- Wednesday 5/6 confirmed discharge plans for Noon — 2:00 PM discharge
- No need for oxygen
- Still has slight cough because his lungs are still healing (can treat with PRN cough medicine)
- Heart rate controlled on Metoprolol 25mg. 1 times/day
- Follow-up with cardiologist
- Discharge meds have been ordered

Post-discharge follow-ups

- PCP-2 weeks
- CD-1 month
- Pulmonologist-2 weeks

Tuesday 5/5 @ 9:15 AM

I spoke with Nurse Jill.

- This is Tee's last full day, we're all super excited!
- Next check-in with AM Nurse
- Vital signs great
- Completely off oxygen
- Last therapy sessions

Side Note: Today is our fifth anniversary, Tee has been telling everyone all week that he needs to get home TODAY to celebrate our anniversary. I actually need the extra day to plan his surprise Welcome Home celebration, including media coverage, equipment deliveries, etc.

<u>**Tuesday 5/5 @ 10:13 AM**</u>

I spoke with Emily (OT) about ramping up discharge prep.

- Ordered pain patch (Robaxin 500mg)
- Flex well muscle relaxer
- Noted spasms in trapezoid and rhomboid muscles
- Right side is the weaker side of his body
- When Tee sits on the side of the bed, prop up his arm on the pillow
- Can order "Pain Terminator" patch on Amazon
- Use (heat/ice daily) muscle relaxer
- Clarify frequency for muscle relaxer and pain patch

<u>**Tuesday 5/5 @ 11:09 AM**</u>

I spoke with Dr. April Pruski.

- She says, "Your husband is a Superstar — Doing very well!"
- Possible nerve damage to right arm
- May need EMG nerve conduction study — outpatient
- Musculoskeletal pain trapezius muscle — 1 times dose of Robaxin; — If so, will take PRN, Chacan makes him sleepy
- Pain Terminator patches — can try Lidocaine — may not work for muscle pain
- Freeze water bottles-rhomboid and trapezius — roll water bottle on muscles

<u>**Paperwork still underway to be done by today**</u>

- Discharge Noon — 1:00 PM (call beforehand)
- Doesn't think he needs anything else for cough

- Follow-up with outpatient pulmonary
- Can send muscle relaxer to Walgreens
- Probably no therapies tomorrow on discharge day

Homestretch preparation time

- Inquire about cough medications
- Discharge time
- Social worker home care referrals

Tuesday 5/5 @ 2:06 PM

I spoke with Brittany (SLP therapist).

- Tee has come a mighty long way since extubation of ICU
- Keep an eye on drinks causing cough or clearing throat; coughing while eating can be a sign of aspiration

SLP planning to come tomorrow for final session and discharge

- Small sips, no gulps or successive sips
- No straws when drinking
- Progressing with cognitive tests from last week
- *Recommends continuation of SLP, can do telehealth
- Signs and symptoms of aspiration:
- Cough (clearing throat)
- Small sips
- If persistent, notify doctor and SLP

Tuesday 5/5 @ 4:25 PM

I spoke with home care coordinator to confirm all.

Today is Day 46: Homecoming Day!

Wednesday 5/6 @ 6:06 AM

I spoke to Nurse Jill.

- Good night, Tee slept well
- She paged doctors for Noon pickup, I WILL BE THERE!

Special thanks to all of the Johns Hopkins staff for their wonderful care and detailed timely updates.

Appreciation

First and foremost, to our Lord and Savior Jesus Christ, we acknowledge and love You for seeing us through time and time again; especially for allowing us to live through COVID-19 to share this story. We know You have a plan for our lives, so we wait diligently for You to continue to show us Your mighty will.

To Terri Liggins, our amazing Editor, for lending us your brilliance toward this outstanding masterpiece highlighting our trials, triumphs and testimonies.

To our adopted uncle, Dr. David Nyanjom, for being an incredible person, doctor, spiritual minister and friend and for your invaluable medical advice and guidance.

To the wonderful doctors, nurses and other medical professionals, for the stellar care given my husband and assistance to me from March through June 2020. There are too many people to name individually, but please know you ALL hold a special place in our hearts forever. There aren't enough words to express our gratitude and appreciation for the extraordinary level of care, thoughtfulness, and professionalism you rendered to Tee. He is alive and well because of answered unified prayers, and your outstanding life-saving efforts! You and your colleagues everywhere are more than the "frontline coronavirus hero" distinction given to you during this pandemic; you are God-sent angels for all times!

To Patient First Columbia MD, for the great patient care and skillful professionalism you provide to our community. It was made evident, through the service rendered to us by nurse Amy and staff (including

Sharon and Danielle), that you live up to your name, truly putting your patients first.

To Johns Hopkins Howard County General Hospital—especially Dr. Sarkar and nurses Kelly and Sean—for your quick-thinking measures that kept Tee alive, and for the selfless, hard work you put forth every single day in the Emergency Room.

To the many amazing souls at Johns Hopkins Main Hospital, for preserving Tee through the worst health struggle of his life and for allowing him to come home to me completely preserved and on the road to being fully restored. To Dr. Pruski and the amazing PM&R staff Tara, Emily, Melanie, etc.. To all of the fabulous nurses including but not limited to Kasum, Jenny, Julie, Linda, Tracy (Charge Nurse), (PA's) Michael, Kathleen, Drs. Liz Carstens, Megan Hosey, and all the countless others, thank you, thank you, thank you!

To everyone outside of the hospitals who assisted in restoring Tee's health and strength, for your diligence and selfless attention to his every need for several months under your care. To Elise, MedStar PT; Chris Edou, Ram @ Oula of Home Health; Mark, Maria, Melissa of Bayada Homecare; and any others we may have regretfully forgotten to mention, we cannot ever repay you for your contribution to Tee's long term health results.

To Tee's coworkers known as the APKS family, for your love and support toward Tee, especially during his time away from the workplace. Janet Robin, in particular, we cannot express how grateful we are for the help, support, and consideration you and your staff have given to us!

To Bishop Walter Scott Thomas, Sandra Draper Stewart (my spiritual mom) and the entire New Psalmist family, including Donnell and Priscilla Burrell and our Couples class clique, for your ongoing prayers and support. Our hearts are so full of gratitude to the Burrell's for building our garage stairs and bathroom railings in preparation for Tee's return home! And you may never know, Bishop Thomas, how extremely grateful we are for your divine leadership and ministry. Without a doubt, your consistent teachings of faith over the last 23 years are what helped me make it through one of the toughest periods of my recent adult life!

To the mighty "TC Prayer Warriors," including all our weekly prayer group participants, and particularly our amazing prayer leaders, Jon and Kristi Gray and Jared and Danielle Perry, for your loyalty and consistency through one of the hardest times of mine and Tee's lives. Your relentless, united prayers were the key to our survival!

To the Myles siblings (Too many to list lol-inside joke) We love you forever and a day. Thanks for your collective love and prayers!

To our little sisters, Kellie (Kel) and Dakota (Didi Cakes), for your contributions to the book—Kel for your shared archived texts and Didi for your beautiful digital invitations. We cannot thank you both enough for helping to keep contributing matters related to this book organized and on point.

To my big brother Darrell, for your much-needed spiritual insight that was shared in this book. I love you, and my specific prayer for you is that you forever acknowledge and walk in your marvelous anointing.

To my lovely, loyal, and faithful Aunts Diane (Auntie Mom), Bunny, Marilyn, Mom Boonie, Aunt Joy, God-mom Polly (in heaven), for always, without fail, being in my corner. For my Uncles and their continued support (including but not limited to Uncle Johnny, Mervin, Stan, Freddie, etc.)

To Kaelyn and Bud, for your unconditional love toward your dad from up close (Kaelyn) and afar (Bud). No doubt, his strength to pull through was largely due to your strong bond. You really grew up during this time, Kaelyn, and I'm so proud of you! Thank you, Marcus, for always being Kaelyn's pillar of love and strength but especially during this difficult time for her. Your help with getting Tee home and situated was also invaluable.

To our Phila area family (Beloved Myles, Overton, Johnson, etc.) and to my Jones Family (Uncle Merv and Aunt Joy, aka the Huxtables), for showing us the true meaning of marriage (60 years for Merv & Joy), and family. You have set the perfect example for us!

To our beloved and faithful cousins Marshall "Jamie" and Josephine "Jo" Blackston for your unwavering love and support. Thanks for loving us and for always looking out for our Gmom.

To our lovely cousin LaWanda (first responder to the ER) during Tee's initial emergency at JH-HCGH. We love you unconditionally and we're so grateful that God sent you to us during our time of need.

To Our MD/VA family (beloved Clarks, Jeffreys family *i.e.,* Aunt Mary, Uncle Jack, Aunt Barbara Ann (cook extraordinaire), etc. for being who you are in mine and Tee's lives, always showing us much love.

To Mom Lulu, sisters Vera and Anita (Byrd), Bro-in-laws "E" and Kevin, for being there for us. Thanks, also, for sending the wonderful homecooked meals during Tee's transition back home. Kevin, thank you for helping with the household tasks (you know Tee trusts your handy-man and professional skills wholeheartedly in his absence).

To, all the media outlets (NBC WBAL TV, BNC, WIIN, Baltimore Sun, CBS-WJZ, Fox-Baltimore, AARP, etc.), for having shared our story on your broadcasts. Special thanks to Ava Joye Burnett and CBS Baltimore, for a great job in covering Tee's departure from Johns Hopkins and follow-up stories about his progress.

To Renee Bobb "The Book Publishing Lady" and remarkable book marketing coach. Thanks for your professional leadership through the process.

To Marie Therese, my "personal chaplain," for being the faithful and powerful praying saint that everyone needs in their life. I am so grateful God assigned you to me! I love you my sister friend!

To all our family and friends who stuck by us during this time. Thank you immensely for the food, the supplies, your time, love and prayers! Special thanks to Rick & Elena Link, Jeff and Stacey White, and countless others for looking out for me in Tee's absence.

To my brothers in life and in Christ, Pastors Brian Murray and Julius Renwick, for joining in on our prayer calls and for your continued effervescent prayers during our time of need. Brian thanks for your wonderful written contribution to our book. To my adopted Big brother and sister Ken & Lynn Shareef, thanks for the love and support over the years. Most recently thanks for introducing us to Terri L, our amazing Editor and friend.

For my beloved Sister Girls: Camille, Bri, and Big sisters Glenda and Dee-Dee (aka my Philly girls), Stacey, Risa, Monica, Shkari, Sondra, Miki, etc. Thanks for the mutual loving friendships, and Amazing memories over the years. Thanks for always having my back then and now, and of course you know its reciprocal!

To the many Angels God has assigned to me throughout various seasons of my life (Loleeta S, Donna V, Mark M, JG Bell, and too many more to name), Grateful Thanks for all you've done for me. You are forever in my heart, even in our separation of space. I've tried my best to pay it forward, as well as reach back to help others.

Marcy's Special Tributes:

To my beloved big brother cousin, TV producer and creative talent extraordinaire, Merv Jones ("my Temple University cousin") who lost his battle with cancer during this coronavirus pandemic. Thanks for encouraging me to write this book. You told me to write my own story because no one could tell it better than me, and that you would review it for me upon completion. Well, cousin, here it is for you to review from heaven. I hope you approve! (Smile)

To my beloved big sister cousin Angela Jones (whom I affectionately referred to as "Judge Angie"), who recently took her Heavenly flight just before the final publishing of this book. Cuz, thanks for your continuous love, and support over the years, and for being an Outstanding person and role model. It pains me to think that you are no longer here, and like your brother Merv who predeceased you only 8 months ago, you are tragically gone too soon!

Seeing cousins Merv and Angela's lives cut short like my sister Maryann's and my brother Carl's (all of whom never made it to age 60), helps us to further re-evaluate the importance of life. We will cherish each day, and we have a renewed commitment to enjoy our lives to the fullest, as this last year has TRULY showed us that tomorrow is not promised! Hold down the heavenly skies family, until we meet again.

To my parents in Heaven, the late Mar'Cia and Carl E. Myles Sr. I think of you every day. I thank you for giving me life and love in your special way. God has made me a perfect blend of the two of you. I'm reminded of your precious legacy whenever I look in the mirror.

To Mom, I always vowed that the perfect guy for me was one with all of daddy's good characteristics. I just never imagined God would send me a complete replica—just younger. I'm convinced you had something to do with this. Dad, they say girls marry their dad. Well, I can never forget you because I married the best of you. I thank God for you both and I wish you'll were here on earth with me longer, but God had another plan. I feel your ever-present spirit, and know you are smiling down on us. Eternal love, until we meet again!

To Grandma (Arlyne Craig), our family matriarch. You're 95 now and still hanging in there, lady! Throughout my young life, you were the first successful black woman I knew who owned her own business. You were way ahead of your time with your gifts and talents. You're also a historical legend as "Pennsylvania's Board of Cosmetology—First Black State Examiner." Personally, you have been an amazing provider and pillar of strength, teaching me how to be a "Boss!" I definitely attribute my strength and entrepreneurial aspirations to you. It gave me great comfort to know I could always count on you, and that you were always just a phone call away. Now, our roles have been reversed and you can always count on *me*! While you've outlived your children and your husband, you still have Tee and me, and we couldn't be more grateful! May God continue to bless and keep You! I love you more than words.

Forever Our Lady C

Appendix – Photos

Our life in pictures – before COVID-19

Celebrating Marcy's Birthday

Celebrating Philadelphia Eagles in Aruba

Plane Trip to our Aruba Wedding

(Son) Bud and Family

Our Kids and their Mates

Beach Time in the Dominican Republic

Tee on his way to work

Cruise Ship Photo

70's Party (Rick James & Teena Marie)

Aruba Beach Wedding

DJ Tee mixing it up

Our life in pictures – after COVID-19

Tee's 57th Drive-up Birthday Celebration

Johns Hopkins Honors Tee with a White Doctors Coat

Praying Wife, Healed Husband

About the Author

Marcy Myles-Clark is an Inspirational Author and Financial Entrepreneur who loves traveling almost as much as she loves offering her spiritual gift of helps to her family and friends near and far. As a member of New Psalmist Baptist church (Baltimore, MD) since 1998, she serves diligently under the leadership of Bishop Walter Scott Thomas, to whom she largely attributes her spiritual growth, development, and leadership.

Marcy has championed through numerous traumatic experiences and losses in her life, starting with witnessing her young 32 year old mother having a life changing stroke at 8 years old, and losing a young 37 year old sister (Maryann) to Breast cancer. She has transformed these events into insurmountable faith and draws on that faith as a source of encouragement to others. It is her belief that hardships are designed to craft one's strength that makes way for unwavering faith and affective prayer.

Marcy wrote this book to tell her and her husband's story of illness survival. Her story is a proclamation of how her unyielding faith led to the formation of a massive prayer group which then lead to her husband's miraculous healing. She hopes to be a beacon of light, and a source of encouragement, to others who may be facing similar challenges. Marcy has 20+ years of combined experience as a Pharmaceutical Representative, and Entrepreneur. She utilizes this knowledge in the book to give others spiritual and practical ways to position themselves to WIN in life (both in and outside of a pandemic).

Although Marcy is a native Philadelphian, she's resided in Maryland for the last 23 years. She has a BA from Temple University and an MBA from University of Phoenix. She and her husband of five years, Theirrien "Tee" Clark, reside in the Howard County, Maryland area. They are empty nesters of two adult children.

About the Co-Author

Contributing Author, **Theirrien A. (Tee) Clark** is a Senior Manager at an International Law Firm based in Washington, DC. Tee has more than 30-years' experience successfully promoting and providing dedicated service to the legal industry.

Tee is a powerful force in the workplace and uses his positive attitude and tireless energy to encourage others to work hard and succeed. His leadership was celebrated by his law firm's immense support of him and his family through his most recent tribulation.

Tee is inspired daily by his wife Marcy, their two children and twin grandchildren. In his free-time, Tee a wife proclaimed "busy body/superman" has developed several relationships with Wedding Planners, and freelances as a wedding DJ.

Tee experienced a death-defying experience in March, 2020. He is now part of a demographic that has been devastated by the coronavirus since the start of the pandemic. He believes that it is unconscionable that Black people are, in many ways, bearing the brunt of COVID-19. The impact of this pandemic will last for years to come; not only because of the morbidity and mortality caused, but also because of the economic devastation suffered by these families. His survival is nothing short of a miracle, prayer and good health care. This experience has inspired him to co-author this book and share his experiences so that it can be a beacon of light for others who are in the fight or may suffer from this coronavirus.

Tee is a native Washingtonian and now resides in the Howard County Maryland area with his wife Marcy. Tee holds a BS from The University of Maryland and he is very proud of his two children who have managed successful careers in the United States Marine Corp and Veterinarian medicine.

To learn more about Marcy and Tee, please visit:

www.PrayingWifeHelps.com

CPSIA information can be obtained
at www.ICGtesting.com
Printed in the USA
BVHW041741311021
620407BV00008B/32

9 781736 554050